BUILDING BETTER SOCIETIES
Promoting social justice in a world falling apart

Edited by
Rowland Atkinson, Lisa Mckenzie
and Simon Winlow

D1612787

P

First published in Great Britain in 2017 by

Policy Press
University of Bristol
1-9 Old Park Hill
Bristol
BS2 8BB
UK
t: +44 (0)117 954 5940
pp-info@bristol.ac.uk
www.policypress.co.uk

North America office:
Policy Press
c/o The University of Chicago Press
1427 East 60th Street
Chicago, IL 60637, USA
t: +1 773 702 7700
f: +1 773-702-9756
sales@press.uchicago.edu
www.press.uchicago.edu

British Library Cataloguing in Publication Data
A catalogue record for this book is available from the British Library

Library of Congress Cataloging-in-Publication Data
A catalog record for this book has been requested

ISBN 978-1-4473-3203-9 paperback
ISBN 978-1-4473-3202-2 hardcover
ISBN 978-1-4473-3204-6 ePub
ISBN 978-1-4473-3205-3 Mobi
ISBN 978-1-4473-3201-5 epdf

Cover design by Hayes Design
Front cover image: Charlotte Atkinson
Printed and bound in Great Britain by Clays Ltd, St Ives plc
Policy Press uses environmentally responsible print partners

Contents

Notes on contributors   vi

one   Who would not be for society?   1
Rowland Atkinson, Lisa Mckenzie and Simon Winlow

Part 1: Problems   **13**

two   The social question and the urgency of care   15
Iain Wilkinson

three   Better politics: Narratives of indignation and the possibility   27
of a prosocial politics
Keith Jacobs

four   Valuing and strengthening community   39
Lisa Mckenzie

Part 2: Ideas   **53**

five   Confronting the roots of violent behaviour   55
Anthony Ellis

six   In defence of the public city   67
Martin Coward

seven   Artfully thinking the prosocial   81
Deborah Warr, Gretel Taylor and Richard Williams

eight   Re-visioning exclusion in local communities   95
Kate Pahl and Paul Ward

nine   Putting 'the social' back into social policy   111
Steve Corbett and Alan Walker

Part 3: Futures   **125**

ten   Progress through protest   127
Samuel Burgum

eleven   Cities, crises and the future   141
Sophie Body-Gendrot

twelve   Policy steps towards a better social future   155
Michael Orton

thirteen   The (in)visibility of riches, urban life and exclusion   165
Rowland Atkinson

fourteen   The uses of catastrophism   179
Simon Winlow

Conclusion   **193**

fifteen   Thinking prosocially   195
Rowland Atkinson, Simon Winlow and Lisa Mckenzie

Index   201

Notes on contributors

Rowland Atkinson is Chair in Inclusive Societies at the University of Sheffield, UK. His work is primarily concerned with the spatial consequences and form of inequality in cities. His work focuses on issues of social exclusion, gentrification, gated communities and the disordering impact of the very wealthy on urban life. He is author (with Sarah Blandy) of *Domestic fortress: Fear and the new home front* (Manchester University Press, 2016).

Sophie Body-Gendrot is Emeritus Professor at Université Paris-Sorbonne (Paris IV), France, a researcher at CESDIP-CNRS-French Ministry of Justice, the author of *Public disorder and globalization* (Routledge, 2016) and co-editor of *The Routledge Handbook of European Criminology* (2013).

Sam Burgum is a researcher with interests in social theory, power, resistance, urban politics (including squatting) and social movements. He is based at the Department of Sociology at the University of Warwick, UK. His three-year ethnography with the Occupy movement in London will be published with Routledge in late 2017.

Steve Corbett is a lecturer in Social Policy at Liverpool Hope University, UK. His research interests include social quality, participatory democracy, alternatives to neoliberalism, and empowerment. He has written on the social implications of Brexit in the *International Journal of Social Quality* and has contributed to *The Post-Brexit Declaration on Social Quality in Europe* (with Alan Walker).

Martin Coward is a reader in International Politics at the University of Manchester, UK. He works at the intersection of International Political Theory and Security Studies and is particularly concerned with questions of war, violence, (in)security, identity and community. To date, his research has focused on the conceptual understanding of (in)security and organised violence in an urban context, particularly the 'urbanisation of security', attacks on critical infrastructure and urbicide.

Anthony Ellis is a Lecturer in Criminology and Sociology at the University of Salford, UK. He is the author of *Men, masculinities and violence: An ethnographic study* (Routledge, 2015) and several other journal articles and book chapters addressing issues of gender, violence, alcohol consumption and deviant behaviour.

Professor Keith Jacobs is based in the School of Social Sciences at the University of Tasmania, Australia. Keith is currently an Australian Research Council Future Fellow, working on a project investigating contemporary housing affordability issues, and was co-author, with Rowland Atkinson, of *Housing, home and society*, published by Palgrave in 2016.

Lisa Mckenzie is an ethnographer and currently a research fellow at the London School of Economics and Political Science (LSE), UK. She has worked extensively as an activist around housing and social issues more broadly. Her PhD on life in a marginalised urban neighbourhood produced the best-selling *Getting by: Estates, class and culture in austerity Britain* (Policy Press, 2015). Her interests are in working-class identities, progressive politics and social change, and the means by which inequalities can be addressed.

Michael Orton is a senior research fellow at the University of Warwick, UK. Prior to academia he worked for over 15 years in the voluntary sector and local government. His work focuses on core issues around poverty, work/welfare and inequalities, with emphasis on consensus building around solutions.

Kate Pahl works at the University of Sheffield, UK, with a focus on arts, literacy and co-production as a methodology. She is the principal investigator of the ESRC-funded 'Imagine' project, which is concerned with imagining different communities and making them happen. She is the author, with Keri Facer, of *Valuing interdisciplinary collaborative research: Beyond impact* (Policy Press, 2017), which looks at ways of knowing and researching with communities, and across disciplines.

Gretel Taylor is an artist and researcher at University of Melbourne, Australia. Through a broad enquiry around relationships to place, Gretel creates performances, facilitates art projects and is engaged in research exploring potentials at the juncture of site-specific art and community cultural development.

Alan Walker CBE, FBA is Professor of Social Policy at the University of Sheffield, UK. He directed the New Dynamics of Ageing Programme and chaired the Sheffield Fairness Commission.

Paul Ward is Professor of History at the University of Huddersfield, UK, and researches national identities in the UK since 1870. He explores co-production of historical knowledge and public history. Author of four books, including *Britishness since 1870* (Routledge, 2004), he is currently co-writing another, called *Co-producing research: A community development approach*, as part of the ESRC-funded programme Imagine: Connecting Communities Through Research.

Deborah Warr is a sociologist based at the University of Melbourne, Australia. Her research focuses on diverse circumstances associated with poverty and socioeconomic marginalisation. She uses diverse methodological approaches, including social network analysis and qualitative, ethnographic, visual and arts-based methods, combined with a longstanding commitment to participatory and collaborative methods.

Iain Wilkinson is a reader in Sociology at the University of Kent. His publications include *Anxiety in a risk society* (Routledge, 2001), *Suffering: A sociological introduction* (Polity, 2005), *Risk vulnerability and everyday life* (Routledge, 2010) and (co-authored with Arthur Kleinman) *A passion for society: How we think about human suffering* (University of California Press, 2016).

Richard Williams is a sociologist whose work is informed by long experience in delivering services to poor and marginalised communities. He is interested in how people interpret and adapt to public policy initiatives, and the implications of this for policy formation and institutional design, and on research collaborations with local communities.

Simon Winlow is Professor of Criminology at the Teesside Centre for Realist Criminology, UK. He is the Vice President of the British Society of Criminology. His primary research interests are in violence and criminological theory. He is the author or coauthor of *Badfellas* (Berg, 2001), *Bouncers* (OUP, 2003), *Violent night* (Berg, 2006), *Criminal identities and consumer culture* (Willan, 2008), *Rethinking social exclusion* (Sage, 2013), *Riots and political protest* (Routledge, 2015), *Revitalizing criminological theory* (Routledge, 2015) and *The rise of the right* (Policy Press, 2016).

ONE

Who would not be for society?

Rowland Atkinson, Lisa Mckenzie and Simon Winlow

> If you have a garden and a library, you have everything you
> need. (Cicero, *Ad Familiares IX*, 4, to Varro)

Who would say they are not 'for' society? Society shapes our
expectations of life. It informs our values, our behaviour, our dreams
and our ambitions. The communities and networks that form an
integral part of society give life colour and connect us emotionally
to others. It is almost impossible to construct a positive vision of our
lives without these things. What kind of life would we imagine for
ourselves as individuals without such affective relationships, without
obligations to others, and without affiliations to the various networks
and groups that form the fabric of our daily lives? What would it be
like to deny ourselves as individuals – and 'ourselves' as a collective
– the advantages generated by health, education and other public,
social or municipal services, such as roads, police forces or parks? It is
clear that our lives would be reduced or impoverished without them.
When faced with calls to break collective identities and to roll back
the frontiers of the state, we should pause for a moment and think
about the various kinds of damage that are wrought upon the lives of
others, our own lives, and the life that we all share together when we
are told to focus only on our individual interests and when forms of
public provision are withdrawn.

The central argument of this book is that these kinds of taken-for-
granted shared privileges are being increasingly disremembered, and
often actively dismantled, by the current ascendancy of social and
political ideologies that celebrate individuality and achievement as
though they can somehow be extracted from their social, political and
economic contexts. Such ideologies, often drawn together under the
banner of neoliberalism, can be understood ostensibly as celebrations of
individual autonomy. However, the call to increase individual freedom
by decreasing the size of the state has, since the 19th century, acted
to cover up a cruder concern to extend the economic freedoms of
those who have already amassed significant wealth and privilege. On

the surface of things, we are all supposed to benefit from tax cuts and a reduction in state spending. Once we have severed the fetters that restrain us and bond us to the mediocrity of the herd, the dynamism and innovation of the best among us will act to drive our species to ever greater heights and improve the lives of all. Of course, beneath the surface, reducing taxes on wealth and income and decreasing the size of the welfare state benefits only a small percentage of the population, and these benefits are accrued at the expense of everyone else.

Neoliberalism reinforces, reproduces and exacerbates economic inequalities over time (Harvey, 2011). Its advocates argue that economy and society should be managed as a business, but they fail to understand or appreciate just how reliant businesses are on civil society and a functioning tax-dependent state (Hay and Payne, 2015). They fail to acknowledge that it is civil society as such that makes businesses viable, and that it is the state that establishes and maintains the security and order that businesses need to operate and to grow. The core principles of neoliberalism have achieved unrivalled supremacy. Their obvious ideological character has been stripped away, and these principles are now presented to us as basic common sense. Yet the broader tragedy generated by the victory of these ideas is that they encourage a carelessness for those without investment capital, for those without the wherewithal to help themselves, and for those at the margins who are unable to find reasonably remunerative employment. Our attitude to the suffering of others, and our willingness to intervene in the world to put an end to that suffering, tells us much about what has become of our society and where it appears to be heading. Now, in the midst of staggering wealth, technological dynamism and relative cultural freedom, we continue to see genuine poverty and want, searing distress, hardship and loneliness, and the total unwillingness to act now to prevent the accumulation of threats and harms into the future if it means sacrificing our time, energy or even the smallest facet of our consumer lifestyles. What are we to make of all this? What has happened to our commitment to a just and inclusive society that valued all equally?

The post-war social democratic context produced many of the greatest achievements of collaborative human behaviour: a welfare state, full employment, incremental improvements to the lifestyles of the vast majority, free education for all, a massive expansion in the quantity and quality of public and private housing, and other forms of public infrastructure that benefited many millions of people. It also equipped the citizenry with a sense of security and stability that enabled forms of togetherness and common purpose to grow and to heal the nation's wounds after years of war. How could it be that such collective achievements might come to be recast as tainted and inefficient bureaucracies that inhibited freedom? How could it be that those who depended on these services would be cast as skivers, shirkers and layabouts? Our attention must fall on the market and those who gain the most from its dizzying fluctuations. The market has been invigorated by a significant sale of public assets.

The prevailing view often espoused by the elites in business, politics and the media is that these kinds of social investment and insurance are too expensive, that recipients are not 'deserving', and that market models are more efficient and effective (see, for example, Mason, 2016). The real limits of this vision and the poverty of its thinking are increasingly revealed to us – both by a crisis generated by the risk-taking of private banks shored up by government bailouts[1] and a decade of austerity measures to shore up public finances. These decisions have been costly to those with already very little of the rewards of work and wealth, and also served to insulate the risk to the financial services sector by unleashing austerity programmes that defunded almost all forms of social investment and support (Blyth, 2013).

Neoliberal political administrations in the 1980s and 1990s pursued a very basic but highly effective divide–and–rule strategy. They cultivated individualism, and sought to fragment established social groups. They encouraged 'hardworking taxpayers' keen to boost their spending power to believe that welfare-dependent families were stripping the welfare state bare, frittering away the taxes paid by the employed, and generally acting as a drag on the nation's economic competitiveness. By slight contrast the new raft of austerity programmes now driving significant social distress were given apparent legitimacy by the 2008 global financial crisis that was identified by elite figures as presenting no other options, least that of helping the wealthy originators of the crisis, the banks, to make some contribution to the fiscal reconstruction package. Like the 1980s, however, governments were also able to suggest that it was the public domain that had become overly costly and a drag on efficiency and economic potential. This state of affairs led to the charge that what was being presented as logical was, in reality, an ideologically charged attack on the weak who had long been cast as unwilling to work or engage within right-wing framings of what lay at the root of society's troubles. Worse, it became clear that these explanations concealed the deeper purpose of enabling wealthier constituencies to be insulated from the deep economic shock that this crisis, like others before it, had generated. This was nothing less than a quite staggering reversal of existing narratives around culpability and the source of social and economic malaise – one that was furthered by compliant corporate state media systems (the BBC in the UK, Fox News and many others in the US, for example). In the UK, fearful for its own financial future, the BBC asked 'what would you cut', seemingly finding it difficult to present other possible futures and proposals in the name of balanced political coverage.

It is important that we remember that forms of social insurance (such as welfare benefits and pensions) as well as universal provision (a national health service, public schools and so on) were hard-won projects designed to address the problem of what happens to us as individuals and families if we fall on hard times or experience personal crisis. Many of these systems are now under attack, have been damaged, or have gone entirely. These changes go to the heart of debates about social justice and social protection, but they also signal the relative position and status of what we think of as the social or society today. In that sense, how can we understand these kinds of attacks on systems put in place to offer support to those most socially vulnerable? What has been cast as a question for economics, efficiency and rationality belies a deeply moral issue – even if these things are expensive, they might surely be seen as a non-negotiable feature of a civilised society? Perhaps for those at the top civility mattered little if it was possible to escape to gated communities and fortress homes in leafy districts (Atkinson and Blandy, 2017)?

What is happening to the public domain more broadly? Here we see public spaces, city streets, universities and other public institutions increasingly identified as over-priced or unnecessary facilities that many affluent countries now claim to be unable to maintain. Among the many risks of this feeling of a closing down of public spaces is that the possibility of circulating knowledge, forms of education and resistance is also prevented. These issues have been highlighted by an increasing focus on new forms of inequality and privilege by many analysts of our current situation. For example, plans to demolish public housing have occurred alongside crises in affordability and housebuilding that now generate intense public anger as, in the background, cities like London and some in the urban north have seen real estate assets secured by international wealth funds and the wealthy themselves. How are these, and many other, outcomes fair? Who benefits and who loses? How is it possible that we cannot plan for, amend or re-craft these changes to prevent their negative impact on many individuals and communities? The sense of cynicism and fatalism throughout the social body, and the general absence of hope that we can, in fact, create the society we want, is now quite palpable. We are told over and over again, in both subtle and unsubtle ways, that we currently occupy the best of all available systems. We are told that if we abandon the logic of markets our lifestyles will fall back with breath-taking speed. We are told that we must retain capitalism, because if we do not, we will be returned to the horrors of totalitarianism and dictatorship. If you're dissatisfied with any aspect of the system, we are told, use your vote to change things. And we tend to go along with all of this, even though there has not, until recently, been a great deal of difference between our major political parties. Rather than sticking to the democratic ideal and positively endorsing the political party that appears to express our views, we often vote negatively. We vote for the political party we least hate. More than this the rise of new publics and spaces of dissenting voices within social media not only seem to be essentially passive forms of dialogue that substitute for more deliberative and engaged forms of action, but are locked into exchanges within like-minded communities whose anger or ideas do not challenge others.

Our society and many others are now experiencing forms of social fragmentation in which social precariousness is met either with disdain or hand-wringing apologies that the public coffers are empty while the richest are subjected to historically unprecedented low tax rates or evade them by both fair means and foul (Shaxson, 2012). Yet these problems are not only the symptoms of our current crisis, but also evidence of the tendency to crisis and chaos offered by the economic and political systems we inhabit. These features are, in fact, part of much longer-run phases of economic calamity and periodic attacks on poverty. What is remarkable today is the triumph of what is essentially an antisocial vision of market logics, individualism, the naturalisation of inequalities and the theft of common spaces and resources by the few. Worse, these features of our economy are often presented to us as the very means by which a fairer and more productive society might be created (Friedman, 1993, 2002). In such views lies the sense that common resources should be plundered in the name of the common good (such as the privatisation of public resources like the UK postal service) and which then might allow greater economic security by generating one-off injections of cash to governments already committed to projects of public demolition. The real tragedy of such thefts is not only that pension funds and the wealthy benefit from subsequent share sales, but that hard-won and slowly built enterprises that had a social mission or vital function are let go in an instant with little or no prospect of their reassembly. Rather, it is in this context that the poor are attacked for their theft of the wealth of the hardworking (for which, given recent analyses, we should, in fact, read the rich) as they drain benefit systems and health services instead of being seen as the worthy recipients of relatively modest forms of wealth or income redistribution (Meek, 2016).

More trenchant critique from political economists regarding our contemporary plight highlights how a capitalist world (a market-based system with the distinctive feature of being predicated on unending expansion) produces and reproduces vast wealth inequalities that continue to grow now as they did in the early part of the 20th century. Now the welfare state, public services and lower income inequalities appear as an unusual blip in social history in the post-war period as the otherwise business-as-normal position of gross inequality has been renewed since the 1980s (Harvey, 2011; Piketty, 2013). In this context Keith Jacobs' chapter in this collection (Chapter Three) argues that this neoliberal project has become a complex and all oppressive power that forces despondency on all of those engaged or disengaged by it. As many now recognise, the force of these ideas as a kind of social normal are not met with strong and coherent counter-narratives that envision a radically different or clearly reformed version of our current social system.

As C. Wright Mills (1959) argued in *The sociological imagination*, there is a need to locate personal troubles and broader social issues and move forward to identify how social science can offer programmatic alternatives and ideas. In the current context, the dismantling of social projects and erosion of what were the otherwise softening effects of taxation systems that levelled out such relative excesses are likely to be at the centre of any future projects, and are represented by the massive popular interest in the functions of the economy, in questions of tax justice and the teaching of economics itself (Earle et al, 2016). One of the clear points of such work is that, as Freire (1970), pointed out many years ago, the design of education systems in ways that prevent a full awareness of the sources of inequality represent a form of oppression and mystification that must be challenged for greater social justice to be driven forward. Even for those on the political right, as the implications of a national economy at the whims of foreign capital have become increasingly apparent, the sense of rapid change, loss of many traditional ways of life and erosion of paternal hierarchies generates significant anxiety and often a retreat into nationalist and xenophobic dogma. Yet in many ways there are large sections of those who might identify as being on the political left or right to whom the sources of such anxiety and dejection are, in many ways, shared.

Costs of social fragmentation

One way of indexing the cost of the many transitions of the past decade can be located in the deepening senses of alienation and anxiety that has come to predominate the lives of many across social class, occupational and wealth spectrums. Precariousness of existence is experienced by many, even in what would traditionally have been deemed 'jobs for life' (Winlow and Hall, 2013). In this context, Lisa McKenzie's chapter (Chapter Four) analyses the growing precariousness of the poorest families in the UK, in particular, those who rely on social housing. The race to own a home and the offer of finance has produced higher house prices that require chasing and long hours in contract occupations to try and secure a base for a social and private life, and that of the new generations of children to be nurtured in these homes and communities. Very few people are in any meaningful sense either 'winning' or satisfied under these conditions. We are over-worked, over-stimulated into sleeplessness by work stress or distracting technologies, unsure of what social life means in the face of rampant consumption that forms the core of increasingly hollowed-out social identities, and face a gnawing realisation of the finality of life, often without any guiding myths or transcendent belief systems to offer guides to morality, how to live or to manage the stress of daily social life. In all of this we can see what might be described as an economistic model of social life that has triumphed – notions of efficiency and profit are the logic of more and more aspects of social life. Later on in the book Kate Pahl and Paul Ward's contribution here (Chapter Eight) argues that there is and has to be a community resistance through local grass-roots practice, although this community logic is too often de-valued by local and national governments who instead seek the justification of economists in a 'value-for-money' expectation that there is a number one can place on matters of the social.

The advantages generated by combining the resources of those around us, whether this is at the level of the locality, the city or nation, is rarely contested as an 'academic' thesis. Nevertheless, separating out the question of whether it is possible to imagine being without these resources and connections is more difficult. Surely the response must be that social bonds of numerous kinds not only express forms of connection and interaction, but also resources and positive influences in our lives. Rowland Atkinson's chapter (Chapter Thirteen) suggests that the increasing excesses and resources of a growing large group of the wealthy are founded on the belief that life without reciprocity or mutual obligation to those around us is possible, enviable for its sense of freedom and autonomy. Research tells us that close and meaningful connections influence our health and wellbeing in deep ways – from issues like obesity to our psychological health. Those who feel isolated and withdrawn from social interaction experience deeper forms of distress, depression and anxiety. In this context there is a need to develop ideas that challenge the desirability and emulation of the privileges and privacy of celebrities and the wealthy.

Who is for the social?

All of this brings us to the question of social bonds and institutions as being more than simply connections; they are resources by which, in a critical sense, together we are better and more able to develop and do more in our lives (see, for example, Halpern, 2010). To speak of these resources we also need to acknowledge a profound and recurring feature of social life – this is the idea of social inequality and can be expressed in multiple ways. One of the key problematics underlying the question of inequality is that of what can be understood as fair, within certain limits or boundaries. If someone earns twice as much as someone else is it because we (society) somehow value their work more deeply, is it because their skills are scarce (the question of a market) or is it untenable and unwarranted – a product of simple luck or, worse, a rigged system? Of course even such a simple thought experiment belies the reality that those at the top of many corporations often earn hundreds of times the pay of the lowest paid of their workers, and this is now generating increasing scrutiny and anger. What many sociologists try to disentangle, and forms the focus of much of this volume, is to consider the ways in which many inequalities are damaging to society, groups and individuals, and the degree to which they are reproduced and engrained in social structures and relations.

For many people the odds are against them, even as they lie as babies in their mother's arms in hospital at birth. This sense of pre-destination has added energy to debates and condemnation of the excessive kinds of inequality and, thereby, harm that exist in our society today. Appeals to the idea of fairness have, in this context, been effective in drawing fire onto those who seek to defend or reproduce the kinds of inequality and damage we see around us today. Perhaps one of the most critical questions we may ask today is whether our political system is inherently antisocial given, whether right or left, it has produced regressive outcomes for particular communities, localities and the less well-off. Perhaps even two decades ago we might have suggested that this question of politics relates to the way that power and influence is linked to those who own our media, and the means of production. We can call this a Marxist position, or we can describe it more accurately as a critical perspective and understand the need to go beyond the surface reality of the social and economic system around us. It is the duty of social science and social researchers to consider whether life around us is working, that social outcomes are the best they can be, as C. Wright Mills understood more than half a century ago. Social science must be allied with those who have less voice or control and who are damaged by the directed or emergent properties of the world around us. Without critique, social science is merely the handmaiden of the powerful, telling us that there is nothing to see in the wreckage of the great economy and society around us, moving us on and back to complacency. Yet what is clear to many analysts is that inequalities are growing, that many people are, in fact, damaged by life in a market economy that undervalues social skills and connections, and the weight of such analyses is growing and is being relayed globally in ways that elites and the powerful are little able to control or influence.

Antisocial acts

What many commentators, researchers, scholars and even some politicians are suggesting is that what we call 'the social' has been damaged, evacuated and hollowed out by a sustained assault. Here we need to distinguish between markets and capitalism – one can permit or use markets without seeing the fundamental role of the economy only to grow and serve those with money and influence. A progressive although often empty cry is that 'something must be done to protect society, to help people, rather than money, to thrive', although imagining what kinds of social, economic and political arrangements we need to design or engage that might help to dig us out of the antisocial moment we live in is proving more challenging. The term 'antisocial' has come to signify individuals and groups making choices to damage the lives of others – 'neighbours from hell', noisy parties or loitering youth. Yet there is another way of using the term 'antisocial', and this is in relation to the way that our social and economic systems have been set in pursuit of goals and outcomes that are antagonistic or oppositional to a more thriving, cohesive, enriching and just society. Used in this way, to talk of what is antisocial is to provoke a kind of systemic thinking about the deeper structural, ideological and planned ways in which the workings of the economy have been set against human needs (for education, good health, security from harm and thriving communities) of the bulk of society, whether conceived nationally or globally. In recent years it has become clear that the gains of social solidarity, relative material inequality, social insurance and improving wellbeing must be defended

The root of changes in the degree of social inequality that lie in a deep market orientation promoted and orchestrated by national governments, by international elites and other systems of economic governance, has yielded the demand that private wealth and unregulated corporate action is the preferred means by which society should be managed. The result of this commitment has not only been almost historically unprecedented levels of wealth held by a few, yet growing, fraction of society, but also a resulting social condition in which welfare supports are seen as outmoded or wrongheaded, while the poor are seen to have made the wrong choices or are accepted as a kind of underclass that must be corralled and maintained in subsistence conditions. Put bluntly, this market orientation is a thinly veiled means by which wealth is enlarged and protected for the very few, while the wider implication of these conditions is a withering of support for moderating and supportive mechanisms.

What is needed to think prosocially?

This book was born of an anger at the levels of social injustice that now prevail, nationally and globally, the absence of social researchers' voices, and the shutting down of social imaginations by compliant media services. We desperately need a positive social science, not in the sense of one that pretends to be value-neutral, but one capable of offering dispassionate analysis and robust research with a passionate commitment to social justice.

Social researchers often spend significant time considering problems of inequality, crime, poverty, ill health and related questions so that they rarely have time to pause in order to offer more utopian, counter-factual ideas, to step outside the 'realities' and constraints of needing to be policy-relevant or palatable for other audiences. Many of us act in ways that are self-disciplining, if not self-defeating – we make careful pre-judgements about who will listen, and this often prevents us from making proposals or running ideas that might make the world a, dare we say it, better place. This has long been the case, but in the context of contemporary forms of unparalleled inequality, ecological crisis and economic instabilities, the role and perhaps duty of social researchers is to draw on their evidence and intervene effectively in helping social conversations about these issues. The contributions you will find on the pages to follow were generated by a call to action on social problems, and a request to write in an accessible way that could also be seen as offering ideas, if not solutions, for how we might see improvements in these areas. In our conclusion (see Chapter Fifteen) we return to these ideas again, and offer some further reflections on how we might achieve a more prosocial imagination.

Note
1 It is worth noting that the ideological divide on this issue was, in fact, complex – many of those on the apparently free market right had similar views to many on the left that bailouts would enable the risk taking of these institutions again in the future, and that they should have been left to 'go to the wall'.

References
Atkinson, R. and Blandy, S. (2017) *Domestic fortress: Fear and the new home front*, Manchester: Manchester University Press.
Blyth, M. (2013) *Austerity: The history of a dangerous idea*, Oxford: Oxford University Press.
Earle, J., Moran, C. and Ward-Perkins, Z. (2016) *The econocracy: The perils of leaving economics to the experts*, Manchester: Manchester University Press.
Freire, P. (1970) *Pedagogy of the oppressed*, London: Penguin.
Friedman, M. (1993) *Why government is the problem*, Washington, DC: Hoover Institution Press.
Friedman, M. (2002) *Capitalism and freedom*, Chicago, IL: University of Chicago Press.
Halpern, D. (2010) *The hidden wealth of nations*, Cambridge: Polity.
Harvey, D. (2011) *The enigma of capital*, London: Verso
Hay, C. and Payne, A. (eds) (2015) *Civic capitalism*, London: John Wiley & Sons.
Mason, R. (2016) *Postcapitalism: A guide to our future*, London: Penguin.
Meek, J. (2016) 'Robin Hood in a time of austerity', *London Review of Books*, vol 38, no 4, pp 3-8.
Mills, C.W. (1959) *The sociological imagination*, Oxford: Oxford University Press.
Piketty, T. (2013) *Capital in the 21st century*, Cambridge, MA: Harvard University Press.
Shaxson, N. (2012) *Treasure islands: Tax havens and the men who stole the world*, London: Vintage.
Winlow, S. and Hall, S. (2013) *Rethinking social exclusion: The end of the social?*, London: Sage Publications.

Part 1
Problems

TWO

The social question and the urgency of care

Iain Wilkinson

In the 19th century 'the social question' held currency as a term denoting the misery of the poor, downtrodden and underprivileged members of society. It also represented a call to debate with the bounds our social responsibilities and our dispensation to care for the social needs of others. Those asking 'the social question' were morally and politically concerned to alleviate the 'social suffering' experienced by people forced to live on low wages and in poor housing conditions. It was further understood to signal a commitment to combat the social causes of people's poor health conditions. 'The social question' was taken to express a shared understanding that there was something deeply wrong with the material conditions under which many people were made to exist; and further, that there was an urgent need to set social arrangements in place to make their lives worth living.

We are living through times where, as Tony Judt puts it, the social question has been 'reopened' (Judt, 2010, pp 174-8). Britain is now one of the most economically and socially divided countries in the world. The net income of the top 10% of households is around 10 times higher than that of the poorest 10% (about £80,000-£90,000). Around one-fifth of the population live in poverty (living on 60% or below of the UK median disposable household income of £25,400), and for children, this rises to 28.6% (Cribb et al, 2013; ONS, 2016). For the vast majority of people (about 95% of the population) disposable incomes are either in decline or stagnating, while among the richest top 1% of households they are rising at an ever-accelerating rate. The best-off (top 1%) currently have a minimum annual household income of around £190,000, and among these the average personal annual income is estimated to be £253,923 (Dorling, 2015; see also The World Wealth and Income Database at www.wid.world).

Such pronounced levels of income inequality are accompanied by significant health inequalities. According to the most recent studies the gap in life expectancy between the most materially advantaged and most deprived parts of Britain is around 8 years (79.1 to 71.2 years) for men and 6 years (83 to 77.7 years) for women, while differences in health life expectancy (the number of years in which an individual can expect to live in relatively good health) are even more pronounced, at 16.7 years for males and 16.8 years for females (ONS, 2015). Data from the London Health Observatory reveal that differences in life expectancy could be as high as 25 years when comparing the mortality rates of some of the richest wards in Kensington and Chelsea to the poorest wards of Southwark. It is anticipated, moreover, that on current trends, these differences are all set to increase.

Some of the most alarming evidence for the declining living standards of the poorest sections of society is identified in the numbers of people experiencing conditions of food poverty. Over the last financial year The Trussell Trust handed out 1,109,309 food supplies to people who have been left hungry due to poverty (The Trussell Trust, 2016). Moreover, a recent survey by the Food and Agriculture Organization (FAO) of the United Nations (UN) on the prevalence of food insecurity experienced by adults throughout the world reveals that while as many as 4.7 million British people are now regularly going a day without eating a meal, an additional 3.7 are also classified as 'food insecure', where they are experiencing difficulties gaining access to food because of their monetary poverty (FAO, 2016).

These are among the conditions that lead some commentators to note the resemblances between contemporary British society and that of the 1920s. Income and wealth inequalities and allied social variations in life expectancy are now akin to those of the early decades of the 20th century before the creation of the modern welfare state. On many accounts, moreover, the British welfare state is in a pronounced state of crisis. It is understood to be abandoning its mid-20th century commitments to provide social security for those in need, and no longer holds that the goal of social justice should be pursued through the reduction of socioeconomic inequalities. The ever more precarious human consequences of some 30 years of unbridled neoliberalism and free market fundamentalism are all too plain to see. There is no shortage of lamentations for the loss of an earlier more mutually concerned and more caring society. There is plenty of protest being issued against the state to which we have been reduced, and the 'dog-eat-dog' values we are made to live by. There is an all too obvious need for movements of progressive social change.

In this chapter my interest lies in the contribution that sociology might make to this. We are living amidst social problems that C. Wright Mills famously portrayed as foodstuff for the 'sociological imagination'.

Following other sympathetic critics of his work, I hold that, while we should still take seriously his contention that this is a 'most needed quality of mind' for enabling us to 'grasp history and biography and the relations between the two within society', there are many deeply vexed and unresolved methodological and political problems that remain when it comes to understanding how people's 'personal troubles' might be transformed into 'public issues' (Mills, 1959, p 6). We should read Mills as operating with a vision for sociology that invites us to debate with its practices, aims and value. The arguments developed in *The sociological imagination* require much more refinement, and in some important aspects, they also need a considerable amount of updating and revision.

I offer a contribution to inquiries into the ways in which the sociological imagination might be fitted to equip us with the moral wisdom and practical initiative to involve us in creating more humane forms of society. In this, the public value of sociological research and thinking is held up for debate. I argue for an alliance between sociological inquiry and practices of caregiving. I review Jane Addams' model of 'doing sociology' as a pioneering example of what might be possible here. At the same time, I attend to some of the ongoing institutional obstacles and cultural constraints that are set to deny and oppose this. I further contend that, insofar as sociology remains divorced or disconnected from caregiving, on the model advocated by Mills, it risks leaving people frustrated with no more than a potentially demoralising critique of the structural conditions that bring harm to human life.

I begin by reviewing some of the critical debates surrounding the legacy of C. Wright Mills that have taken shape in the context of the current vogue for 'public sociology'. I then move on to make the case for a return to the types of social inquiry and sociological learning advocated by Jane Addams. I conclude by outlining some of the critical and practical challenges that are hereby set for a sociology that approaches the task of being 'prosocial' as involving the practice of care for others.

Public sociology and the frustrated legacy of Mills

One of the more significant movements in early 21st-sociology is that which seeks to advance a 'public sociology'. Following Michael Burawoy's 2004 Presidential Address to the American Sociological Association, there has been widespread and heated debate over the cultural character of contemporary sociology (Burawoy, 2005a). Here, many share in the understanding that as far as any involvement in shaping the contours of public debate over how we should live and what we should do is concerned, sociology is mired in a crisis of relevance. It is argued that professional sociology is largely divorced from any concern with communicating its findings to the public at large, and as a result, takes place as a purely academic exercise. At one level, 'public sociology' is understood to involve a commitment to render sociological knowledge communicable in a jargon-free and accessible manner so that publics might better appreciate its insights and grasp its value. At another level, it is heralded as a movement to re-politicise sociology and regenerate 'its moral fibre' (Burawoy, 2005a, p 5). It is taken to involve sociologists in normative commitments where they make open declarations of values to promote social justice and equality, and here it has come to be associated with initiatives to involve sociology in the promotion of 'democratic socialism' (Burawoy, 2005b).

C. Wright Mills is widely recognised as the 'champion' of such an approach, and it is often the case that commentators identify 'public sociology' as a movement to consolidate his legacy and advance his ambition (Burawoy, 2005a, p 9). On Mills' account sociology should provide us with a critical 'quality of mind' that enables us to link the frustrations borne in our personal lives to the wider social forces and institutional arrangements that govern our fate. He further holds that where this is achieved, it promises to transform problems experienced at an individual level into collective social issues. He contends that where sociologists are mainly preoccupied by projects of 'grand theory', methodological dispute or with marketing their expertise as data gatherers and analysts to government or industry, they are set to deny the moral relevance of sociology and to compromise its human value. He declares a commitment to sociology as an emancipatory form of critical thinking and as a humanitarian practice. Mills abhors the careerism, bureaucratisation and marketisation of academic sociology. By contrast he seeks to advance the sociological imagination and its promise as vital elements in the pursuit of progressive social and personal change.

It is in these respects that many declare themselves to be inspired by his writing to follow his example. It is argued, however, that Mills fails to provide his readers with an adequate demonstration of how to set sociology on this mission. It is frequently observed that what Mills achieves by way of his critical attitude and style is not matched by an adequate demonstration of how 'the sociological imagination' should be used as a guide to action. For example, Mills' account of the 'craft' of sociology is perceived to be dismissive of the attempt to understand how people actually experience the day-to-day trials and tribulations of their lives. He appears to be more concerned with packaging sociology so that it can occupy a space in the critical magazine culture of 'New York intellectuals' than with making it relevant to society at large (Burawoy, 2008, p 372). It is argued that Mills' sociological standpoint is that of the maverick outsider, who, as an independent intellectual, occupies a vantage point from which he is better able to grasp what is really going on the in the world. He is more concerned with writing to provoke debate among the intelligentsia than with documenting 'ordinary' people's experiences so that we can hear their voices and empathise with their personal contexts. In this regard, moreover, it is suggested that Mills sometimes appears to be proceeding as though direct association with people caught up in the immediate problems of milieu would diminish his critical effectiveness and contaminate his thoughts. While arguing for a critically engaged sociology, he takes the position of a critical outsider operating above the many practical difficulties, moral confusions and inherent messiness of everyday life.

It is further argued that his sociological imagination lacks political imagination (Burawoy, 2008, p 369). He is perceived to be more concerned with advancing a value position than with developing a praxis; that is, Mills does not offer much by way of practical guidance on how to turn social problems into public issues. His main advice to sociologists concerns their manner of writing. Mills contends that in order to be relevant they must be concerned to craft a style of writing that is broadly accessible and that works to communicate sociological insights beyond the confines of the academy. He holds that sociologists should commit themselves to developing a new 'politics of culture' where texts operate to provoke moral disquiet among their readers so as to stoke their political concern. He is essentially concerned with advancing a critical sociology that operates as a catalyst for change. He does not offer much, however, by way of instruction or advice on how to practically change society so as to make possible a fuller experience of humanity and benevolent community.

When it comes to the vital question of 'how, then, should we live and what should we do?', Mills' sociological imagination lacks moral relevance. While advocating a standpoint of moral concern he does not offer much by way of advice on how to proceed in terms of moral action. While encouraging sociologists to declare value positions that stand critically opposed to the dehumanising conditions under which many people are made to live, Mills does not appear to be concerned with equipping sociology to move beyond a position of protest. On his model, sociology is chiefly concerned with proclaiming value positions that are set against the ways we live now; he does not appear to be worried by the need to practically demonstrate how we should live differently so as to realise more humane forms of society.

Above all else, Mills is preoccupied with the production of critique. However, what he achieves by way of a critical rebellion against 'mainstream' academic sociology is not matched by an adequate demonstration of an alternative form of emancipatory practice. In this regard it might be said that his appeal lies more in his status as a radical outsider than as a model social reformer. He has more to say about what he is against than what he is for. Insofar as he is taken as an example for 'public sociology', there is a risk that this is cast more as a means to sound alarms over what is wrong with the world than as a commitment to develop sociology for the purpose of realising alternative and better social arrangements. In an earlier account of 'public sociology', and one from which Mills claimed to draw inspiration, this was explicitly recognised as a risk that should be faced head on. Here, moreover, it was held that, properly conceived, and so as to better understand our human social condition, sociology should be troubled by an active engagement with how human social life is made possible through committed practices of care.

Jane Addams and the first public sociology

In order to grasp the intellectual currents and tensions running through Mills' thought, it is important to understand that he is seeking to reinvigorate a classical tradition of American pragmatism, and especially the components of this that are committed to advance models of social democracy along the lines advocated by John Dewey. It can be argued that Mills understood the critical spirit of American pragmatism to have been curtailed by its failure to develop a sufficiently elaborated theoretical analysis of presiding structures of inequality within modern capitalism, and that this was the reason that he devoted himself to producing works of critique. If this is the case, however, one might argue that he travelled too far in this direction, for Mills appears to have lost sight of some of the founding premises on which pragmatist traditions of social inquiry are based, and by which they aim to promote more effective forms of social democracy. On this view, those concerned with 'public sociology' might worry not so much about the character of their critical thinking, but more about their conceptions of how to set sociology in practice. Moreover, this is the ground on which Jane Addams sought to locate her approach to 'doing sociology'.

Recent attempts to rehabilitate the status of Jane Addams as a major figure in classical sociology have underlined the ways in which her activities in the Hull-House settlement on the Near West Side of Chicago between 1889 and 1935 were expressly concerned with an attempt to realise the practice of social democracy along the lines advocated by John Dewey. Indeed, it is noted that Dewey credited Jane Addams with demonstrating how his philosophy should be carried out as a practicable 'way of life' (Seigfried, 1999, p 219). From her writing in works such as *Democracy and social ethics* (2002 [1902]), moreover, Addams' sociology is recognised as being founded on a deep reflection on Dewey's ideal of a democratic community that seeks to solve its problems and promote its interests through a quest for mutual sympathy and shared experiential understanding.

Addams holds that, when set to work in universities as an academic discipline, sociology not only evades its object of study, but also distances itself from the means to acquire adequate knowledge of society. On her model, sociology should operate within social settlements with the aim of putting theory to the test in action. She argues:

> The most pressing problem of modern life is that of a reconstruction and reorganization of the knowledge we possess.... The settlement stands for application as opposed to research, for emotion as opposed to abstraction, for universal interest as opposed to specialization. (Addams, 1965 [1899], pp 186-7)

Addams is concerned with far more than an attempt to apply sociology to the attempt to improve the lives of people forced to live in disease-ridden slums on the low wages of sweated labour. In this respect, her aims and objectives are misunderstood where she is cast as a pioneer of 'social work' (Wilkinson, 2013). Indeed, as Eric Schneiderhan (2011) points out, she is concerned to distance her activities from any state-sponsored initiatives to govern the poor. Addams is not only inspired by humanitarian concern, but also by a commitment to actively involve herself and her associates in the perplexities endured by others whereby they are set to learn from conflicted social experience. She advocates a sociology that requires an active participation in the problems of a community, on the understanding that the acquisition of knowledge of society requires one to be involved in enactments of human value whereby the life of society is made possible.

In her seminal biographical work, *Twenty years at Hull-House* (1998 [1910]), Addams explains that, as far as any attempt to understand 'the social question' is concerned, caregiving should be set as a core purpose of sociology. While Hull-House was initially set up as a settlement house to provide educational opportunities for the local community, Addams quickly found that many other problems were brought to her door. She writes:

> In addition to the neighbors who responded to the receptions and classes we found those that were too battered to care for them. To these, however, was left that susceptibility to the bare offices of humanity which raises such offices to a bond of fellowship. From the first it seemed understood that we were ready to perform the humblest neighbourhood services. We were asked to wash new-born babies, and to prepare the dead for burial, to nurse the sick, and to "mind the children". (Adams, 1998 [1910], p 75)

She then describes how, having made space available in Hull-House for a kindergarten, a public bathhouse, a public kitchen and coffee house, along with colleagues such as Ellen Gates Starr, Annie Marion MacLean and Florence Kelley, she was involved in more concerted political campaigns against insanitary living conditions and for improved wages, workers' health and safety and shorter working days. Addams' sociological approach was founded on an embodied openness to the experiences of others and on material acts of care. By actively caring for the needs of particular individuals, she was drawn into a caregiving commitment to the betterment of society. This required a work of 'active listening' to others (Hamington, 2004). It was also carried out with the aim of cultivating the moral solidarities, practices of civic participation and friendships through which 'caring knowledge' was applied in action both for the care of people and for promoting the good of society. Here caregiving is identified as a phronesis, that is, a means by which one might acquire the moral and practical wisdom to pursue the art of living socially. The pursuit of sociological understanding is taken to require the pedagogy of caregiving, and all the more so if this sets a priority on being a prosocial endeavour.

For discussion

In his call for sociologists to engage in 'public sociology', Michael Burawoy holds that insofar as this is presented as a critical 'intervention' in the contemporary culture and practice of sociology, it exposes the beleaguered state of this discipline in contexts where neoliberal market values now command the organisation and ethos of the academy. Insofar as sociology is divorced from activism, this is not only a consequence of concerted drives to 'professionalise' its practice so that it operates as an academic science above the fray of politics, but also a result of the ways in which it is packaged and sealed for the delivery of marketable degree courses. At one level, the call for a more 'public sociology' challenges sociologists to critically reflect on the ways in which their research activities, practices of knowledge production and adopted modes of teaching are disciplined by the presiding values of the modern academy. Is it possible to engage in 'doing sociology' in institutional settings where its practice is conformed to the rules of bureaucratic procedure and the sale of education as a mass commodity?

Addams did not see any need to associate herself with the University of Chicago's Department of Sociology, and further feared that the meaning and value of her work would be corrupted if it was cast as some kind of 'laboratory experiment'. Addams declined Albion Small's invitation to take up a faculty position on the grounds that she could not conform to its philosophy of education. She further held that, if the funding arrangements of Hull-House got caught up with those of the university, her activities were likely to be compromised and disciplined by capitalist business interests. Moreover, as Hull-House became more involved in the activities of the trade union movement, especially following the violent state suppression of the Pullman strike of 1894, Addams' 'fellowship with trade unions' was one of the reasons for the University of Chicago taking steps to distance itself from her activities (see Wilkinson and Kleinman, 2016, pp 170-4). Mary Jo Deegan (1988, pp 167-90) contends that if Addams had been employed by the University of Chicago, it is very likely that she would have been sacked from her post, as at this time this institution moved to dismiss radicals that upset their funders, and many of the latter were drawn from local industrialists and business leaders who were in conflict with the trade unions.

Given the renewed emphasis on civic engagement, community-based learning and community-based research in some contemporary North American universities, it might be argued that Addams would find a more welcoming response to her work in the current century. Certainly it is the case that some of those working in these new initiatives are inclined to trace their lineage back to the activities of Hull-House. At the same time, however, these remain largely divorced from academic sociology, and here the very fact that a debate exists on whether, and if so how, sociology should hold public relevance is understood to bear testimony to the extent to which it is now is overrun by career values and reward structures that militate against its practitioners setting a priority on civic engagement. Indeed, in a recent article, Emily Kane (2015) writes from the premise that while a dialogue between sociologists involved in 'the public sociology debate' and those involved in community-based research may be desirable, for the most part, the latter have no need for this, while the former remain mired in an intradisciplinary dispute of their own making. Indeed, if one was to take a cynical view here, one might highlight the extent to which 'the public sociology debate' has operated more to create a frenzy of peer-reviewed article writing on the vexed state of academic sociology than it has to clear a space for new sociological practices of civic engagement.

The 'public sociology debate' has drawn renewed attention to the agonised state of sociology. Arguably, as a discipline, sociology has never been at ease with itself; many of its theoretical and methodological developments have thrived on its propensity to generate disagreements over its guiding values and domain interests. It is a deeply conflicted field of study. There has never been any agreement within the discipline on how to think sociologically or on how sociological research should be carried out in practice. If those advocating a 'public sociology' aim to persuade their peers to fall into line beside them, no doubt they shall fail. It has been readily dismissed as a 'populist fad', 'fast-food social science' and as an argument for a 'partisan profession' that is set to achieve little besides an undermining of the legitimacy of sociology as a professional practice (Holmwood, 2007).

There can be no doubt, however, that many of those associated with sociology have either lost sight of 'the social question', or rather, see no need to address this as a prime concern. In our times 'the social' has become a fuzzy concept and an abstraction that seems far removed from real persons who possess real needs and do real things. It has been morally neutralised. C. Wright Mills responded to this with protest, but arguably this left us with no more than a position of protest. While the 'public sociology debate' has served as a context in which to review Mills' legacy and to refine his account of the conditions and tendencies within the sociological field, arguably it amounts to yet another reprise of his complaint. It is a lament for moral relevance.

Addams held that, when pursued as an end in itself, critique lacks human value and social commitment. A critical sociology that occupies a position above the fray makes no advance towards realising the conditions that might enable people to make life worth living. As a critical pragmatist she held that the value of our sociological thinking should be sought in its 'cash value', that is, in the experiences that it makes possible and in the ways it is mobilised in action. She not only operated in moral disagreement with sociologies that evaded this test of value, but also believed that insofar as sociologists have no foundational concern in the inherently perplexing, morally conflicted and practically frustrating experience of social life, they are evading their object of their study, at least, that is, in terms of how society matters for people. Through her practice of caregiving she not only sought to make sociology hold moral relevance, but also have it equipped with an understanding hewn from conflicted moral experience of social life.

As we take stock of the way we live now and where we venture to ask 'what is to be done?', I urge us to take seriously Addams' (1965 [1999], p 186) contention that 'the most pressing problem of modern life is that of a reconstruction and reorganization of the knowledge we possess.' For sociologists, this must incorporate a sociological self-understanding that continually works to clarify the social conditions under which they operate and by which their work is set to be valued. Addams argues, moreover, that this cannot be accomplished through bookish contemplation, but rather, requires forms of thought forged in commitments to social care in action. The sociological imagination needs to locate its promise in what is made possible for people through 'doing sociology'. We need to question once again how this can be done, and where it is possible, do it.

References

Addams, J. (1965 [1899]) 'The subjective necessity for the social settlements', in C. Lasch (ed) *The social thought of Jane Addams*, Indianapolis, IN: The Bobbs-Merrill Company.

Addams, J. (1998 [1910]) *Twenty years at Hull-House*, New York: Penguin.

Addams, J. (2002 [1902]) *Democracy and social ethics*, Urbana and Chicago, IL: University of Illinois.

Burawoy, M. (2005a) 'For public sociology', *American Sociological Review*, vol 70, no 1, pp 4-28.

Burawoy, M. (2005b) 'The return of the repressed: Recovering the public face of US sociology, one hundred years on', *The Annals of the American Academy of Political and Social Science*, vol 600, no 1, pp 68-85.

Burawoy, M. (2008) 'Open letter to C. Wright Mills', *Antipode*, vol 40, no 3, pp 365-75.

Cribb, J., Hood, A., Joyce, R. and Phillips, D. (2013) *Living standards, poverty and inequality in the UK: 2013*, IFS Report R81, London: Institute for Fiscal Studies.

Deegan, M.J. (1988) *Jane Addams and the men of the Chicago School, 1892–1918*, New Brunswick, NJ: Transaction Books.

Dorling, D. (2015) 'Income inequality in the UK: Comparisons with five large Western European countries and the USA', *Applied Geography*, vol61, pp 24-34.

FAO (Food and Agricultural Organization) of the UN (United Nations) (2016) *Methods for estimating comparable prevalence of rates of food insecurity experienced by adults throughout the world: Technical report*, Rome: FAO.

Hamington, M. (2004) *Embodied care: Jane Addams, Maurice Merleau-Ponty, and feminist ethics*, Urbana and Chicago, IL: University of Illinois Press.

Holmwood, J. (2007) 'Sociology as public discourse and professional practice: A critique of Michael Burawoy', *Sociological Theory*, vol 25, no 1, pp 46-66.

Judt, T. (2010) *Ill fares the land*, London: Penguin.

Kane, E. (2015) 'The baby and the bathwater: Balancing disciplinary debates and community engagement to advance student interest in publicly engaged sociology', *Humanity & Society*, vol 40, no 1, pp 43–63.

Livingston, J. (2009) 'Their Great Depression and ours', *Challenge* vol 52, no 3, pp 34-51.

Mills, C.W. (1959) *The sociological imagination*, Oxford: Oxford University Press.

ONS (Office for National Statistics) (2015) *The effects of taxes and benefits on household income: Financial year ending 2014*, London: HMSO.

ONS (2016) *Household disposable income and inequality: Financial year ending 2015*, London: HMSO.

Schneiderhan, E. (2011) 'Pragmatism and empirical sociology: The case of Jane Addams and Hull-House, 1889-1895', *Theory and Society*, vol 40, no 6, pp 589-617.

Seigfried, C.H. (1999) 'Socializing democracy: Jane Addams and John Dewey', *Philosophy of the Social Sciences*, vol 29, no 2, pp 207-30.

Trussell Trust, The (2016) 'Latest stats' (www.trusselltrust.org/news-and-blog/latest-stats/).

Wilkinson, I. (2013) 'With and beyond Mills: Social suffering and the sociological imagination', *Cultural Studies <-> Critical Methodologies*, vol 12, no 3, pp 182-91.

Wilkinson, I. and Kleinman, A. (2016) *A passion for society, How we think about human suffering*, Berkeley, CA: University of California Press.

THREE

Better politics: Narratives of indignation and the possibility of a prosocial politics

Keith Jacobs

My motivation for writing this chapter is that we require a truthful understanding of politics that admits the complex and at times very contradictory subject positions that we adhere to. For all of us concerned about the *modus operandi* of politics and the seeming unwillingness of governments to ameliorate widening inequality or mitigate the impact of climate change, there is always a temptation to disengage from contemporary political struggles and instead expend time postulating what a 'post-neoliberal' future might entail.

In an exploration of neoliberalism, the politics of resistance and prosocial forms of engagement, I argue that a useful starting point is to interrogate the subject positions we adopt to understand the contemporary political era. Often these rely on a depiction of an economic and social crisis accentuated by neoliberalism, a sense of moral outrage and the attribution of culpability on to those we consider responsible. While such subject positions might assuage our yearning to feel indignant about what we don't like, they fall short as a starting point for the development of an adequate sociological understanding. Drawing on psychoanalytical literature and other sources, I consider the risks of relying on an abstracted form of neoliberalism and a defensive strategy of resistance as a foundation for the development of more prosocial forms of politics.

Among the arguments set out in this chapter is that our despondency at the magnitude of the prevailing economic and societal challenges, such as global warming, inequality and social isolation, encourages us to rely on an overly simplistic understanding of a neoliberal hegemonic project and accompanying binaries of 'good' and 'bad', 'us' and 'them'. Furthermore, we assume that a strategy of resistance is a radical position, even though it may eventuate in a defensive posture that requires only 'others' to change, or even result in a form of disengagement from prosocial forms of politics. Rather than see neoliberalism as something concocted by 'others', we must reconcile our own complicity in neoliberal practices. It may be seductively appealing to apportion blame on to all things 'neoliberal' and adopt a defensive form of resistance, but ultimately they are futile responses.

Neoliberalism

Is our current preoccupation with detesting forms of neoliberalism a badge of identity and a celebratory endpoint? Should we instead view resistance as a necessary starting point for prosocial interventions but not a sufficient one for its attainment? In this opening part of my chapter I attend to the 'neoliberal' thesis that is now the dominant explanation for an understanding of the contemporary era. It has become *de rigueur* for those critical of the current era to cite neoliberalism as a driving force, and the key writers most identified with this critique include David Harvey (2010, 2014), the late Stuart Hall, Doreen Massey, Jamie Peck and Mike Rustin (see Hall et al, 2013 and Peck et al, 2014).

Neoliberalism is often used by these and other scholars to denote the political settlement secured in the 1980s by finance industries and wealthy elites who articulated a 'common-sense' ideology purporting that generous welfare provision and trade union power were responsible for economic malaise and that a restoration of market-based principles was required to restore economic prosperity. Proponents of neoliberalism purport that governments should weaken the bargaining capacity of trade unions, dismantle regulatory controls imposed on financial industries and establish opportunities for commercial agencies to deliver welfare services. Powerful media conglomerates determined to maintain their influence on the political class also play an important role in the reporting of news and provision of commentary sympathetic to neoliberal ideals.

The neoliberal ascendency has been documented and researched by writers such as Joseph Stiglitz and Thomas Piketty, who have noted the widening gap between the rich and poor and the way in which inequality has affected our sense of identity and limited our political imagination. There is plenty of scholarship that has drawn out the dysfunctional components of neoliberalism and how governments have been orchestrating the advance of wealthy elites. Doreen Massey, drawing on the work of Karl Polanyi, has claimed that the existing neoliberal settlement has been achieved through state activity, in rules, regulations and administration, while 'the market has been the outcome of a conscious and often violent intervention on the part of government which imposed the market organisation on society for non-economic ends' (Massey, 2013, p 17).

Opposition to neoliberal government policies is often constituted on the premise that, up until the mid-1970s, governments were more willing to redress social and economic inequality. It has been claimed, for example, that from the mid-1940s to the mid-1970s, governments adhered to the ideal of forms of universal welfare provision and Keynesian-informed economics. The late Tony Judt is one of many writers who argued for a return to the social democratic forms of politics that prevailed during the 1970s. As he wrote in his book *Ill fares the land*, the 1970s, despite obvious shortcomings, was a period when there was less social inequality and governments were more disposed to maintain wage levels. Judt, while perhaps overly nostalgic about the political settlement in place for most of the 1970s, recognised the importance of engagement with state institutions. Increasingly, we adhere to the fantasy that some form of crisis is inevitable and the neoliberal order will collapse. My misgiving with this 'crisis-is-inevitable thesis' is that it commits us to focus primarily on future-orientated matters rather than attending to challenges that confront us now.

Bob Jessop (2013, p 134) provided a more nuanced view of what a crisis entails. In his words, 'crises are multifaceted phenomena that invite multiple approaches from different entry points and standpoints.' His description serves as a reminder that any attempt to establish a singular response to the crisis of neoliberalism is likely to fall short. Jessop's notion of crisis is relevant when we consider the standpoint adopted by many on the left who view neoliberalism as a totalising political project. It is not unusual, then, to see neoliberalism as a Leviathan operation that we have little influence over. We link up different variegated happenings and understand it as features of a 'system'. Whatever happens we call it 'neoliberal'. Contradictory forms of politics and inconsistencies are all seen as a feature of the system. This may be one way to understand the contemporary era and the interconnections between different aspects of the economy and the connections to the social, but it is a limited explanation.

While 'neoliberalism' is helpful for a description of the broad direction of government policy, there are other problematic aspects in seeing all of what is taking place within society as somehow reducible to a system (Peck, 2013). While not wishing to go so far as to suggest that the very notion of a system constitutes a categorical error, it is, like all sociologically based concepts, a construction that we devise and then deploy to understand and connect different events and practices.

'Neoliberalism' also performs as a naming device that we rely on to negotiate aspects of what we don't like socially and politically, and to avoid accepting our agency within such social and political happenings.

If we accept that neoliberalism is a concept that we use to make sense of politics and to understand our frustrations, we can consider a more nuanced version of contemporary society that dispenses with the idea of neoliberalism as some autonomous system. As stated earlier, we invest great store in these abstracted systems for they enable us to carry on as we have always done as well as to serve as a construct we can channel our indignation and disillusion towards. It is our way of making sense of and living in the world. It is a construction but, psychically speaking, a necessary one.

There are a number of scholars who have attended to the problematic aspects of framing neoliberalism as an abstract entity. Here my argument overlaps with the work of Barnett (2005, 2010), who has argued that while criticisms of neoliberalism offer a compelling moral narrative, they often 'remain chronically constricted in their capacity to reflect seriously on questions of institutional design, political organisation and economic coordination' (2005, p 10).

The constriction that Barnett identifies may be because scholarship has been too attentive to the symbolic and ideational aspects of neoliberalism, and this distracts us from attending to its specific practices. Discussions of neoliberalism that are not connected to a location or point in time may inadvertently mislead us about the actual possibilities for reform. The attempt to posit a singular reality of 'neoliberalism' encourages us to seek reforms that are broad-ranging and lacking specificity.

Being stuck in the present?

Ruth Levitas (2013) argues for a form of utopian thinking. Without a consideration of alternative social futures, she argues that we risk being stuck in the present, unable to get beyond the day-to-day issues that permeate the political landscape. Of course, Levitas is making an important point – there is always a need to consider the type of society we would like to forge, and without this mode of thought we remain 'stuck'. And yet there are risks in moralistic denunciation and not speculating as to what the future might entail. Not only is this form of futurist thinking often opaque, but it also falls short in terms of specificity. Consider, for example, Enroth (2014, p 71), who is not untypical when he wrote that 'we need a sociological imagination that stretches beyond societies and a political imaginary that can do without the presuppositions of collectivities.' Yet Enroth provides no detail as to what this sociological imagination entails or what will eventuate. Another vision of what a political imaginary should entail is set out by Massey and Rustin (2015, p 220), who write that:

> ... the challenge, after these years of neoliberal ascendancy, is to develop ways of thinking and feeling which can bring about connections between those engaged in them. There needs to be both respect for diversity, for the specificities of each sphere of life, and a recognition of need to be fundamental guiding conceptions of fairness, equality and 'deep democracy'.

Again, it is difficult to take issue with this aspiration, but Massey and Rustin, like Enroth, are unable to provide any pointers as to how this might be achieved.

Perhaps a more useful way to proceed is to focus on the practices that are enacted rather than neoliberalism's symbolic effects. Consider, for example, Featherstone (2015), who points out that too often critics of neoliberalism have constructed a narrative about how economic and political elites partake in a hegemonic political project that is intended to exploit the poor and dispossessed. We are enticed to think that the task for those critical of neoliberalism is to resist this hegemonic project through critique and to posit alternative political strategies. The problem with this construction of neoliberalism is that it casts the public into two distinct camps: those who are upholders of the neoliberal project and those who are oppressed by or opposed to neoliberalism. Clearly we require a less abstracted account of the neoliberal project that attends to what Featherstone (2015) has termed the 'practices' of power. Such an account, while not entirely dispensing with neoliberalism *per se*, does emphasise the diverse local struggles that are a feature of all aspects of politics.

Expending too much time setting out a vision of the post-neoliberal future may detract from what I consider to be more pressing challenges. Envisaging a post-neoliberal world takes us away from some of the more difficult and immediate concerns of the present, but more importantly, such future-orientated thinking hinges on a framing of politics that presupposes the existence of a neoliberal entity or system. Here the work of Gibson-Graham (2006, p xxii) is helpful. Gibson-Graham point out that such thinking about the need for some future revolution is in some way flawed, as it presupposes that it would 'occur in a time-world discontinuous with this one, so it was not possible to talk about steps and strategies for getting there.' Gibson-Graham make a compelling case for a politics of the *here and now* that is connected to existing struggles.

Framing neoliberalism as an entity that is constituted and enacted by others is, psychically at least, helpful, because it enables us to disassociate from what we don't like, see ourselves as not complicit or responsible for contemporary problems, and allows us to expend time and energy in a strategy of resistance. It is the bankers, we say, that are culpable for the financial crisis, the Conservative government for the housing crisis, and ruthless business leaders for the precarious employment conditions many people now endure. We reconcile our fears and frustrations by apportioning the blame on to others, whether they are bankers, politicians or media owners. I don't want to suggest that these 'others' are not in some way responsible; they are. My point is that this attribution is an easy response as it assuages feelings of guilt and helps us to feel more comfortable about adopting cynical or detached positions.

Such a subject position has appeal as it enables 'us' to separate ourselves from what is happening and continue as before without due consideration of our own agency to change or influence current problems and what this agency might entail. If we reject the narrative that posits all that is bad can be offloaded on to a system that we term 'neoliberalism', there are two standpoints we might consider. We can accept that we are in part responsible for what is happening and take steps accordingly. Alternatively, we can convince ourselves that we are not responsible in any way and continue to indulge in a form of resistance where everyone else is expected to change but not ourselves.

The lens of psychoanalysis

What would happen if we desist from seeing politics through the lens of a neoliberal explanatory frame? Would our forms of political engagement alter? In a recent essay on psychoanalysis, Pick (2015, p 125) writes about how political critique can all too easily rely on 'complacent occlusions of reality'. For Pick, these occlusions apply both to left-orientated forms of 'liberal cynicism' as well as 'self-congratulatory capitalism'. The important point here is that what we think of as politics to some extent rests on our preconceived fantasies about our role in the world and our engagement with others.

For the purposes of this chapter I am not interested in the normative aspects of psychoanalysis or any of the specific claims by its exponents as to its therapeutic value. Rather, my interest is in whether its conceptual vocabulary might offer us a way to understand our contemporary reality. However, I recognise that there is a normative component that underpins much of the psychoanalytic literature, and we should always be cautious of any universal claim made by its advocates in relation to its efficacy. This noted that, at its best, the concepts of psychoanalysis can serve to encourage us to question rigid or long-held subject positions as well as the limitations of seeing political 'reality' as somehow entirely 'outside' of ourselves.

An exploration of psychoanalysis and its utility for an understanding of politics was the focus of Jacqueline Rose's 'States of fantasy' (1996). In this essay she argued that we rarely consider the role performed by our fantasies and how they function as a psychic defence to enable us to disassociate from all that we don't like. As Rose writes, 'in psychoanalytical language, resistance as a concept is far closer to defensiveness than to freedom; you resist when you don't want to budge' (Rose, 1996, p 5). She went on to write, 'it is a form of redemptive fantasy in itself to believe that, in a world of publically engaged action, you can step forth free of mental embarrassment' (Rose, 1996, p 8). Rose, if I understand her correctly, is suggesting that our fear of mental embarrassment is often our motive here. In other words, our desire to rid ourselves of any feeling that we may be complicit in what we don't like encourages us to adopt a defensive form of resistance.

Zizek (2012) offers a similar perspective. He suggests that we frame progressive politics in terms of production and the economy rather than our own subjectivities, and engage in a form of solipsism where we disassociate our connections with others. As Zizek has written, 'the stepping out of (what we experience as ideology) is the very form of our enslavement' (Zizek, 2012, p 6). For Zizek, the 'stepping out' is what we think will provide us with personal freedom, but it has the opposite effect. It confines us to a solitary form of engagement with the political. Zizek is suggesting that our disavowal diminishes our capacity to engage in the here-and-now of political struggle.

Both Rose and Zizek suggest that our stand of resistance is a necessary subject position for psychic survival in the modern world. We can also draw from the writings of Stephen Frosh (2010), who has written that 'the resistive power of the "other" is what makes the subject's existence possible, marking out a space which is "real" in the sense of being beyond the subject's control. This continuous process of assertion and resistance is what constitutes the possibility of a stable kind of life' (Frosh, 2010, p 166). Frosh helps us to see that 'resistance' is not simply a passage to freedom, as assumed by many on the left, but also linked to our inclinations to repeat, act obtrusively and stay stuck in a mode of resignation. Perhaps we have to attend to our defensive modes of engagement and recognise that resistance is not such a radical form of politics as we would like to believe. As Frosh writes, resistance 'is both an obstacle to change and an indication of where change is most needed' (Frosh, 2010, p 167). Resistance should be seen both as a positive starting point but also as a form of defensiveness that can lead to inaction.

The writings of Rose, Frosh and Zizek attend to our troubling thoughts, our unconscious drives and the ease to which we appear to hold on to contradictory beliefs. Most importantly, their work foregrounds the ways that we are internally divided and unstable subjects who can identify with and at the same time resist change. It is in foregrounding the unconscious as a concept for understanding action that differentiates psychoanalysis from other forms of critically inspired theory. We do not wish to know too much about our own culpability in what is happening, but choose instead to attach ourselves to systems of belief that offer us comfort or allow us to blame others and attribute all that is 'bad' on to them. Yet, as psychoanalysis attests to so well, these are ways in which we might avoid facing up to difficult realities by projecting on to others all the things we don't like, and seeing ourselves as a victim of others' actions.

The modern university

One way to illustrate my argument is to consider the neoliberal ideology that has taken hold of many working in universities. Marina Warner, in an article for the *London Review of Books* (Warner, 2015), has described her experiences of attending to the changing requirements of senior administrators while employed at the University of Essex. Warner argues that contemporary universities are jettisoning long-established values about independent forms of scholarship and collegiality in favour of competition and other neoliberal practices. Yet, while Warner's account of her experiences may ring true for many, is it not the case that the 'neoliberal' university survives because of the tacit consent of those who work in it? I am aware that my own response, and of others I know, is to 'manage' experiences by displaying opposition, but at the same time operating in accordance to the expectations of the university. It is as if I believe that what is happening has little to do with me because others have imposed it. This internalisation serves as a survival mechanism, making it possible to vent my disquiet but at the same not put at risk my position within the university. The example might offer us an insight to a larger political context, that is, 'we' (people in privileged positions) rarely want to act on the power we have, choosing instead to dwell on our lack of influence and to turn this into an excuse that our own actions would make no difference. The argument I have put forward is that for the privileged, moral indignation serves as an endpoint that prevents us from taking appropriate action.

Conclusion: advancing prosocial politics

Up to this point in this chapter I have considered the limitations of an abstracted form of neoliberalism, and given an explanation of resistance as a standpoint for reform. In this conclusion I attend (albeit briefly) to setting out the forms of engagement that might advance the prosocial. We can dispense with managerialism and the old-style bureaucratic forms of government, as both are too unwieldy as instruments of change. As the editors of this volume point out in their introductory chapter (Chapter One), altruistic-inspired interventions that seek to challenge neoliberal and market-based practices can be termed 'prosocial'. The challenge for those seeking to pursue prosocial inventions is to move beyond an expression of indignation and attend to scoping the political alternatives that have a chance of becoming actualised. A useful lead is provided by Simon Critchley (2012), who writes that we can rethink our way of seeing the world. Rather than configure ourselves as atomised individuals set aside from each other, we might instead dwell on our shared aspirations and the ineluctable truth that our survival depends on a collective response to the challenges that confront us all. Other vantage points can be transformative, as it is through acts of care and reciprocity that provide us with our best hope for more prosocial forms of engagement. Privileging our sense of agency enables us to rethink not only what constitutes neoliberalism, but to disregard the notion that it somehow operates independently of our actions.

Solidarity and trust is established through reciprocity and relational forms of care, and this can be found within existing institutions such as the health services, welfare providers and other caring agencies. Williams et al (2014) alert us to the opportunities for progressive reform within these agencies and our need to be vigilant to these. As they write, 'any dismissal of those grasping the opportunities at hand to work interstially and symbiotically towards progressive ends is itself a potential undermining of progressive potential – it is buying into a false dichotomy in which participation equals accommodative compromise, whilst resistance equals non involvement with the state' (Williams et al, 2014, p 2804). A similar argument has been set out by Wright (2011), who highlights the need to attend to institutional design and strategies that are a prerequisite for reform. Yet he also offers precautionary advice by suggesting that we avoid the temptation to be a cheerleader, uncritically extolling the virtues of promising experiments (Wright, 2011).

A valuable contribution is made by Gibson-Graham in the book *A postcapitalist politics*, arguing that:

> … we were originally trained to see and represent a social object (the capitalist economy) structured by concentrations of power and qualified by deficiencies of morality and desirability…. We have more recently come to understand that its repoliticisation requires cultivating ourselves as subjects who can imagine and enact a new economic politics. (Gibson-Graham, 2006, p xxviii)

Gibson-Graham also suggest that the political action must be in the 'here and now in myriad projects of alternative economic activism' (pp vi–vii), seeing the tendency 'to constitute "the" economy as a singular capitalist system or space rather than as a zone of cohabitation and contestation among multiple economic forms; and the tendency to lodge faith in accurate representation that guaranteed and stabilised the prevailing substantive framings.'

My chapter addresses how we make sense of politics, what can be termed the 'ideology of neoliberalism', and the consequences of political disengagement. Among the arguments I have put forward is that the current global configurations are not unified but are instead a multitude of variegated practices that we choose to label 'neoliberal'. Furthermore, disengagement, often in the form of 'resistance', provides a base for psychic survival by enabling us to apportion blame on others and absolve ourselves of responsibility. Such a position often encourages us to adopt a cynical response leading to withdrawal. We should avoid simplistic characterisation of politics and so, too, we should be weary of binaries that categorise politics in terms of resistance and oppression.

As to the political possibilities for prosocial forms of engagement set out by Williams et al, Wright and others, we have to be attentive to the *here and now* of politics and also be vigilant to the ways that large corporations and governments pursue regressive ends in forms of language that mask intent. Consider, for example, the way that collective and environmental ideas are often appropriated by commercial businesses for their own ends. Finally, the need to pursue prosocial politics is clear. The consequences of political involvement camouflaged under the banner of resistance are far-reaching. While the pursuit of a celebratory mode of resistance enables us to apportion blame on others and absolve our own responsibilities, it ends up as a response that is likely to lead to disengagement. Both the assignation of blame on to all things 'neoliberal' and proclamations of 'resistance' have a seductive appeal, but they are ultimately futile gestures. Confronting and living with the psychic discomfort of our complicity in problematic policies and practices, as well as the nature and scope of our agency in confronting and changing such problems, is a necessary precondition for establishing more enduring prosocial forms of politics.

Acknowledgements

The arguments set out in this chapter were first presented at 'A conversation on the prosocial' Annual Inclusive Societies Meeting that took place at the University of Sheffield, 6-7 July 2015. My thanks to Rowland Atkinson for his invitation to present a paper, and also to Kesherie Gurung for her helpful suggestions on a first draft.

References

Barnett, C. (2005) 'Critical review: The consolations of neoliberalism', *Geoforum*, vol 36, pp 7-12.

Barnett, C. (2010) 'Publics and markets: What's wrong with neoliberalism?', in S. Smith, R. Pain, S. Marston and J.P. Jones III (eds) *The Sage handbook of social geography*, London: Sage Publications, pp 269-96.

Critchley, S. (2012) *Infinitely demanding: Ethics of commitment, politics of resistance*, London: Verso.

Enroth, H. (2014) 'Governance: The art of governing after governmentality', *European Journal of Social Theory*, vol 17, no 1, pp 60-76.

Featherstone, D. (2015) 'Thinking the crisis politically: Lineages of resistance to neo-liberalism and the politics of the present conjuncture', *Space and Polity*, vol 19, no 1, pp 12-30.

Frosh, S. (2010) *Psychoanalysis outside the clinic*, Basingstoke: Palgrave Macmillan.

Gibson-Graham, J.K. [Julie Graham and Katherine Gibson] (2006) *A postcapitalist politics*, Minneapolis, MN: University of Minnesota Press.

Hall, S., Massey, D. and Rustin, M. (2013) 'After neoliberalism: Analysing the present', *Soundings: A Journal of Politics and Culture*, vol 53, no 1, pp 8-22.

Harvey, D. (2010) *The enigma of capital*, London: Profile.

Harvey, D. (2014) *A brief history of neoliberalism*, Oxford: Oxford University Press.

Jessop, B. (2013) 'Recovered imaginaries, imagined recoveries: A cultural political economy of crisis construals and crisis management in the North Atlantic financial crisis', in M. Benner (ed) *Before and beyond the global economic crisis: Economics, politics and settlement*, Cheltenham: Edward Elgar Publishing Ltd, p 234.

Levitas, R. (2013) *Utopia as method*, Basingstoke: Palgrave Macmillan.

Massey D. (2013) *Landscape/space/politics: An essay* (https://thefutureoflandscape.wordpress.com/landscapespacepolitics-an-essay/).

Massey, D. and Rustin, M. (2015) 'Displacing neoliberalism', in S. Hall, D. Massey and M. Rustin (eds) *After neoliberalism*, London: Lawrence & Wishart, pp 191-221.

Peck, J. (2013) 'Explaining (with) neoliberalism', *Territory, Politics, Governance*, vol 1, no 2, pp 132-57.

Peck, J., Massey, D., Gibson, K. and Lawson, V. (2014) 'Symposium: The Kilburn Manifesto: After Neoliberalism?', *Environment and Planning A*, vol 46, no 9, pp 2033-49.

Pick, D. (2015) *Psychoanalysis: A very short introduction*, Oxford: Oxford University Press.

Rose, J. (1996) *States of fantasy: The 1994 Clarendon Lectures*, Oxford: Oxford University Press.

Warner, M. (2015) 'Learning my lesson', *London Review of Books*, vol 37, no 6, pp 8-14 (www.lrb.co.uk/v37/n06/marina-warner/learning-my-lesson).

Williams, A., Goodwin, M. and Cloke, P. (2014) 'Neoliberalism, big society and progressive localism', *Environment and Planning A*, vol 46, pp 2798-815.

Wright, E. (2011) 'Real utopias', *Compass*, vol 10, no 2, pp 36-42.

Zizek, S. (2012) *Mapping ideology*, London: Verso.

FOUR

Valuing and strengthening community

Lisa Mckenzie

There is a growing and distinct group of people in the UK who are faring badly in this period of advanced capitalism. As inequality rises and the gap between the top and the bottom of society widens, their lives are becoming more precarious (Savage, 2015). The people struggling the most are working class, but unlike previous generations, they have little in the way of self- or state-organised stability, from trade unions, political parties or from identities connected to their employment. It is this group of people at the bottom of society who have been harmed the most by capitalist economics and who have traditionally relied on 'the social', whether in their employment or in their communities, to thrive, and we cannot ignore the connections between widening inequality and the de-valuing of the social.

The post-war consensus in 1945 put social goods at its centre education, social housing, state pensions, child benefit and the National Health Service (NHS). These social goods have always been important to working-class people, but over the last 30 years there has been a marked retreat from the post-war consensus, and a definite policy of 'rolling back' public-owned and public-run social services. The de-industrialisation and loss of manufacturing industries, and the privatisation of those industries that were once publicly owned, have devastated working-class communities, economically and also culturally, socially and symbolically. Housing policy has shifted over the last 30 years towards the homeowning democracy and away from a large social renting culture. Consequently, changing the way that the population view housing, from a 'home' to an 'asset', has serious implications for how communities organise and operate (Gough et al, 2006; Hodkinson et al, 2013). Simultaneously, removing state support for further education for all adults over the age of 25 and introducing and raising fees within higher education has ensured that even the myth of social mobility is now unbelievable (Bathmaker et al, 2013; Holmwood, 2014).

Because of these factors, the debate in the UK has moved from how we use the 'social' in tackling poverty and inequality to the usefulness of an individual, their productivity, their behaviour, their culture and their values (Skeggs, 2004, 2014; Welshman, 2006). However, this is not an entirely new phenomenon: there have been institutional and moral judgements regarding the poorest for as long as there has been a 'poor law' naming them (Welshman, 2006). Consequently, naming and identifying the poor has been used to divide them into two distinct groups – the 'deserving' poor, those deemed 'the respectable', doing their best and perhaps becoming 'unlucky', as opposed to those who are 'undeserving', the deviant, dangerous and criminal.

This chapter focuses on those who have become the most precarious, those who have historically used many forms of collectivism within their employment and also within their social lives, in order to get by. This group now appears to be struggling in an ever-competitive jobs market, rapidly changing faster than they can accumulate the skills required. Added to this is the rolling back of many state social programmes as governments follow the ideology of a neoliberal market-driven economy for both its public and private services. Public services have been hollowed out, yet there has been little in the way of empathy towards those working-class communities and the struggles they face; instead, they have been demonised, stigmatised and ridiculed for their apparent failure. Subsequent government policy for almost 40 years has compounded this with rhetoric that has shifted the focus from the market to the individual by looking specifically at the culture and the practices of the poorest. Policy and rhetoric from the full spectrum of British politics have followed the undeserving/deserving mantra from the Conservative government's theories of the underclass during the 1980s (Levitas, 2005) to New Labour's social exclusion agenda and back to the current Conservative government's concept of a 'Broken Britain' (McKenzie, 2015, p 7).

By simultaneously naming the poorest through negative narratives, there has been a removal of class struggles, class politics and class inequality from the public consciousness to the point where the British Labour Party has eliminated 'class' from its vocabulary, preferring the hollow terms 'working people' and even worse, 'hardworking people', suggesting there is another group of people who are not hardworking. Removing the language of class, and removing the struggles of class from our politics, is to de-politicise inequality, removing the critique of the system and instead placing that critique onto the individual through a narrow understanding of failure or success.

Market value

The debate around value during this period of advanced capitalist ideology is central within the prosocial argument because 'the market has become God' (Frank, 2001, p 19), dominated by the logic that capital is to make capital, wherever, whenever, from whomever. The concept of value becomes central – who we value and why we value them has to some extent replaced the debate around class struggle. Rather than understanding inequality as structural with collective beneficiaries at the expense of collective losers, we attribute value to an individual (Sayer, 2015). The debate is often subtle, and can be addressed in many ways, for example, 'the hardworking families' rhetoric used in Westminster political language. This is subtle but effective in removing the concept of class and also removing the critique of social structure, making distinctions between 'hardworking' people and others we must assume are not hardworking. Bev Skeggs' (2014) recent research on 'value' argues that this forceful logic opens out, and:

> … commodifies every aspect of our lives, making everything: every person and every interaction subject to a value that can be bought, sold or exchanged. Consequently over the last 40 years this intense neo-liberal project means there has been a naturalising and normalising of capitalism that has reduced the ideas of social interaction into rational action and a self-interested calculation. (Skeggs, 2014, p 176)

This is apparent in the current 'crisis' for homes in London, but also in specific 'hotspots' across the UK where people and communities have been reduced to their wealth value and the cost of the land they live on. Recent research undertaken by the estate agent Savills (2016) has calculated that London is now the most expensive city in the world to live and to work in. Savills is an estate agent that is also at the forefront of several regeneration projects across the UK aiming to turn unproductive land into productive land. According to Savills and to the many local councils around the UK, unproductive land is known as 'brownfield', although many brownfield sites are actually council estates with a resident population. Productive land, on the other hand, is where private development can be enabled; consequently, land and property can be valued appropriately to market value.

The terms used for this process by private developers is 'place making' (Savills, 2016), where they specifically look for high-value land that is close to improving infrastructure so they can 'value uplift', meaning pushing up land and property value. Savills also noted in their report in January 2016 that the cost of space an individual needs for accommodation and work in London totals £80,700 a year per person. This reduces people to a 'market value' figure of their earning power, as Skeggs says, only seeing value 'from within the blinkers of capital's logic' and removing all recognition of 'the values that live beyond value' (Skeggs, 2014). The consequences of this 'place making' by private developers is that poorer residents have been socially cleansed out of their communities, where there might be good or improving social infrastructure, to places further out of the city, where the infrastructure they need is lacking.

This logic has had severe consequences for working-class people through stigmatisation, and re-branding them as of a lesser value, and in some cases, valueless. This connection between an individual's market value and their moral value has been central in producing new ways of exploitation through the fields of culture and media, strengthening established forms of class differentiation and also inventing new forms of class prejudice. This process of differentiation is subtle, moving among society unseen, but has terrible consequences for those whose social value is being undermined, a process that Pierre Bourdieu (1986) would term 'symbolic violence'. An act of violence that is symbolic and often difficult to detect through the normalisation process of everyday practice that is inflicted on a less powerful group by a more powerful group, this can be demonstrated in the way that social cleansing is being used by cities to ensure that land and property have 'value uplift' with the 'common-sense' notion of deserving and undeserving, through reducing people to their market value.

The social in the community

A way we can demonstrate the difficulties in recognising and naming acts of symbolic violence is to show how working-class and middle-class cultural capitals are not seen as equal but different. The difference that working-class people display is 'made into inequality' through a de-valuing process. We can see this in the ways that working-class people are regularly ridiculed and despised within popular culture. Defining working-class people as valueless has taken on new forms in recent years, in often very negative ways. This has manifested itself into a growing genre of popular television programmes that 'watch the poor' in pseudo-documentary formats, a phenomena known as 'poverty porn'. This trend of 'watching the poor' has produced programmes like Channel 4's 'Benefit Street', and my favourite, 'Dogs on the Dole', and a whole host of the genre on Channel 5 that are shown nightly at prime time; even the BBC has cashed in with 'We Pay Your Benefits'. This genre has become an outlet for those 'hardworking families' that Westminster politicians have helpfully differentiated for us against 'Benefits Britain' to vent their anger, giving them someone to blame for the rising inequalities in Britain, and the continued precarity that millions of families are experiencing. These are based on simple but well-used narratives, the benefit-claiming young single mother taking too much from the state, or the lazy benefit family with no intention of ever working. These are myths and stories, rather than coherent narratives, but are still extremely damaging and hurtful to these communities and individuals – a type of violence that is not physical but symbolic. Symbolic violence hurts families and has severe consequences on communities because the removal of social goods, either through 'brownfield' regeneration or through austerity measures, can be justified because the poor can be blamed for their poverty.

However, recent and rigorous research by Shildrick et al (2012) clearly shows that poverty in the UK is caused by an insecure employment market where people move from no-pay to low-pay, to zero hours contracts, and to welfare benefits. In addition, the crisis for homes that has been purposefully orchestrated by successive government policy on housing has meant that there has been an inflated property market, a lack of genuine affordable rented accommodation and a rise in 'buy to let' private landlords (Dorling, 2014). Consequently, social goods that the poorest in society have needed and relied on are being removed and justified through the narrative of value: who is of value and who is not.

Drawing on my own ethnographic research in Nottingham in the East Midlands and in Bethnal Green in London's East End, I argue that despite the naturalising of the market, and the normalising of all 'value' being linked to an exchange value within the market, working-class people in both locations resist this neoliberal model of society through placing their own understanding of value firmly located within and among their families, friends and local communities.

Narratives from the bottom

It is July 2014 and I am sitting in the backyard of a local pub in Bethnal Green with a group of people who have lived within staggering distance of this establishment for either all or most of their lives, as have their families and friends. We are talking about the local neighbourhood, the gossip, the news and, of course, and as always, the fears of the residents about the rapidly changing nature of the community. Today's talk consists of a new film being made about the Kray Twins, the notorious East End gangsters, which is being filmed in the cafe two doors down from the pub; the rise in popularity of 'loom bands' among their children; and the Elvis Presley tribute act that is on on Saturday night. Peppered among this conversation are the personal worries and the public state of the severity of inequality in Britain today. This seems remarkable – most of the people who drink in this pub in the East End did not vote in the 2015 General Election, and would be known as the 'politically disinterested'.

Although conversations change daily, the constant is talk about how difficult it is to make ends meet in London – this conversation never changes, and never ends. The people I am sat with in this pub are finding themselves in increasingly precarious positions regarding their work – the men are on very precarious contracts within the building trade, sometimes a day at a time, and the women mostly work cleaning the offices and homes of the more affluent, and are unlikely to earn the London living wage. They are also worried about their ability to stay in this community, with rents rising, and tell me that the local council are putting more and more pressure on local people to move out of this part of London and to move further east into Essex, or even north as far away as Birmingham or Manchester. The talk in this pub is what will happen to them – will they be allowed to stay in this neighbourhood? And if not, what will happen to their relatives, particularly the elderly, who have more secure social housing and are more difficult to move? One woman in her 80s, 'Mary', told me she was stranded "among the yuppies". Her daughter had been moved out when the private landlord raised the rent well beyond her minimum wage job. New pressures had been placed on this family by Mary's grandson moving in with her in order to get work and to stay close to the building sites in central London. Their positions are unstable and precarious, not knowing whether they will be in work, not knowing where they might be living in a year's time. Constantly changing cuts in welfare keep them precarious – they never know what new cuts will be implemented and how it will affect them.

This is particularly salient regarding housing benefit capping and the cost of renting privately – the benefit just doesn't fit the rent. Whole communities that have been stable for generations are being forced to move further out of London. The value of 'the social' and of family, and of community, is becoming increasingly diminished and overridden by the needs of a capitalist system extracting as much market value as possible out of each and every relationship, interaction and person.

This method of devaluing low-income working-class people is not subtle; it is extremely blunt. If you live in Bethnal Green, and within walking distance of the City of London and the financial district, and you are not worth the £80,700 that Savills has calculated the cost of the space you are taking up, you need to leave, as no value can be extracted from you. This type of blunt and simplistic logic is having a severe effect on working-class families within London and wider within the South East, as rents rise and house prices sky-rocket. The bottom line to whether you are allowed to stay in a neighbourhood where you have perhaps lived most or all of your life, where you have a job, a family and a connection, is based on whether you are worth it. In this case, the social is sacrificed, and with a mercilessness and unapologetic ideology, as Mary told me, "you ain't worth it, mate."

Sharon's story

The East Midlands has been hit for over 30 years with total de-industrialisation by the closure of the mining industry, the large engineering industries and the textile industry. The de-valuing process has been more culturally pitched because of the levels of unemployment and the extremely low-paid work it has fixed on a moral worth. I was undertaking research during the mid-2000s with a group of women in the local community centre where it was very clear that the de-valuing process was strategic and purposeful, and focused on what the women did, and also who they are.

Out of the eight years of ethnographic research in this neighbourhood, I spent almost every day for two years in a community centre in St Ann's council estate in Nottingham. This community had, for generations, suffered high unemployment, low wages and increasing amounts of class prejudice (McKenzie, 2015). It was home to almost 15,000 people in predominantly social housing still controlled by the local council. The estate itself had no real aesthetic value for gentrifiers or property developers, being built in the 1970s using grey concrete pre-moulded or pre-cast sections, with uniformly small, square, terraced houses. The neighbourhood had a local reputation as a dangerous place where you should never go. It was where there were drug dealers, single mothers, gangsters and the poor. Throughout Nottingham the estate was known as pretty lawless, but also ugly, with nothing worth going to within the neighbourhood. Consequently, over several generations, both place and people have been de-valued and stigmatised as valueless.

I lived on this estate for more than 20 years, and spending a lot of time with local women highlighted to me how stigmatised the neighbourhood was, and also the effects of stigmatisation on the community. I visited the community centre most days, and sat around talking, drinking tea and coffee with the local women; there was always a lot of gossip and a lot of laughing. The women used this community space as a meeting point, usually after dropping their children off at school during term time. At 9.30 every morning it was very busy – usually 10 or 12 mums would turn up and sit for a few hours laughing and talking with toddlers and pushchairs. At lunch time the space was used by older people – the community centre had a kitchen run by a local social enterprise, and provided very cheap hot meals every day, two courses for £2.50, with a cup of tea only 50p. The community centre was busy and vibrant, often very noisy, and was well used.

There was one woman, 'Sharon', who volunteered in the kitchen every day; she would arrive at 9.15 after dropping her own children off at school, and she made all the drinks, cleaned up the tables, and did some washing up. Her constant presence at the community centre was comforting; she knew everyone by name and made everyone feel welcome. Feeling welcome is important in a community; it allows a sense of belonging, and a sense that you are not entirely on your own. Sharon knew everyone's names, and she also knew about their families, and their illnesses – the doctor's surgery and the chemist was next door, and people would often call in for a cup of tea and a chat afterwards. She also had a knack of bringing other people into a conversation; she was a lightning rod for local social capital. Sharon had been central within my own research, introducing me to people and vouching for me, including me within the conversations, the gossip and the laughing. Her contribution to the community was enormous, although her contribution to wider society was de-valued. Sharon claimed full state benefits to live, she received Income Support for her two children and herself that amounted to £110 per week, she lived in a three-bedroom council house on the estate, and received the full rental amount in housing benefit of £52.50 a week. Consequently she was costing the taxpayer approximately £8,500 a year in living and subsistence costs. Sharon worked in the community centre approximately 16 hours a week but received no pay. I remember asking her whether she wanted a paid job:

> '... yes, I want to work in the community ... something like
> a youth worker ... working with the youth on the estate
> ... although I kind of do that already. That's the kind of
> job I want ... as long as it pays enough ... enough for the

rent and that ... it would be nice to have a car and perhaps a holiday ... but mostly I want to stay in the community.'

I then went on to ask her about qualifications and what she thought she might need by way of training:

> 'Well I haven't got any official qualifications; I weren't very good at school ... since being here, errr, three years now since [son's name] went to nursery I've done a health and hygiene course in catering.... I kind of enjoyed that ... yeah, more stuff like that I would like, although being here you get loads of experience [laughing].'

Although Sharon's voluntary position at the community centre is really important for the community, and the centre advertises volunteering positions as ways to 'build up your CV', Sharon has had minimum support from the community centre. This, however, doesn't stop her being hopeful and optimistic for the future, that she might find her way into a paid job within the community.

I conducted this interview early in 2008. Two years later, in 2010, I met with Sharon again. Things had really changed for her personally; global financial and political events had affected her life and this small community centre on a council estate in Nottingham. A few months after I had interviewed Sharon, the then Chancellor of the Exchequer for the Labour government, Alistair Darling, agreed a bank rescue package totalling £500 billion in response to the instability of the British banking sector. This measure, according to all politicians within the British Parliament, was crucial in safeguarding the stability of 'our' economic future following a global banking crisis born out of a reckless banking industry that had borrowed and traded on the debts of others. Similar measures were subsequently introduced by the US and the European Union (EU) in response to the financial crisis. The developed world went into recession, and most governments in Europe and the US applied austerity measures to their finances, warning their citizens that there would be significant cuts in public spending.

The poverty lifestyle and the 'life of Riley'

In May 2010 the UK government had held a general election and a coalition government was formed as no political party had secured an outright win. The coalition between the Conservative Party and the Liberal Democratic Party immediately began new and much harsher austerity measures, with an estimated loss of 500,000 public sector jobs, mainly from front-line services. In addition, tougher welfare measures in the forms of reduced entitlement and capping of benefits were also introduced. Job centres and benefits agencies throughout the UK were instructed to carry out more frequent work capability assessments in order to ensure that benefits were only given to 'the right people'. Simultaneously, government language and rhetoric regarding unemployment and worklessness became harsh and punitive. The new Chancellor of the Exchequer made much political capital in the old trope that lazy people receiving benefits were living the 'life of Riley' on the backs of hardworking families. In September 2010 he announced £4 billion worth of welfare cuts, with this rhetoric:

> People who think it is a lifestyle to sit on out-of-work benefits … that lifestyle choice is going to come to an end. The money will not be there for that lifestyle choice. (Osborne, quoted in Wintour, 2010)

We know, however, the reasons why people claim welfare benefits are complex, as the research undertaken by Shildrick et al (2012) shows, and people are not living the 'life of Riley', as my own research in Nottingham shows (2015). The Chancellor's statement clearly shows that by reducing the message to one of morality – a person is good or bad, hardworking or work-shy – you don't need to explain fully why spending cuts fall onto one group of people over another. It is simply a matter of value – who is valuable and who is not.

About this time I met with Sharon again, and she told me that she had received a letter telling her go to an appointment at the local benefits agency. During the interview she had been questioned about her availability to work, and she told them she was working, albeit without pay, in the community centre. The adviser asked her whether she thought it was about time she stopped taking from society and gave something back, in the form of paid work. Sharon wanted to work in the local community, but Nottingham City Council had just sent out thousands of 'under threat' redundancy letters to current public sector workers, put a freeze on recruitment, and announced that they had been forced to make public sector spending cuts of £28 million. The benefits agency pushed on with Sharon's case that she needed to get a paid job and contribute to society. Sharon was eventually sanctioned, her benefits cut from £110 per week to £30. Needless to say, she didn't manage well, and admitted defeat, taking the offer of 'help' that the job centre extended to her in putting her forward for a job in a cheese-packing factory 6 miles away. This meant that Sharon could no longer volunteer at the community centre and had to leave her two children, then aged 7 and 12, alone from 6.30 in the morning to get ready for school themselves. Sharon earned £177 before stoppages for a 30-hour week in the cheese-packing factory, and with the changes in her housing benefit and council tax benefit, she was £9 a week better off financially, although her health very quickly deteriorated through working in a freezing cold environment, and the constant stress of leaving her children alone. After three months Sharon had to quit the job through ill health and depression.

Sharon's story is not unique; if you look you can find thousands of these stories in many of the mainstream press, although they may be told in many different ways, depending on the politics of the editor and the readership. In the *Daily Mirror* and *The Guardian* the stories might be more sympathetic; in the *Daily Mail*, *The Sun* and *The Express* the focus would be on the 'lazy and undeserving' morally bankrupt families taking too much from the state.

In 2015 Mary O'Hara collected stories from around the UK for her book *Austerity bites*, criticising the austerity measures and policies in the UK as cruel and irrational. John Hills' (2014) research shows that austerity measures actually transferred funds from the poorest to the pockets of the better-off, with single-parent families being hardest hit. While the very richest in the top 1% of the most wealthy lost some of their wealth, Hills notes clearly that austerity measures made no net effect on public funds. The economic argument for cutting social services and public goods has not been made, although that has had little to no difference at all in public policy, which continues to find new ways to cut social services.

Critiquing the economic arguments against the social is important, but simultaneously we must also critique the way that culture is used to prop up the economic argument. Television programmes such as 'Benefits Street' and 'Skint', discussed earlier, develop the already stigmatised view of the poor for a new era, as does the work of austerity . These tropes that are peddled through the media perpetuate and strengthen the neoliberal rationale that value can only equate to a person's wealth and their monetary value. This work is done subtly by linking moral worth to monetary worth. As Sharon found out, her position in the community as a volunteer in the community centre, ultimately prosocial work, was valueless and instead, in order for her to become 'useful' and a recognised part of society, a paid job in the private sector was her only way of 'redemption'. The people who live in East London know that they are not worth the land they live on, and are waiting, one by one, to be 'cleansed out'. Being part of the community, a mother, a volunteer or a low-paid worker is no longer good enough. If you are in a position of economic deficit, you are also morally deficit; your connection and care to your family, community or fellow human is valueless.

References

Bathmaker, A., Ingram, N. and Waller, R. (2013) 'Higher education, social class and the mobilisation of capitals: Recognising and playing the game', *British Journal of Sociology of Education*, vol 34, no 5-6, pp 723-43.

Bourdieu, P. (1986) *Distinction: A critique of the social judgement of taste*, London: Routledge.

Dorling, D. (2014) *All that is solid: How the great housing disaster defines our times, and what we can do about it*, London: Allen Lane.

Frank, T. (2001) *One market under God: Extreme capitalism, market populism, and the end of economic development*, New York: Doubleday.

Gough, J., Eisenschitz, A. and McCulloch, A. (2005) *Spaces of social exclusion*, London: Routledge.

Hodkinson, S., Watt, P. and Mooney, G. (2013) 'Introduction: 2013 Neoliberal housing policy: Time for a critical re-appraisal', *Critical Social Policy*, vol 33, no 1, pp 3-16.

Hills, J. (2014) *Good times, bad times: The welfare myth of them and us*, Bristol: Policy Press.

Holmwood J. (2014) 'Beyond capital? The challenge for sociology in Britain', *The British Journal of Sociology*, vol 65, no 4, pp 607–18.

Levitas, R. (2005) *The inclusive society* (2nd edn), London: Macmillan.

O'Hara, M. (2015) *Austerity bites*, Bristol: Policy Press.

McKenzie, L. (2015) *Getting by: Estates class and culture*, Bristol: Policy Press.

Savage, M. (2015) *Social class in the 21st century*, Harmondsworth: Penguin.Savills (2016) *London mixed use development* (http://pdf.euro.savills.co.uk/uk/residential---other/spotlight-london-mixed-use-development-2016.pdf).

Sayer, A. (2015) *Why we can't afford the rich*, Bristol: Policy Press.

Shildrick, T., MacDonald, R., Webster, C. and Garthwaite, K. (2012) *Poverty and insecurity: Life in low-pay, no-pay Britain*, Bristol: Policy Press.

Skeggs, B. (2004) *Class, self, culture*, London: Routledge.

Skeggs, B. (2014) 'Values beyond value? Is anything beyond the logic of capital?', *The British Journal of Sociology*, vol 65, issue 1, pp 1-20

Welshman, J. (2006) *Underclass: A history of the excluded, 1880–2000*, London: Continuum International Publishing.

Wintour, P. (2010) 'George Osborne to cut £4bn more from benefits', *The Guardian*, 11 September (www.theguardian.com/politics/2010/sep/09/george-osborne-cut-4bn-benefits-welfare).

Part 2
Ideas

Part 2
Ideas

FIVE

Confronting the roots of violent behaviour

Anthony Ellis

... it would be absurd to claim that rage's best days are behind it. (Sloterdijk, 2011, p 227)

Introduction

Any conversation about humanity's capacity for cruelty, destruction, sadism or 'evil' is a difficult one, and the conversation I engage in during this chapter on confronting violence is no exception. I want to argue that we must confront an uncomfortable and sad truth – the cold reality that it is currently not possible to imagine a world fully free of human violence and aggression. Every day we are bombarded with new stories of human cruelty, viciousness and sadism from across the globe, many of which we seem unable to adequately explain. The seeming inexplicability of much violent behaviour may often generate a sense that the times we live in are in some way bereft of a common morality or mutual sense of compassion. Certainly our internet, print and TV news media are often fixed on unsettling stories of murder, gang violence, riots, sexual assaults, child abuse, domestic violence, civil war and terrorism. In addition we find ourselves immersed in films and video games containing numerous images and interactive experiences of extreme violence and human suffering. Even some children's television programmes and toys make frequent reference to the utility of aggressive behaviour for 'getting things done', such as Ben 10, Transformers, Marvel's Avengers or Teenage Mutant Ninja Turtles, in which violence is regularly used by the heroic central characters, and is always portrayed as justifiable and righteous. The seeming ubiquity of violence in society, and the apparent appetite for it when packaged up as a consumer product, might help us to understand why many people hold the view that violence is ingrained in our nature, that we are naturally wicked, selfish, competitive animals, and that any attempts to dispel hostilities, anger and rage are therefore futile and pointless.

How, then, can we begin to understand and challenge these aspects of our culture and behaviour?

As a scholar with a long-standing interest in violence and having spent several years researching it, I feel obligated to be optimistic about the possibility of more peaceful social relations. However, in offering an honest assessment, I would also confess that I rarely do feel a sense of optimism. My extensive contact with those who regularly experience and perpetrate violence is important in understanding these feelings. As discussed in the introductory chapter to this collection, it appears that the horizons of academic thought and scholarship have narrowed in recent years. The injunction to be quick thinkers or to fall into step with the whims of current policy ideas or frameworks certainly appears to be a hindrance to the kinds of deeper analysis and more searching conclusions that are needed to address various social problems. In this narrowing of critical thinking has emerged the sense that liberal capitalism and parliamentary democracy represent the pinnacle of our social, economic and political evolution (Winlow and Hall, 2013). In this context it has become increasingly difficult to mount alternatives and critical ideas that might focus on and change the structural foundations of our economic system. For the most part we make piecemeal policy suggestions that represent minor alterations and tweaks to the existing system, in an attempt to make it work slightly better, despite the systemic prevalence of violence globally.

In the spirit of this collection what I offer here is based on an attempt to cast off a cynical approach and reflect with conviction on possibilities, despite the obvious charge of simplification and naivety. In this short chapter it is simply not possible to address fully the various forms of human behaviour and action deemed to be examples of violence, ranging from the act of one person pushing another, to large-scale armed conflict affecting millions. This, of course, only covers those acts that constitute physical force perpetrated by a clearly identifiable individual(s) and that our society readily identifies and thinks of as violent. Philosophical thought on defining violence reveals that there are many kinds of violation that cause human misery and suffering, which often do not stem from the identifiable and intentional physical action of humans, but which, nevertheless, can, and should, still be conceived of as violent (Zizek, 2008). In other words, human bodies and potential are often damaged by living in societies in which the emergent quality of corporate and political acts (such as foregoing payment of taxes, fraud or neglect in working practices) or of the deeper system itself (such as forms of poverty and inequality) generate real harms. My focus here is primarily on UK society and particular groups of men known to habitually engage in physical violence, often with other men. However, in addressing concerns about the conduct of these men I also want to reflect more broadly on the roots of violence in our society, how to confront it, and to look at the wider system that has shaped the conditions and lives of these men.

A history of violence

To engage in a serious conversation about how we might reduce violence and create a more peaceful society, particularly at this time in our history, is to attract dissention and possibly derision from various quarters. On the one hand there are those who will no doubt point to the apocalyptic visions regularly conjured by our violence-obsessed 24-hour news media, as evidence that violence will always be with us, that it is somehow natural and inevitable that some human beings will physically harm others, while other potential critics are likely to draw on recent results from the Crime Survey for England Wales (CSEW, formerly the British Crime Survey), and respond with the strong retort of 'rates of violent crime are down', 'Britain is safer now', and 'we are experiencing a crime decline'.

Each anticipated response is understandable based on the sources of information that document violence in our society. The second anticipated response in particular is an understandable one, as, for almost 20 years now, police-recorded crime statistics and data from the CSEW have indicated a gradual decline in violent crimes, a trend mirrored in several other Western states and that continues the long decline of lethal violence in Western Europe that available historical records indicate began roughly at the end of the Middle Ages. So the 'history of violence' has been written as one of decline.

However, what I find problematic about such a position is that it often fails to problematise the actual historical context to this decline, as well as the social and economic conditions that have accompanied it. The evidence that suggests violence is declining has prompted some scholars to claim that the 'better angels of our nature' (Pinker, 2011) are finally prevailing in the battle against humanity's barbaric potential, that we are becoming genuinely more civilised and peaceful. Democracy, human rights and incremental rises in living standards in Western liberal states, like the UK and the US, are frequently held up as evidence of this growing civility, as if we need do no more than simply sit back and let the minimally regulated economy and parliamentary democracy continue the good work of slowly 'civilising' us while delivering a better quality of life for all. An immediate issue here is that those who are often in support of this position fail to acknowledge the violence that has been required to reach this unique historical position, as well as the violence that must continue in order to sustain it (see Zizek, 2008). While evidence for the decline in lethal physical violence is particularly strong, what this decline supposedly tells us about Western societies and humanity has been, I would suggest, somewhat misconstrued by some. The idea that liberal capitalism has helped to generate an onward civilising of humanity needs careful evaluation. Violence is multifaceted and, although addressing physical violence perpetrated by individuals is important, it is but one aspect of humanity's relationship with violence. For example, little of the discussion of the violence decline has engaged with its relationship to unprecedented levels of incarceration, state surveillance and control, particularly in the US and the UK.

The suggestion that we are entering a unique historical period of generally more peaceful, restrained and harmonious social relations, in which the motivation to physically harm others is waning, should not be accepted uncritically. Those that propagate the violent crime decline thesis often tend to neglect the geographical and social unevenness of this decline and the continued difficulty of life in high crime and dangerous localities (Ellis, 2015; Currie, 2016). Rapid social and economic transformation in the late 20th century was accompanied by some rises in serious violence in de-industrialising, poor communities, trends that have persisted in some of these communities (Wilkinson and Pickett, 2010; Hall, 2012). More importantly, the continued general decline in violent crimes over the past 20 years in England and Wales has actually reversed of late, with slight increases in several categories of violence (Travis, 2016). There is, of course, the issue of how these crimes are recorded by the police and researchers that must be factored into any conclusions we might draw, but these complex patterns should not lead to straightforward assumptions that we are therefore much better people living in improved societies.

When examining the statistical evidence we have available it is also important to bear in mind that there is an unknown, potentially large, number of incidents of violence that are never reported and that do not end up in either police-recorded crime or self-report crime survey data. This is particularly likely in the kind of violence that occurs in the home, workplaces, among criminal populations (see Currie, 2016) and within some institutions, such as prisons. Of course, the location of violence is also complex and variable, but an examination of the evidence we do have indicates that violent crimes tend to be more greatly concentrated in areas and groups of individuals experiencing various forms of disadvantage. Wilkinson and Pickett's (2010) work on the relationship between material inequality and a range of social problems, including violence, demonstrates quite strongly the potentially damaging and socially corrosive effects of un-checked gulfs in wealth and access to resources between social groups. There is little, if anything, redeeming in the experience of suffering material hardship (see Zizek, 2016), and being made acutely aware of the material advantages that are enjoyed by others. These conditions, that are likely to foster feelings of strain, envy, humiliation and desperation, are implicated in the complex roots, causes and contexts of interpersonal violence between individuals, and add significant layers of complexity to the broad relationships mapped by Wilkinson and Pickett. Yet their work does offer an important social and economic context for thinking about violent crime. Although we must remain aware of the complex distribution of violent crime throughout society, research and evidence tells us that inequalities in their various guises need to be addressed if we are serious about confronting the roots of violent behaviour (Currie, 2016).

Lives of violence

That most violence, particularly serious violence, is perpetrated by males has become something of a truism, and for some time now a large number of scholars have wrestled with the clear associations that exist between men and violence in recorded crime statistics, but also within culture. Much content in film genres, media and video games certainly reflects the strong cultural associations between men and physical aggression. In this sense, violence is often posed in these numerous mediums as an acceptable resource for males, and very often as a righteous response to being humiliated, slighted or victimised. Yet the ubiquity of tough masculinity in Western popular culture, and its utility for righting perceived wrongs and injustices, should not be seen in a directly causal relationship with actual male violence, but is mediated by a range of cultural influences, norms and economic conditions. The strong evidence that the majority of men do not habitually engage in physical violence is indicative of why mediated links, as opposed to directly causal ones, need to be better understood.

Available research evidence points strongly towards a quite specific demographic profile of men that are more likely to use physical violence persistently and for whom it can potentially provide an important part of their self-identities: men that hail from communities experiencing social and economic exclusion. These are communities that were historically fairly stable, economically functional and socially included. But the demise of manufacturing and extractive industries in the UK at the latter end of the 20th century had a devastating impact on them, reducing job opportunities, social capital and communal ties, eventually leading to the gradual demise of the socialist politics that had once provided vociferous political bargaining power for the working class.

The point I make here is not to suggest that all men of this social background are violent. Rather, what social scientific research on this complex issue consistently finds is that some men from such communities and social conditions tend to display a deeper appreciation of the possibilities and reality of physical confrontation, and to see this as the root to greater respect or social success in these areas. They are often taught to recognise that violence actually exists, that it is real, that one day they may have to face it, and that it is vital to be able to retain some dignity and self-respect from encounters with it (Winlow and Hall, 2009). For them, violence happens; it is not an alien force, or a form of behaviour that they have become aware of through reading newspapers or watching the television. It happens in the immediate spaces they occupy, and they know that sometimes you have to be prepared to deal with it or offer it when necessary. These men know that to make sustained eye contact with other men, especially in a public place, is likely to be construed as a challenge and may result in a physical confrontation. They know that another male often sees significant females in his life as in need of protection, and that an inappropriate remark or advance aimed at them may trigger a violent response. They tend to know who the local 'hard men' are within their communities and that you should take steps to avoid them and that you must be cautious in their presence. They know that these men's identities are connected to violence and an ability to use it competently.

In the course of my own research on male violence I have spent many hours in the company of such men and the physical spaces they occupy day to day, men whose personal reputations are partly built on their potential to use violence against others and who are prepared to inflict physical harm if the situation is felt to require it (see Ellis, 2016). During the extended periods of time I spent in their company, many of these men spoke continually about the importance of being both physically and mentally 'tough', ready, and prepared to deal with individuals they believed threatened their safety. This acute sense of fatalism about the possibility of violence was so deeply ingrained in their lives and their sense of who they were as men that it was difficult for many of them to imagine a situation where a potential to use violence would not be required. For as far back as they could remember, violence, and the possibility of it, had been a feature of their lives. It was a genuine possibility that they had learned to accept. They found that what was most appropriate in such circumstances was to demonstrate a willingness to fight back. Although their biographical histories were often unique in many ways, what united them was that they had all, to varying degrees, experienced what is often referred to as a 'toughening up' process. This process often resulted in them witnessing and being subjected to physical abuse, being instructed and forced to use violence, and, importantly, being encouraged to recognise the value in 'taking a beating' from someone.

The various physical scars on their bodies from fists, sharp implements and firearms, served as stark and important reminders that the world is a dangerous, unforgiving and deeply competitive place. Their attempts to psychologically make sense of such brutalising experience resulted in a view that the presence of violence was unfortunate, but nevertheless important to ensure they were adequately 'prepared' for what they perceived was a life filled with inevitable and unavoidable confrontations, and where one should be suspicious of others' intentions. As might be expected, much of their experience in later life did confirm these harsh injunctions to them, with many becoming both the perpetrators and the victims of serious, physically injurious violence. They were painfully aware of the humiliation and anger they would feel if they failed to respond to a personal slight or insult aimed at them by someone else. If they were physically assaulted or lost a fight, it would occupy their thoughts for weeks, months, and sometimes years afterwards. The humiliation of defeat, of being made to look foolish, meant social insignificance and worthlessness. So, in some cases, violence represented a physical and social survival strategy, pure and simple.

When faced with individuals who sought to harm them, these men had to sometimes make split-second decisions, where passivity would have resulted in serious injury, even death. They simply did not have time to 'think' or consider the consequences of their behaviour as their attackers attempted to punch, kick, stab or shoot them. In making these points I am not attempting to, in some way, justify their violence, and nor am I suggesting that they are innocent victims; only that there have been situations with no easy choices when they, literally, had to fight for their lives. Of course, there were also many occasions when these individuals used violence that, to an outsider, would be considered totally unnecessary and unjustifiable, and much of it certainly was. The level of violence these men had inflicted on others in some situations was appalling and without justification, but so was violence that they, too, had been the victims of.

A violent reputation can be perceived as beneficial. It can represent a means to recuperate a sense of dignity and respect in places where legitimate sources of these can often be in short supply. It may be difficult for some readers to comprehend this, but for some of the men I have worked with over the years, their willingness to use violence in certain situations makes them feel good about themselves. They feel that they are individuals who are in some ways rather unique, because they are prepared to go further than most other men would dare. They are prepared to do what is sometimes considered necessary, prepared to 'stand up for themselves', even if that meant breaking the law and all the risks associated with this. They were prepared to fight for what they thought was right, and therefore felt entitled to hold their heads up proudly, with their self-respect intact. For some of them violence, and a reputation for being able to use it, represented more than just a source of reputation and dignity, but a means to make a living in areas where opportunities for well-paid, secure and rewarding work are often scarce.

It is easy enough, of course, to simply dismiss the experiences and views of such men as products of damaged subcultures and ways of life that have little connection to mainstream society and its values. We seem to feel more comfortable with ourselves when we can individualise violent behaviour as a product of biological or genetic abnormality, faulty socialisation, poor parenting or simply as a kind of social 'evil'. Such means of explaining violence allow us to distance ourselves from it and these modes of explanation tend to be taken as more 'credible' and acceptable within our society because they leave unacknowledged the social, cultural, political and economic conditions in which physical violence takes place. Such brutal experience, although confined to minority populations of men, should not be understood in the ways that we commonly 'think' about violent behaviour and those who use it. As morally unpalatable as this may be in a society that prides itself on being tolerant, inclusive and 'civilised', violence is, for some individuals, and these men in particular, a resource that still carries a kind of power in the communities they come from, yet the communities and the individuals I describe here are not immune from society's 'mainstream' values; indeed, they are profoundly shaped by them.

The uncomfortable truth in all of this is that for some people and some specific groups of men in particular, violence is a resource, one that can help to 'get things done'. But this doesn't apply to just violent criminals, as Bufacchi (2005) has perceptively argued; violence is, of course, a social problem, but it is also the solution to the problem of maintaining order and thus a political solution too. Philosopher Slavoj Zizek (2008) points to the violence that must happen to maintain order and the sense of calm that physical violence perpetrated by individuals perturbs and threatens. Zizek draws our attention to a violence that he describes as akin to what physicists term 'dark matter': the mysterious, unseen force that affects more visible and tangible matter in the Universe. Zizek's metaphor in this context was used with the intention of offering us a means with which we might think more clearly about 'violence', challenging us to examine the structures that function to ensure our everyday lives operate smoothly and effectively. Our obsession with violence that is physical, and therefore visible, prevents us from critically examining the often unseen, catastrophic circumstances that enable and maintain the serenity enjoyed by large proportions of most Western populations, serenity, Zizek argues, that is enabled and made possible by systemic violence and the exploitation of powerless and vulnerable groups.

What do we do now?

Inevitably, we have to move now towards the conclusions of this difficult conversation on violence and ask the question, 'what should we do now?' We can focus, as politicians and policy-makers often do when faced with a social problem such as violence, on having stronger deterrents, such as tougher punishments and sentencing. In addition we can talk about having better policing, better social services, improved rehabilitation programmes, more positive diversionary activities, and more jobs. Current community-based approaches and rehabilitative interventions to prevent violent crime, and crime in general, such as positive diversionary activities, community projects and education, do have the potential to make significant impacts on some individuals' lives. In my previous employment as a researcher for a charitable organisation, I was involved in the evaluation of an alternative educational programme for vulnerable young people excluded from school, some of who were involved in criminal and violent behaviour. This project had been successful in re-engaging some of these young people in prosocial behaviour.

As discussed previously in relation to my own research with men who use violence, it is important that we recognise and understand that an attachment to violence and its persistent use has something to do with particular biographical experiences, the problematic ways in which notions of masculinity can be expressed, and the abject conditions within economically and politically abandoned communities. As much as positive interventions and rehabilitative work carried out with persistently violent individuals must attempt to address those 'feelings' at the individual level that motivate violence, there is also much that can, and must, be done at the broader social, cultural and economic level. Despite the various successes of the previously mentioned alternative education programme and its evident value to the young people and the practitioners delivering it, the large private corporation that funded it through its social responsibility agenda discontinued the programme after several years. So as valuable and as important as many interventions can be to those in receipt of them, their shelf-life is so often limited to the good will of philanthropists, hard-up local and national government budgets and finite corporate social responsibility programmes whose purpose is perhaps, cynically, more about maintaining brand image and loyalty rather than a genuine attempt to intervene in and alter the underlying conditions of various social problems. Interventions have the potential to make significant impacts on some individuals' lives, but in a world of cost-benefit analysis, value-for-money and high-speed mobile capital, these have the tendency to disappear quickly in more straitened times. They represent small islands in the choppy, unpredictable waters of advanced liberal capitalism, the current social and economic context we now find ourselves in.

So, if we are going to address what it is that actually drives violence so that we might effectively reduce it, as opposed to simply threatening greater punishments and throwing a little money into those places lacking resources, we have to perhaps think rather more carefully and critically about the complexity of violence itself, and the important function it actually serves in maintaining conditions of stark inequality and injustice. We have to have very difficult conversations about the role and functions of violence, and not just for those groups of men discussed in this chapter, whose use of it is effectively 'othered', reviled and morally condemned by the media, public and politicians alike. Of course, their use of it should not escape condemnation and attention, but crucially they are not the only ones who recognise the utility of violence and benefit from it; merely they are the ones whose violence is problematised and obvious to us. So we must also think about the violence that has been used historically, and contemporarily, to further specific political and economic goals, as well as the way of life that Western populations so often take for granted (Zizek, 2008).

Conclusion

Recent global economic crises and the response of our politicians to these provides strong evidence that capitalism, in its current state, cannot be tamed or made prosocial with gestures to its better nature or a little more regulation (Winlow et al, 2015). If anything it appears to have become anathema to the idea of the prosocial as discussed in this volume. Capitalism has been exposed as an economic system that is utterly incapable of integrating and including huge swathes of the global population in its activities, and arguably more so now than at any other point in our recent history (Winlow and Hall, 2013). It effectively no longer needs sections of the human population. It can exploit and discard them, relatively safe in the knowledge that they are thoroughly politically disorganised and simultaneously so deeply incorporated into its value systems to represent little threat to its continuation. As much as we can feel repugnance at the 'violence' of those men discussed in this chapter and the violence that fills up our media coverage, perhaps we need to recognise the violence of capital, the way it dominates the lives of all, and violates the lives of many. For Zizek (2016), various incidents of physically harmful behaviour cannot be understood in isolation from this systemic violence of global capitalism: the socially corrosive envy, hostilities, anger, rage and the vulnerability that its stark inequalities engender. So perhaps the first step towards better addressing violence in all its forms is to identify the violence that is inherent to our economic system and to name it as such. The second is to begin the hard work of exploring how we might alter problematic local and regional conditions created by capital's general disregard of its impact on human life and that continue to profoundly shape the lives of particularly disadvantaged groups. The second step cannot be fully effective, though, without the first.

This short chapter has problematised the ways in which we commonly think about the roots of violence. While we are regularly, and rightfully, horrified and morally outraged at physically injurious behaviour committed by individuals, the way in which we think about violence prevents us from fully making sense of it and from acknowledging its multifaceted nature. Although we may talk of 'civility' and frame our discussions of violence in terms of a minority of pathological individuals who do not abide by our values, at some point we have to push past this simplistic narrative and engage with the evident complexities of this. If we truly desire to explore possibilities for more nurturing, supportive, prosocial relations that are less violent, we have to be prepared to move beyond the parameters of these current debates that locate violence purely within the realms of individual physical action. We have to be prepared to engage in difficult conversations about the consequences of our current political and economic arrangements, the violence these generate and the benefits that we, too, accrue from 'violence'.

References

Bufacchi, V. (2005) 'Two concepts of violence', *Political Studies Review*, vol 3, pp 193-204.

Currie, E. (2016) *The roots of danger*, Oxford: Oxford University Press.

Ellis, A. (2015) 'Hard evidence: Crime rates are down but is the world a less harmful place?', *The Conversation* (https://theconversation.com/hard-evidence-crime-rates-are-down-but-is-the-world-a-less-harmful-place-46654).

Ellis, A. (2016) *Men, masculinities and violence: An ethnographic study*, London: Routledge.

Hall, S. (2012) *Theorising crime and deviance: A new perspective*, London: Sage Publications.

Pinker, S. (2011) *The better angels of our nature*, New York: Viking.

Sloterdijk, P. (2011) *Rage and time*, Chichester: Columbia.

Travis, A. (2016) 'Homicides in England and Wales up 14%', *The Guardian*, 21 January (www.theguardian.com/uk-news/2016/jan/21/england-wales-homicides-rise-knife-gun-crime).

Wilkinson, R. and Pickett, K. (2010) *The spirit level*, London: Penguin.

Winlow, S. and Hall, S. (2009) 'Retaliate first: Memory, humiliation and male violence', *Crime Media Culture*, vol 5, no 3, pp 285-304.

Winlow, S. and Hall, S. (2013) *Re-thinking social exclusion: The end of the social?*, London: Sage Publications.

Winlow, S., Hall, S., Treadwell, J. and Briggs, D. (2015) *Riots and political protest*, London: Routledge.

Zizek, S. (2008) *Violence*, London: Profile.

Zizek, S. (2016) 'The Cologne attacks were an obscene version of carnival', *New Statesman*, 13 January (www.newstatesman.com/world/europe/2016/01/slavoj-zizek-cologne-attacks).

SIX

In defence of the public city

Martin Coward

Introduction

If we want to understand how to create better societies our thinking must inevitably touch on the predominant locus of human settlement and organisation – the city. In 2006 UN-Habitat, the United Nations' urban programme, announced that the majority of the world's population now live in cities (UN-Habitat, 2006). In doing so they underlined the common perception that global life in the 21st century is predominantly urban. As a consequence, it has become common to claim that we live in an 'urban age'. While scholars have questioned its city-centric premise, what might be described as the 'urban age thesis' expresses a widespread perception that global urbanisation represents an epochal shift in the nature of human settlement (Brenner and Schmid, 2014). Global urbanisation could thus be described as a process of structural transformation on a planetary scale, the emergence of a distinctive global condition characterised by agglomerations of urban fabric.

What characterises this urban shift? At the heart of urbanisation – as urban theorist Louis Wirth noted long ago – are density and plurality. Urban life is characterised by encounters with others who are different to us. Density of population and interconnection encourage ever-greater numbers of such encounters. The spreading of the urban fabric and the swelling of the populations dwelling in its spaces or connected by its infrastructures raise the question of how we negotiate the diversity of social encounters that city life generates. At the heart of urbanisation there is thus a profoundly social question about the ways in which we encounter, are connected to, and live with, others. Ultimately, this question asks us to consider how we can co-exist with others, in spaces of close proximity and, frequently, significant inequality. The prospect of a global urban condition invites us to speculate on the nature of the prosocial and whether, in fact, we may find this in the world's cities.

The city faces many challenges to its social fabric, many ways in which encounters with others can be disrupted and collective solutions for co-existence avoided by reticent national and local political actors. Whether it is the erosion of traditional commitments to collective goods as part of austerity programmes, or the insecurity of land tenure and provision of services in the Global South, the various negotiated settlements that support a sense of social collectivity in the city are often precarious. Perhaps one of the most serious challenges to urban social life is the destruction and erosion of spaces that make encounters and shared political action in urban life possible. Accusations of deliberate destruction of the shared space and connective infrastructures of the city have long been levelled against peacetime urban planning. Marshall Berman (2014), for example, highlighted the way that the Bronx Expressway not only segregated – and thus disconnected – New York, but also destroyed the shared spaces of long-standing communities. Under conditions of market-oriented urban governance these concerns have only been further amplified by accusations of a more wholesale privatisation of public spaces.

However, it is organised violence against, or in, the city that starkly illustrates what is at stake in the destruction of the urban fabric. War, terrorism and state security measures against these dangers increasingly threaten the connective infrastructures and shared spaces of the city. Without connection or shared space it is not possible to encounter difference and plurality withers, leading to an impoverished co-existence. Under such an assault, urban society itself (conceived of as a kind of plural social co-existence) is threatened. The question of organised violence in and against cities thus offers us a distinctive opportunity to think about the prosocial in an era of urbanisation. I want to argue in this chapter that the response to these threats should be a defence of the public city against those forces that would destroy the urban fabric that underpins shared space and connectivity.

The 'Grad' and 'blackout' bomb

To begin with it is worth illustrating the kind of threat to the shared spaces and connective infrastructures of the city that I am referring to. Attacks on the city come in various forms: bombardment by the armed forces of states using conventional weapons (from missiles to artillery); the deliberate targeting of urban areas by ethno-nationalist forces seeking to ethnically homogenise cities; the use of explosives by non-state actors such as so-called Islamic State to target cultural heritage; terrorist destruction of urban fabric and transport infrastructure such as witnessed in New York (2001), Madrid (2003) and London (2005); as well as suicide attacks on public spaces as witnessed in Mumbai (2008), Paris (2015), Brussels (2015) and Lahore (2016). To this list could be added the increasing risk to energy and data infrastructures from various disruptive cyber-attacks as well as the various 'modernisation' programmes that upgrade urban fabric through destruction. However, across this list, the central threat is one of physical disruption – the destruction of the urban fabric in a way that either erases shared space or that damages connective infrastructures.

There is an arsenal of weapons and techniques available in the 21st century for destroying the spaces and interconnections of the city. Indeed, as the recent campaign focused on the use of explosive weapons in populated areas has shown, the capacity to target the city with lethal violence is a matter of urgent priority (Article 36, 2013). Global urbanisation has led to an increase in the military targeting of, and operations in, the city. These operations give rise to novel weapons and doctrines. On the one hand, then, there is an increase in operations using either weapons or tactics that were originally developed for contexts other than the city. By and large these weapons and tactics were designed to have effects that do not take into account the populated and connected nature of the city. On the other hand, weapons and tactics have been evolved to engage with the city. These weapons seek to exploit the vulnerability of urban fabric to maximise impact. Whether it is the deployment of existing weapons and tactics in urban contexts or the development of urbanised warfare, the effects can be said to be anti-urban and, thereby, antisocial – seeking the destruction of the spaces and everyday connections that characterise city life. In order to see the anti-urban effects of war in and against the city, we might consider the recent history of destruction wrought by two weapons systems: the BM-21 'Grad' multiple-barrel rocket launcher (MBRL) and the BLU-114/B so-called 'soft' or 'blackout' bomb.

MBRL 'systems can launch many rockets (40 in the case of the Grad) within a very short space of time, either in salvos (all rockets at once) or sequentially.... The primary role of long-range MBRLs is in saturating a wide target area with explosive force at a high rate of fire' (Brehm, 2014, p 22). The 'Grad' is designed to deliver multiple warheads over a wide area, and was primarily designed for use against opposing forces out in the open (that is, not in populated/urban areas). It was designed to target massed infantry or mechanised forces, potentially in reinforced defensive positions. The munitions are not controlled in flight and cannot be considered to have any precision.

Indeed, in testimony to the International Criminal Tribunal for the former Yugoslavia it was noted that the

> ... multiple barrel rocket launcher is designed to have a spread pattern of tens of metres, if not hundreds of metres, depending on the type.... It is not possible to fire the weapon and have the shells land in a very small area ... it would be impossible ... to predict ... where the rockets would land. (Brehm, 2104, p 42)

It goes without saying that the use of MBRLs in urban areas will cause widespread destruction. Given that operators will be well aware of the area effect and impossibility of predicting the specific destination of the individual rockets in each salvo, this widespread destruction can be considered both deliberate and indiscriminate.

Grad MBRLs were used to destroy urban fabric in wars in the former Yugoslavia (1992–95) and Chechnya (1994–96) (Human Rights Watch, 1995; Thomas, 1999). In addition to causing civilian deaths, MBRL assaults destroy the buildings that make up the shared spaces of the city. The area effect of such weapons results in the levelling of the city – removing the various markers that define urban space and establish the various shared coordinates of city life. The effect is, therefore, to unmake or decompose the urban fabric, destroying the shared spaces that enable the various encounters with others that make up urban life. This levelling of the city is an erasing of the very foundations for the social plurality that characterises the city and, as such, is an attack on the possibility of such co-existence.

The 'blackout' bomb is aimed at an enemy's electricity infrastructure. A development of the Kit 2 Tomahawk cruise missile that was used in 1991 to destroy Iraq's electricity grid during operation desert storm, the BLU–114/B, was used to incapacitate Serbia's electricity grid during the 1999 NATO bombing of Belgrade (Federation of American Scientists, nd). The weapon disperses graphite filaments over key elements of the electricity grid. As *The New York Times* noted, these 'graphite filaments ... triggered massive short circuits at switching stations and caused power grids to shut down' (Fitchett, 1999). NATO spokesperson Jamie Shae claimed at a daily press briefing that the 'lights went out across 70% of the country' and that this demonstrated that 'NATO has its finger on the light switch in Yugoslavia now and we can turn the power off whenever we need to' (NATO, 1999a). In separate remarks Shae argued that the ordnance

... short-circuits electrical systems without destroying the basic infrastructure which drives those systems ... our key objective is not to deprive the Serb people of their electrical grid but to be able to disrupt and degrade at will the power that drives the military machine so that it is shut off for significant periods of time. (NATO, 1999b)

The 'blackout' bomb thus represents a weapon – and associated tactical thinking – that has evolved to deliberately target the urban fabric. Its apparent precision is a product of deliberately seeking to attack the interconnection that characterises urban life. Shae's remarks underline the way in which such attacks on infrastructure are often regarded as a non-destructive form of warfare. And yet this fails to acknowledge the centrality of infrastructure to urban life and the impact on social conditions within cities affected by such weapons systems. In addition to its key role in supporting contemporary urban life, infrastructure is 'the connective tissue' that forges the various relationships on which plurality is based (Muschamp, 1994). If we are not connected, we cannot encounter others. While targeting infrastructure is seen as bloodless coercion, it has the effect of undermining the very social fabric of the city, atomising its inhabitants.

Urbicide

The destruction of shared spaces and connective infrastructures as a deliberate strategy has been referred to as urbicide – literally, the killing of cities (Coward, 2009). Although the term was coined in the mid-20th century during discussions of urban planning, it rose to prominence in the context of the collapse of the former Yugoslavia. In the context of the shelling of cities such as Sarajevo, Vukovar and Mostar, the perception was that there was a deliberate attempt to destroy the city. Indeed, the destruction of cities in the former Yugoslavia (but particularly in Bosnia) was widespread and deliberate, and extended beyond military objectives and symbolic targets to include the everyday urban fabric, such as apartments, car parks, shops and parks. The subsequent levelling of parts of Grozny by the Russian army (particularly in 1999–2000) reinforced the perception that there was an emerging trend towards widespread, deliberate destruction of urban fabric.

Urbicide has risen to prominence in the post-Cold War period as a military strategy, during a period in which urbanisation has become the predominant form of global life. All major transitions pose profound questions about the way they are reconfiguring life. Global urbanisation is no different – it poses the question of what urbanisation comprises, how it is reconfiguring society and politics, and how we should respond. Urbicide dramatically intensifies these questions. If buildings and infrastructures are destroyed because they are the defining characteristics of the city, urbicide poses the question of what it is precisely that such elements of the urban fabric do that is so important for urban life. Answering this question tells us something about the nature of contemporary urbanity – how the urban fabric that is the environment for the majority of global lives creates distinctive conditions for social life.

Urbicide targets everyday elements of the urban fabric. Such urban fabric divides into two broad categories: the everyday architectures and spaces of the city and urban infrastructures. The former are the office blocks, houses, apartments, shopping complexes, car parks and parks that are the places that orient our daily lives and constitute the spaces where encounters with others happen. The latter are the connective tissues of the urban fabric, the conduits, wires, cables, pipes, roads, rails that transport waste, food, consumer goods, people, data, money, power and so on. Urbicide targets these elements of the urban fabric precisely because they are constitutive of the possibility of social life within the city. Urbicide is aimed at the physical and social constitution of the city itself – the public spaces and the interconnections that make up its characteristic plurality. Urbicide thus attacks plurality by targeting the urban fabric responsible for the two key characteristics that underpin plurality: connection and sharing.

Urbicide attacks plurality in an attempt to control or eliminate it. Cities have long been seen as unruly spaces. Machiavelli, for example, devoted a chapter of *The Prince* to the question of subduing cities. This unruliness derives from the plurality of the city – the visible presence of many different ways of life. As a confirmation that this is the case we only need look at the long history of attempts to segregate this plurality, to confine it (such as in ghettos) or to control access to spaces through architectural, legal or financial regulations (via walls, fences, leases, tariffs). Urbicide comprises a strategy to undermine plurality through deliberate destruction of the urban fabric. It is normally a first phase, prior to the assertion of a homogeneous polity on the space 'cleared' by urbicidal violence. At stake in urbicide, then, is the plural sociality characteristic of the city. Urbicide thus requires a prosocial response.

The threat to urban life highlighted by urbicide – to shared spaces and connective infrastructures – poses questions about how we might better protect and foster urban societies in the contemporary era. We need a response that is not simply conservative in seeking to protect key elements of the urban fabric and repair damage done, a kind of heritage humanitarianism that simply conserves the status quo. We need a response to urban destruction – and the forces and weapons capable of that destruction – that seeks to understand how urban life might be proactively strengthened in the face of threats. This is not a resilience that allows cities to live with – and thus accept the inevitability of – destruction. Rather, it would be a framework – of normative and legal commitments as well as planning guidelines and building regulations – that protects the core attributes of urban life: its spaces and interconnections.

A prosocial response to attacks on the city

Before I turn to specific actions we can take to protect the city against urbicide, I want to suggest that the prosocial response to violence against the infrastructures and shared spaces of the city requires three general commitments. First, a strengthening of legal protections of, and advocacy for, the built environment is required. The built environment and the infrastructure it contains is often assumed to be a secondary concern behind the human casualties of war and development. While we should be outraged by, and legislate against, civilian deaths we should also ensure that we protect the public spaces and infrastructures of the city that make urban lives meaningful. There is a considerable legal machinery available for protecting cities as well as an advocacy network geared towards holding those who violate these laws to account. Key here would not only be protection against destruction, but also against the injustices of poor planning or infrastructural inequality.

Second, there should be an enhanced humanitarianism that values the everyday urban fabric as a constituent part of, not simple support for, social life. A disproportionate focus on symbolic architecture has meant that the importance of everyday shared spaces and unglamorous infrastructures in creating the plurality characteristic of the city has been under-acknowledged. Thus, while it is important to protect key cultural sites, it is equally important not to treat the everyday urban fabric and its associated infrastructures as making a less significant contribution to defining contemporary ways of life. While it is true, of course, that ancient sites should be protected because they cannot be replaced, the perception that everyday urban fabric is less significant because it is replaceable should be contested. Replacing infrastructures and housing takes time and never creates a simple replication of that which has been destroyed. Disruption (and often displacement) and the permanent reconfiguration (which can involve partial or total loss) of certain shared spaces and connections are thus an inevitable consequence of urban destruction. A concern, therefore, for the human inhabitants of cities must also involve a concern for the urban fabric that defines their lives. Similar aspirations might also be enshrined within the principles of urban planning more broadly. Humanitarianism must, therefore, entail a duty of care for that everyday urban fabric.

Finally, there should be a commitment to building and maintaining the urban fabric that underpins the plural spaces that are at stake in – and will ultimately resist – urbicide. Here I am not arguing for the kind of measures that are being taken against threats posed by terrorist attacks on public spaces: hardening, surveillance and increased (and increasingly armed) policing (National Counter Terrorism Security Office, 2014). Indeed, one could argue that these efforts are more likely to disrupt urban environments by restricting the ways in which inhabitants encounter one another and experience the daily life of such securitised cities. Such restrictions are common in contemporary cities – especially those where shared spaces are increasingly privatised and access is controlled to suit the commercial purposes of landowners (Minton, 2006). Under such conditions encounters with others are tightly regulated and plurality – the encounter with those genuinely different to us – is reduced, if not eliminated.

Rather, what we might begin to argue for is the need to recognise the importance of the urban fabric and infrastructure in generating the shared space and connectivity that defines urban ways of life. Such a recognition would start with a prioritisation of sharing and connecting in questions of urban planning, development and justice. Indeed, there would be a normative presumption against urban fabric and infrastructure that represented a reduction in sharing or connectivity.

A right to the city?

Taken together this prosocial response to urbicide comprises a manifesto for an enhanced right to the city: a right to the spaces and infrastructures that create the plurality that is characteristic of urban life. This right to the city is somewhat different to that which has been gaining traction internationally. In its initial formation in the writings of Henri Lefebvre, the right to the city was conceived as 'the right to inhabit the city, the right to produce urban life ... and the right of inhabitants to remain unalienated from urban life' (Attoh, 2011, p 674). Lefebvre's claim is echoed by David Harvey who argues that the right to the city 'is a right to change ourselves by changing the city [which] depends upon the exercise of a collective power to reshape the processes of urbanization' (Harvey, 2008, p 23). Such claims are predicated on a Marxist understanding of the city as a motor of capitalist forces that exploit and alienate those whose labour is productive of urban life. As such the right to the city should be a right to reclaim the city as something that is shared and collectively produced.

In practice, this claim has been taken up in a number of ways, particularly by advocacy groups arguing for the right to public housing.[1] Perhaps most significantly, the right to the city has been translated into the 2001 Brazilian City Statute. The Statute builds on the 1988 Brazilian constitution that established the priority of municipal governments in planning and development, and tasked them with ensuring the social function of urban development (as well as creating a right to the regularisation of informal settlement via a limited right to land title). The Statute develops the constitution particularly to mandate municipal planning and prioritise the use function of urban fabric over exchange value. This Brazilian experiment with the right to the city informed, in turn, the World Charter for the Right to the City circulated at the 2004 World Social Forum and related events (World Charter for the Right to the City, 2005).

Central to the various elaborations of the right to the city has been a concern with contesting inequality and urban exclusion generated by economic exploitation of the urban fabric. At the heart of these claims for a right to the city is the notion that inhabitants of the city should enjoy full use of the city. While this right is sometimes presented as a fundamental right to liberty, it is, in fact, primarily socioeconomic: a claim to enjoy certain collective goods and be protected against exclusion. Such a right, in turn, obligates city authorities to ensure that a legal and political framework exists to ensure that the social use value of the urban fabric is prioritised. In other words, the public use of urban infrastructures and city spaces should be prioritised as far as is possible.

Conclusion: beyond human rights

Rights such as freedom or socioeconomic justice are human rights; they attach to individuals (or collections of individuals) who claim them as requisites for living a full life. I want to argue not for human rights, as important as these are, but on behalf of the buildings and infrastructures that are the background enabling conditions of what is so often today an urbanised form of social life. Before we can live such a full urban life, we must have the spaces and connections that underpin such a life. In other words, while the ability to claim liberty, equality or justice is important, it only makes sense in the context of a right to the things that are the basis of all possible urban lives. Without the distinctive material fabric that makes a city what it is, rights to living certain types of urban life are substantially degraded if not meaningless. This is the threat posed by urban destruction.

Such a claim implies an obligation to provide and protect certain types of urban fabric in order that human rights to an urban life can become meaningful. What might this mean in terms of the defence of the city against urban destruction? In the first place it might involve thinking about the current protection of the city against military aggression. The city is not well protected against attacks. Individuals and communities are partially protected by laws of war and established understandings of crimes against humanity. On the one hand, these establish a logic of proportionality that demands force be applied with some discrimination. On the other, they establish protections for certain forms of group identity. However, proportionality and group rights do not defend against the targeting of the pre-conditions of urban life. While the laws of war can be used to challenge the use of area weapons such as MBRLs in urban environments (insofar as they are likely to have indiscriminate effects; see Brehm, 2014), it could be argued that the concept of proportionality itself has led to devices such as the 'blackout' bomb as militaries seek to legitimise violence in and against urban environments. Indeed, 'switching cities' off has emerged as a tactical choice designed to 'protect' civilians – despite its de-urbanising consequences (Graham, 2005).

We might argue, therefore, that a two-pronged approach is required. On the one hand, it should be recognised – as some NGO actors have argued – that explosive force (particularly weapons that have wide area effects) endangers urban environments. As such the use of explosive weapons with wide area effects should be avoided in urban environments.[2] At stake here is not simply individual life, but rather an urban way of life. A strong case should be made that such a way of life is not compatible with weaponry that seeks to destroy the material fabric and infrastructure that makes possible the plurality that characterises city life. On the other hand, the use of other, apparently discriminating types of force should also be contested on the basis that they strike at the heart of the urban way of life. Weapons that deliberately disconnect or disrupt should be proscribed in the same way as explosive weapons. Seeking to disrupt infrastructure should thus be proscribed as a crime against urban life – at a time when humanity has become urbanised, we could also say it is a crime against humanity.

Given the threats faced by urban societies (for example, paramilitary/terrorist violence and/or malevolent hacking) some will argue that states and militaries must retain the capacity to deploy force in the city. However, this misses the point. In the first place deploying violence that destroys or disrupts urban fabric and spaces is no defence of the city at all. It is a strike at the plural and unruly nature of the city that seeks to provide security through a segregation of the city into enclaves: safety through reduction of encounters with otherness. Such enclaves are a form of negative urbanism. Second, it prioritises armed force over other mechanisms for defending the city, from (de-militarised) policing to robust public contestation of hate speech and other forms of extremism. Indeed, the properly prosocial result of a proscription of the destruction of urban fabric and infrastructure would be an increase in the sense that negotiating provocative encounters with others is a defining feature of the city that should be acknowledged and protected. In turn, a daily encounter with plurality could generate more resourceful responses to those provocations regarded as antithetical to urban and human rights, responses that sought to de-marginalise through extension of justice and equality to those currently denied full urban existences. What is certain is that prosocial stances towards the city require protecting the very conditions of plurality that define urban life. Doing so requires contesting the polarising, de-urbanising effects of military attacks on cities. Only in doing so will we be able to realise the full social and political potential of global urbanisation.

Notes

[1]   See, for example, http://righttothecity.org/

[2]   For NGOs calling for a political declaration committing states to avoiding the use of explosive weapons with wide area effects in populated areas, see Article 36 (www.article36.org/) or International Network on Explosive Weapons (www.inew.org/).

Acknowledgements

My understanding of the campaign to address explosive weapons in populated areas owes much to discussion with Thomas Nash and Maya Brehm – Maya's comments on my discussion of international humanitarian law were immensely helpful. As ever, I am solely responsible for any remaining errors.

References

Article 36 (2013) *Damage to the built environment from the use of explosive weapons* (www.article36.org/wp-content/uploads/2013/09/DAMAGE.pdf).

Attoh, K.A. (2011) 'What kind of right is the right to the city?', *Progress in Human Geography*, vol 35, no 5, p 674.

Berman, M. (2014) 'Emerging from the ruins', *Dissent*, Winter (www.dissentmagazine.org/article/emerging-from-the-ruins).

Brehm, M. (2014) 'Unacceptable risk: Use of explosive weapons in populated areas through the lens of three cases before the ICTY', *Pax* (www.paxvoorvrede.nl/media/files/pax-rapport-unacceptable-risk.pdf).

Brenner, N. and Schmid, C. (2014) 'The "urban age" in question', *International Journal of Urban and Regional Research*, vol 38, no 3, pp 731-55.

Coward, M. (2009) *Urbicide: The politics of urban destruction*, London: Routledge.

FAS (Federation of American Scientists) (nd) 'CBU-94 "Blackout Bomb"/BLU-114/B "Soft-Bomb"', *FAS Military Analysis Network* (http://fas.org/man/dod-101/sys/dumb/blu-114.htm).

Fitchett, J. (1999) 'First use by US short-circuits power grid: NATO knocks out Serbian electricity with new weapon', *The New York Times*, 4 May (www.nytimes.com/1999/05/04/news/04iht-belgrade.2.t.html).

Graham, S. (2005) 'Switching cities off: Urban infrastructure and US air power', *City*, vol 9, no 2, pp 169-94.

Harvey, D. (2008) 'The right to the city', *New Left Review*, vol 53, pp 23-40 (http://newleftreview.org/II/53/david-harvey-the-right-to-the-city).

Human Rights Watch (1995) *Russia: War in Chechnya – New from the field* (www.hrw.org/reports/1995/Russia2.htm).

Minton, A. (2006) *The privatisation of public space*, RICS.org (https://media.wix.com/ugd/e87dab_c893a52a18624acdb94472869d942a09.pdf).

Muschamp, H. (1994) 'Two for the roads: A vision of urban design', Architecture View, *The New York Times* (www.nytimes.com/1994/02/13/arts/architecture-view-two-for-the-roads-a-vision-of-urban-design.html?pagewanted=all).

National Counter Terrorism Security Office (2014) *Protecting crowded places from terrorism* (www.gov.uk/government/collections/crowded-places).

NATO (1999a) Press Conference by Dr Jamie Shea and Major General Walter Jertz, 3 May (www.nato.int/kosovo/press/p990503b.htm).

NATO (1999b) Morning briefing by Jamie Shea, NATO spokesman, 3 May (www.nato.int/kosovo/press/b990503a.htm).

Thomas, T.L. (1999) 'The battle of Grozny: Deadly classroom for urban combat', *Parameters*, vol 29, pp 87-102 (http://strategicstudiesinstitute.army.mil/pubs/parameters/Articles/99summer/thomas.htm).

UN-Habitat (2006) *State of the world's cities 2006/2007*, London: Earthscan (http://mirror.unhabitat.org/pmss/getElectronicVersion.aspx?nr=2101&alt=1).

World Charter for the Right to the City (2005) (http://portal.unesco.org/shs/en/files/8218/112653091412005_-_World_Charter_Right_to_City_May_051.doc/2005+-+World+Charter+Right+to+City+May+051.doc).

SEVEN

Artfully thinking the prosocial

Deborah Warr, Gretel Taylor and Richard Williams

'Little boy running along – Bell ringing – Drill – Stick rattling fence – Orange leaves dancing in wind – Warm sun kissing face – Spring green grass – Bright yellow flower'

'I saw everything green
The sky attracts my thoughts
Same but different.' (translated from Karen Burmese)

'Ants birds burnt house Buddha bus stop breeze dirt dry grass cats & dogs heavy breathing fruit trees cough heavy feet walking stick up hill to vantage point lovely view IGA shop burnout marks on road.'

These words were generated by residents of low-income neighbourhoods who participated in a series of art-based workshops that explored issues of place and identity. Along with images, the words evoked sights, sensations and feelings as we walked together around their neighbourhood, learning to perceive it in new ways. The residents participating in the workshops were of varied ages and ethnic backgrounds, and the activity drew loosely on different practices of 'walking as art', including the Situationists' notion of the *dérive* and the textworks of the artist, Richard Long. We thus invited our participants to observe the features of their surroundings, and to foster awareness of their subjective, embodied, sensory and psychological experiences of our pedestrian passage through familiar suburban environments.

Participants sometimes photographed their observations of the neighbourhood sites, and were again invited to notice and value what they were visually or emotionally drawn to. On other walks, people were invited to bring objects from home that they felt somehow represented their identity. They explored placing these objects in playful relation to the local environment, symbolically claiming their own presence. In one site, residents painted and decorated empty picture frames and took these 'for a walk' to photograph them in the landscapes, performing the idea that what we see is impacted by how it is framed or presented to us. Images that were generated during the walking activities were incorporated into collaborative artworks that were used to present nuanced and textured images of suburbs from residents' perspectives.

The arts-based activities we have thrown at you here form part of an experimental approach for social research that fuses sociological insights with creative practice. In this chapter we explain why we consider this approach might contribute to promoting wider attempts to foster a prosocial ethos and practice. As an ethos, we conceive the prosocial as seeking to promote collective human flourishing, while a prosocial practice is inclusive and imaginative. The potential to flourish is (partly) supported by involvement in diverse social relations that connect us as families, friends, communities, neighbourhoods and nations. Experiences of social collectivity, however, are being shredded through the expanding dominance, and cascading impacts, of market-orientated ideologies. The status of the social as a non-market domain has little value or sense when seen from within these dominant ideological framings. The arts-based project explicitly addressed heightening tendencies to denigrate and stigmatise people experiencing poverty, in particular, residents of low-income neighbourhoods. In this chapter we want to discuss how low-income neighbourhoods can be seen as critical sites for exploring notions of the prosocial because they both bear the brunt of antisocial economic policies while potentially nurturing its incipient counter narratives and possibilities. We suggest here how creative practices might be used to gain insights into these situations and help to generate wider prosocial effects.

The antisocial and the prosocial

For many people living in advanced capitalist nations, a capacity to flourish is being profoundly curtailed by the encroaching dominance of economic calculations and market relations on social life. The effects of this phenomenon in Australian working-class neighbourhoods were recently explored by Dennis Glover in his book, *An economy is not a society* (2015). The sociologist Zygmunt Bauman (1998) was quick to recognise the uneven implications of neoliberal economic policies on social life. He analysed how, in countries that were transitioning from industrial to post-industrial capitalism, processes of de-industrialisation and economic rationalities have served to wipe out the livelihoods of many working-class people and ushered in fundamental changes in values. As free markets and the price mechanism become firmly established as the primary arbiter of value, people themselves have been re-valued in ways that emphasise their roles as consumers, rather than as workers and producers. They are valued as producers only in so far as they support consumption; other roles, as family members, parents, citizens, work colleagues, neighbours and friends, are largely ignored by conventional economic measures. For example, one of the best-known economic measures, gross domestic product (GDP), takes no account of household production, yet current economic activity would collapse without it.

Shifts from production to consumer capitalism have transformed popular interpretations of class in ways that highlight its cultural meanings rather than economic circumstances. Contemporary experiences of being recognised as 'working class' are now likely to involve de-valued identities that are associated with an inability to consume, or consuming in ways that are construed as displaying a lack of taste. This emphasis on what Bauman (1998) describes as 'flawed' consumption practices is associated with heightening tendencies to stigmatise people experiencing poverty and, related to this, the neighbourhoods where they live. Stigma involves negative labelling and stereotyping. In the wake of de-industrialisation and the emergence of structural unemployment, the stigmatisation of poverty in Australia is evident in widespread and pejorative references to 'bogans', akin to the use of the term 'chavs' in Britain. Other countries and regions have their own slang that is used to mark those experiencing poverty as 'other' in ways that convey disgust and contempt.

In combination with the effects of poverty itself, poverty stigma has detrimental effects on personal wellbeing and self-esteem and, similar to the effects of racism, can be associated with internalising feelings of social inferiority with effects of stifling educational and other aspirations. Stigma associated with low-income neighbourhoods leads to forms of 'postcode discrimination' that narrow access to social, economic and cultural opportunities, and afflicted towns and suburbs can be perceived as dangerous 'no go' zones, shunned by the wider community. Loic Wacquant (2008) observed that stigma can also have 'de-solidarising' effects in neighbourhoods when it influences how some residents are viewed by other locals. These circumstances can lead to local friction, diminishing opportunities for interactions between people of divergent socioeconomic status, and contribute to sociospatial segregation in cities and suburbs.

Poverty stigma has proliferated as a result of neoliberal doctrines that have had forceful antisocial effects, if considered against an inclusive interpretation of what constitutes a society. Doctrines promoting the privatisation of state assets, redirection of public spending in favour of market provision, deregulation of economies, shrinking welfare provisions, opposition to organised labour and extending the protection of private ownership are either deliberately or carelessly ruinous of collective welfare. Bauman (2000, p 163) noted that these policies have contributed to a 'fading and wilting, falling apart and decomposing of human bonds of communities and partnerships.' The prosocial can draw attention to antisocial effects that inhibit capacities for collective flourishing, such as intensifying problems of poverty stigma and overlapping issues of social fragmentation, which have been aggravated by neoliberal economic policies. Further, prosocial research practices can be used to develop alternative understandings of the situations of those experiencing poverty that resist stigmatising tendencies.

Although perceptive and impassioned, analyses such as Bauman's can be overwhelmingly bleak. They point to the ways in which social fragmentation has undermined the potential for recognising shared problems and galvanising collective action, and that the capacity of politics to grapple with public issues has been severely eroded. Nonetheless, we must resist giving up struggles to envisage and create conditions that contribute to collective flourishing (see Keith Jacobs' reflections on these issues in Chapter Three). In these efforts, a prosocial ethos challenges antisocial dynamics and promotes inclusive access to material, social and symbolic resources. This requires recognising the commonalities between diverse people and striving to nurture formal and informal social relations that connect us in families, neighbourhoods, communities, cities, nations and a common humanity.

These issues lead us to proffer several reasons why poverty stigma is a useful prism for refracting the possibilities of a prosocial ethos and practice. As we have suggested above, the interlinked antisocial effects of neoliberalism and consumer capitalism are causing social differences to be viewed in less neutral ways, which contributes to conditions that undermine the potential for collective flourishing. Other reasons are more speculative. Neighbourhoods experiencing poverty, socioeconomic marginalisation and stigma can be construed as sites of 'socialisation'. This refers to forms of non-market cooperation by social actors (Gough, 2002). Gough critically interrogates the co-option of forms of socialisation by neoliberal projects. He observes that sites of socialisation, albeit penetrated by neoliberal ideologies and extant patriarchal, class and racial power relations, may nonetheless offer helpful starting points for activating strategies that challenge neoliberal tenets, and the social injustices that are being perpetrated. However, in low-income neighbourhoods and marginalised communities, stigma risks discounting the prosocial qualities needed to realise this potential. Hence such sites need to be perceived in new ways. We explore the power of creative strategies to generate nuanced and reflexive accounts of everyday life in low-income neighbourhoods that are less tinted by effects of stigma.

To unpack these ideas, we recall the work of C. Wright Mills who outlined the task of sociology as making links between individual experience and macrosocial dynamics. He conceptualised this as requiring a 'sociological imagination' that traces the links between 'private troubles' and 'public issues'. Mills' insights, published in his influential book, *The sociological imagination* (Mills, 1959, 2000), deserve revisiting because there are parallels between contemporary times and issues that he was grappling with almost 60 years ago. Drawing on his ideas, we suggest that it is timely to develop a prosociological imagination that is critical and creative. It must explicate the damaging impacts of neoliberalism on everyday personal and community life in ways that embolden us to query, challenge and resist its tenets. Activating a prosocial ethos, however, also requires creativity and experimentation to reveal its significance and potential. We go on to explain how we drew on these ideas to challenge poverty stigma by recovering and revealing the value of the lives of those who have been profoundly disadvantaged by economic and social changes over recent decades.

A prosocial imagination

Mills understood that relationships between the personal and the political are not necessarily evident. He argued that the task of sociology is to link biography (the stories of individuals) to history (their collective situations) and the 'intersections with socioeconomic structures' (1959, 2000, p 143). He perceived that an inability to make these associations leads to apathy and disengagement. He reflected on the ways in which events in the 1930s prompted discussions about the 'crisis of capitalism' that dissipated by the late 1950s into a vague disquiet lacking social and political critique:

> Much private uneasiness goes unformulated; much public malaise and many decisions of enormous structural relevance never become public issues. For those who accept such inherited values as reason and freedom, it is the uneasiness itself that is the trouble; it is the indifference itself that is the issue. And it is this condition, of uneasiness

and indifference, that is the signal feature of our period. (Mills, 1959, p 12)

By the end of the 1950s Mills believed that people were reacting to situations associated with the post-war ascendency of capitalism, but that they struggled to articulate or explain these reactions. He argued that a sociological imagination enabled people to interpret their situations in relation to wider social, economic and cultural dynamics, in ways that can inform political projects. In the wake of the Great Recession in 2008 (or the Global Financial Crisis in some parts of the world), economic shocks and alarming rises in socioeconomic inequalities, both between and within countries, renewed talk of a crisis in capitalism, but this sense of crisis has again subsided into vague feelings of unease, apprehension and anxiety. It seems timely to recover an understanding of the links between personal troubles and public issues, as Mills put it. Arguably, this is a greater challenge than ever before because, as an economic, social and political project, neoliberalism has largely avoided public scrutiny. Its proponents are masterful dissemblers and many of its propositions, its language and its methods have become so normalised that alternatives have been driven out of sight. Although academic scholarship links growing inequalities and undermining of democratic processes to the prevailing influence of neoliberal tenets, these associations have scarcely entered public debate on key economic and social issues.

The covert dominance of neoliberalism suggests that there are tough challenges in developing a prosociological imagination that shows how complex social scenarios, such as rising socioeconomic inequalities and diminishing social security in seemingly affluent nations, are public issues rather than the outcomes of individual failings. As Zygmunt Bauman argued, neoliberalism has forged conditions in which it is increasingly difficult to dispute its social and political claims in ways that can lead to transformative political action. Bauman despaired that rather than private troubles being analysed in ways that bring public issues to the surface, private troubles are simply being made public. This is perhaps unhelpful for grasping the significance of public issues such as widening inequalities, and overcoming these challenges requires methodological and representational approaches that contend with the conditions of contemporary experience. Mills himself was scathing of what he termed 'abstracted empiricism', a decontextualised, atheoretical and depoliticised methodological approach to the study of human life, and advocated a sociological practice that engaged with public and political issues. As familiar categories of sociological analysis are dissolving and reformulating in response to shifting socioeconomic dynamics, new kinds of intellectual strategies, conceptual tools and representational approaches are required. In relation to this, we return to our preamble to suggest how creative methods can enhance a prosociological imagination by broadening the field over which the researcher can range and the perspectives that can be found there.

A need to understand our lives in new ways

Art offers imaginative resources, experimental practices and expressive possibilities that can be used to cultivate a prosociological imagination. This potential encouraged us to explore creative practices within research that aimed to understand and challenge the stigmatisation of poverty. As we have suggested, poverty stigma could be conceived as an antithetical force to that of the prosocial. It divides and creates differentiation, while a prosocial ethos would create encounters to enhance interaction and bring people together – across class, cultural and economic difference.

Our objectives were strongly informed by an awareness of the risks of research for communities experiencing stigma – the possibility of further making the private troubles of these social areas more public. The ways in which poverty is portrayed in the media (as news), in varied forms of cultural production (as stories) and through research (as knowledge) influences public understanding. As this suggests, research has had an influential role in constructing knowledge and representations of poverty and disadvantage through the ways in which it describes, measures and analyses problems of poverty. If anything, poverty is over-researched, albeit from a very narrow range of research perspectives. Of abiding concern to us is that portrayals of poverty, including those generated through research, can have 'reality effects' when they (unintentionally) reinforce negative impressions of people and places in ways that compound situations of social and economic exclusion (Champagne, 1999). The potential for research focusing on situations of poverty to have 'reality effects' is not widely acknowledged by researchers. Indeed, some researchers are likely to believe that highlighting social disorders associated with circumstances of poverty is important for gaining the attention of politicians and fostering public concern. An example of this is evident in a major report on poverty in Australia that included a foreword quoting the Prime Minister at the time in which he responded to alarming data revealing the geographic clustering of socioeconomic disadvantage and resultant social distress:

We need to find innovative ways to break the vicious cycles of poor parenting, low levels of education, unemployment and health problems that can afflict some individuals and communities. We need to find ways of restoring order to zones of chaos in some home and communities – zones of chaos that can wreck young Australian lives. (Vinson, 2007, foreword)

In this interpretation the findings have been de-contextualised, and the uneven effects of economic restructuring, disinvestment and the residualisation of public housing in Australian suburbs are disregarded. Portraying low-income neighbourhoods as 'zones of chaos' risks amplifying stigmatising stereotypes and distorting the everyday realities of residents' lives in ways that imply radical social difference at the expense of their commonality with other neighbourhoods. In his book, *The likes of us*, Michael Collins (2004) pointed to similar tendencies in early 20th-century 'slum fiction' and reportage that focused on the impoverished districts of South London. Much of the writing portrayed people's lives as unrelenting squalor, despair and brutality. Collins argued that this work, invariably produced by outsiders, failed to offer 'a more representative portrait of urban working-class life, in all its quotidian glory ... that touched on but did not dwell on squalor, hooliganism and crime' (Collins, 2004, p 80). His point is important: detached outsiders making fleeting visits often fail to notice the breadth of experiences and local complexities, or to position them within social, economic, cultural and historical contexts.

With these issues in mind, we wanted to find new ways of researching problems of poverty and stigma that avoided misleading portrayals and negative reality effects. Critically, this requires placing value in residents as experts in their own lives and eliciting a phenomenological, site-specific knowledge of place. Integrating creative processes with more conventional sociological research processes offered an exciting potential to work with residents to co-construct representations of their neighbourhoods that were nuanced, insightful, respectful and reflexive. In these aims, we also responded to Les Back's (2012, p 20) call to reinvigorate the possibilities of sociological research, through using 'live' methods that have 'a greater humility about the truth we might touch but not grasp fully, while contesting the realities that others claim with such certainty.' We wanted to explore experiences of place in ways that brought uncertainty, ambiguity and contradiction to the surface and filled out the 'story' of a place beyond fact-based deduction and data.

Prosocial imaginative action

Site-specific art offered stimulating possibilities for a project seeking to use creative approaches to explore place and identity. Miwon Kwon (2002) explains that site-specific art emerged as a movement rebelling against the commercialism of art and the limitations of the gallery system, but has since evolved into an artistic field that has the potential to articulate the changing roles and experiences of place in contemporary worlds. In moving out of traditionally elite cultural spaces, site-specific practice often draws on historical, ecological and sociopolitical dimensions of a place, yielding the potential to democratise both art and space in its location 'out in the world'. In our research, site-specific practice offered approaches to gently interrogate, problematise and represent residents' experiences of their neighbourhoods. This emphasis on making art in response to the site or place was combined with a community cultural development approach that uses proactively inclusive principles. Ideas and practices were integrated via creative processes as starting points to explore key themes, and the artist's (GT) facilitation provided support for resident-participants who may have otherwise lacked confidence or capacity to take part in creative activities. They were guided to reflect on their relationships with place, each other, and wider communities, and to generate creative artifacts that explored experiences of place in locally meaningful ways, and which could also engage wider audiences.

The research involved a series of local projects. Combining excursions, artistic practices and walking activities, these projects aimed to provoke new kinds of encounters with and representations of familiar environments. Each project commenced with an excursion to art galleries. This was novel for many resident-participants, who often have limited opportunities to visit the city and are unaccustomed to visiting arts venues. The excursions offered a supportive introduction to the gallery spaces, social interaction with other residents of diverse cultures and ages, and expanded perceptions of what might constitute 'art'. In an attempt to counter the pervasive perception of the gallery as an elite space, as John Holden discussed in his proposition of 'cultural democracy' (2008), participants were encouraged to notice and photograph things they encountered that they found strange, funny, surprising, shocking and inspiring on the excursion. As co-participants, we all experienced some sense of social and geographic dislocation that could give rise to new possibilities of relating to the people and sights that were encountered.

The excursions were followed up with a series of neighbourhood-based workshops that engaged the participants in photography, sculpture and conceptual craft. The workshops were punctuated by group walks through which local environments were explored via perceptual and embodied experiences. Participants were encouraged to observe and photograph things they were drawn to, and to explore how they might abstractly illustrate their own presence and experiences in these environments as shadows, footprints or reflections (rather than literal representations such as 'selfie' shots). In varied ways these site-specific approaches incorporated participants' multisensory, experiential knowledge into their representations of their neighbourhood.

Walking as art and as a radical pedestrian practice has been extensively theorised by thinkers including Michel de Certeau (1984) and Guy Debord (1958). In *The practice of everyday life* (1984), de Certeau describes walking in the city as a ground-level spatial practice, whereby one is immersed in the city's streets, inhabiting and engaging in a practice in relation to the spaces one traverses. He suggested that walking in cities potentially resists the system of power imposed by modern town planning, by which surveillance from a vantage point above the city aspires to a detached totalising coherence (de Certeau, 1984, pp 91-110). In our project, the walking activities facilitated participants (residents and researchers) to engage with places in an immersed interrelation, valuing insights that emerged from the involvement with the specific features and ambiances of the site. That the researchers were also involved in this close range, 'ground-level' practice is significant in attempting to generate knowledge from an immersed interrelation, rather than an all-encompassing exterior viewpoint.

In addition to gaining this intimate perspective on the neighbourhoods, we adapted the Situationist practice of the *dérive* to connect us in a shared experience (researchers and residents, including residents with diverse backgrounds, abilities and experiences, interpreters and carers) of walking together in an unstructured tour of the neighbourhood. The *dérive* was conceived by Guy Debord in the 1950s as an antidote to the tedium, listlessness and benumbing effects that he attributed to the intensifying influence of capitalism in everyday life. Debord defined the *dérive* as a technique of 'drifting' through varied terrain (usually urban), allowing oneself to 'be drawn' with 'playful-constructive behaviour' and awareness of the effects of the geographical environment on the emotions and behaviour (a theory they termed 'psychogeography') (Debord, 1958). We used it to refresh our senses to what we noticed as we moved through familiar streets, and to open up our sensory, imaginative and thought-provoking responses to the neighbourhoods, realising what the art historian and critic Claire Bishop describes as an 'integration of art and life' (2012, p 83).

On returning from a *dérive*, participants were encouraged to encapsulate their experiences in lists of single words or short phrases. The excerpts at the opening of this chapter offer examples of the textworks that were created, reminiscent of Richard Long's 'Textworks'.[1] The first example suggests experiences of pleasure and beauty aroused through sight, sound and feeling. The second was created by Karen Burmese women, who participated in the workshops with the assistance of an interpreter. The poetic poignancy of their words offered complex insights into experiences of migration – an experience of a present place evoking a distant other. The third example conveys contradictions that are left unresolved (abandoned houses scattered among houses with well-tended gardens) from the embodied perspective of an older participant. The *dérive*, in rendering the local and familiar a site of imaginative and playful interaction, afforded residents the opportunity to reflect on their relationships to their place, and their locational identities.

In another session, participants were invited to bring objects of personal significance from home. They explored placing these objects in relation to the local environment. In one series of workshops, picture frames that were decorated by participants were taken on walks and photographed in situ to suggest a 'reframing' of the familiar environment. In another site, a collaborative work was created as a riposte to disparaging references to a road that bordered the neighbourhood and that was referred to by outsiders as the 'flannelette curtain' ('behind it live the bogans'). Photographs taken during walking activities on the 'wrong' side of this boundary were arranged, designed and printed on a large flag and hung as a curtain in a gallery, as a work entitled 'Curtain call'.

During these workshops, the artist offered participants short presentations on art movements and facilitated group discussions in which participants reflected on external perceptions of their area and the lived realities. The educative aspects of the arts programmes introduced participants to contemporary art as well as encouraging trust in their own aesthetic tastes and interests and value in their existing knowledge of place. The discussions provoked new thoughts and insights that informed creative tasks, and participants' choices about how they represented their relationships to the place were sometimes complicated by these reflections. Follow-up interviews were conducted with participants to explore their motivations for getting involved in the project, perceptions of their neighbourhoods and responses to the workshops. Many participants reported that they welcomed opportunities to explore creative practices, engage with diverse participants in the workshops, and forge ongoing social groups and friendships. Being present in the neighbourhoods we witnessed community-based organisations and residents demonstrate a prosocial ethos through their efforts to foster a collective local flourishing, despite a paucity of resources. This was evident in the themes of creative work, and social interactions that were observed, which displayed the value of neighbourhood connections. In particular, community centres and schools hosted a range of inclusive and cooperative programmes that facilitated exchanges of resources and support, and where we encountered immense generosity and acts of social caring. In these ways, the neighbourhoods offered remnant sites of socialisation within the encroaching influence of neoliberal values. It is important for social research to capture these aspects of community life, in addition to explaining the personal and social harms that are associated with poverty and socioeconomic marginalisation.

The blending of art and research offered the potential for people to express complex ideas in ways that could evoke ambiguity and contradiction, and to navigate around the limitations of language. This included enabling some level of communication between neighbours who may not have a shared language. We describe this approach as a prosocial practice because it responded to situations of socioeconomic exclusion among residents, while valuing the importance of local social relations; it was used to defuse the risks of representing poverty, and to foster empathetic engagement among wider audiences.

Conclusion

Many social thinkers have recognised the antisocial outcomes of rampant capitalism and conceived imaginative and provocative responses to its perils. It is timely to revisit these ideas to extend and adapt them to inform current struggles in which we are pitted against forms of capitalism that are harsher and more assertive and totalising in their effects than 20th-century models. Social research has much to offer by theorising and empirically exploring the local impacts of interlocking social, economic and cultural conditions. Research, however, must be vigilant in mitigating its own potential to have antisocial effects, and must strive to register the breadth and complexity of all lives.

We have suggested that the disciplinary insights of sociology are critical for understanding and responding to the antisocial effects of neoliberalism, and integrating artistic practices into social research offers an exciting potential to represent and advance a prosocial ethos. Claire Bishop (2012, p 7) has observed that socially engaged art can have symbolic effects that are progressive and transformatory. The neighbourhood art project discussed in this chapter suggested some ways in which this potential can be developed. Given enduring concerns among artists with issues of social justice, the relationships between personal, social and political issues, and the latent power of participatory practice, it is surprising that these kinds of collaborations are not more common as they offer mutually fruitful and interesting zones of enquiry. The inter-epistemological fusion of art and social research certainly has much to contribute to the fostering of a prosociological imagination in ways that can generate new insights and rouse us into action.

Note
[1] See http://www.richardlong.org/textworks.html.

References

Back, L. (2012) 'Live sociology: Social research and its futures', *The Sociological Review*, vol 60, S118-39.

Bauman, Z. (1998) *Work, consumerism and the new poor*, Buckingham: Open University Press.

Bauman, Z. (2000) *Liquid modernity*, Cambridge: Polity Press.

Bishop, C. (2012) *Artificial hells: Participatory art and the politics of spectatorship*, London: Verso.

de Certeau, M. (1984) *The practice of everyday life*, Berkeley and Los Angeles, CA: University of California Press.

Champagne, P. (1999) 'The view from the media', in Bourdieu, P. et al. *The weight of the world*, Stanford, CA: Stanford University Press.

Collins, M. (2004) *The likes of us: A biography of the white working class*, London: Granta Books.

Debord, G. (1958) 'Theory of the dérive', *Les Lèvres Nues*, vol 9 (November 1956) (reprinted in *Internationale Situationniste*, vol 2 (December 1958).

Glover, D. (2015) *An economy is not a society: Winners and losers in the new Australia*, Collingwood, VIC: Redback.

Gough, J. (2002) 'Neoliberalism and socialisation in the contemporary city: Opposites, complements and instabilities', *Antipode*, vol 34, no 3, pp 405-26.

Holden, J. (2008) *Democratic culture: Opening up the arts to everyone*, London: Demos.

Kwon, M. (2002) *One place after another: Site-specific art and locational identity*, Cambridge, MA: The MIT Press.

Mills, C.W. (1959, 2000) *The sociological imagination*, London: Oxford University Press.

Vinson, T. (2007) *Dropping off the edge: The distribution of disadvantage in Australia*, Richmond, VIC and Curtin, ACT: Jesuit Social Services and Catholic Social Services Australia (http://k46cs13u1432b9asz49wnhcx.wpengine.netdna-cdn.com/wp-content/uploads/DOTE2007.pdf).

Wacquant, L.J.D. (2008) *Urban outcasts: A comparative sociology of advanced marginality*, Cambridge: Polity Press.

EIGHT

Re-visioning exclusion in local communities

Kate Pahl and Paul Ward

In this chapter we consider ways in which a co-produced approach to research could enable an understanding of how communities might be different. Engagement with communities at all stages of research places collaborative and participatory research methods in a central role to widen the ways community partners and universities can work together. We consider the methodologies that can be used to think about accommodating diverse opinions and tacit knowledge within communities, as well as what this tells us about processes of exclusion and integration in local communities.

When universities work collaboratively with community partners, or individuals within communities, to shape or construct research together, this process develops in different ways. Universities have been conceived of as 'anchor institutions' that contribute to 'place-making', in the words of John Goddard (Goddard and Valence, 2013). Universities can be seen as spaces where people can think, they can provide funding for innovative research projects, they can support ways of knowing and reflective practice, creating 'living knowledge' in the process (Facer and Enright, 2016). They can, in an ideal world, support activist thinking, but they can also be imagined differently, as the 'other' that communities engage with that can sometimes be useful (Facer and Pahl, 2017).

We both come from an activist perspective (Kate as a community outreach worker and Paul as a political activist in parallel with his academic career), and arrived at universities and within our disciplines as people interested in how universities can learn from the outside world to effect social change. Both of us are currently involved in a project called 'Imagine' – a large Economic and Social Research Council (ESRC)-funded project exploring the social, historical, cultural and democratic context of civic engagement, with a focus on imagining different communities and making them happen.[1] Over the past three years we have been working collaboratively with our partners in different communities to do research that matters to them. Kate has been working with community partners in Rotherham to help and support research that re-shapes and re-articulates the landscape of hope after the devastations and hurt of the Jay report into child sexual exploitation in Rotherham (Jay, 2014). Paul has been exploring ways of understanding national identities in the UK and ensuring that they represent histories of ethnic diversity, through working with community groups interested in black history and heritage in Huddersfield.

Together we think that the co-production of knowledge with community groups might be a way of thinking in different ways about, and tackling, exclusion in local communities. In our separate work, with community partners, we have learned to think differently and ask 'hard questions' to work towards more 'hard answers', drawing on the work of Raymond Williams, the cultural historian and theorist:

> Once the inevitabilities are challenged, we begin gathering our resources for a journey of hope. If there are no easy answers there are still available and discoverable hard answers and it is these that we can now learn to make and share. This has been, from the beginning, the sense and the impulse of the Long Revolution. (Williams, 1983, pp 268–9)

This quote illustrates the way in which things in communities are not easily solved. Differences of opinion arise which make the answers 'hard' and the journey difficult. The co-construction of knowledge and the co-production of research involves emotions and feelings in ways that have not been traditionally recognised within the apparently 'objective' space of social science research. Instead, as arts and humanities-defined academics, we recognise the partial, committed and interactive nature of research that we do together. Zanib Rasool, community researcher on 'Imagine', writes that:

> Community research is emotions and we have had a rollercoaster of a ride, emotions bring warmth and passion to academia. Research does not have to be cold, hard like steel and too far removed from human emotions. (Rasool, 2015)

We recognise, from Harding (2015), that the lens we bring to research as academics is itself partial and constructed, and here we want to unpack this in more depth to consider how a co-produced lens might re-frame knowledge about exclusion in communities.

Analysis: co-production and community knowledge

We begin to outline how we have learned from communities, what we have learned about doing research with communities, and describe our different approaches to this way of doing research. Co-production is currently a fashionable term to describe a number of different activities, including the co-production of services within communities, as described by economist and town planner Elinor Ostrom (1990). It has more recently been used in a more generic way to describe processes and practices by which research is done with people, communities and organisations.

Within 'Imagine' we have identified a number of different ways in which we are trying out this new type of research. For some disciplines, such as health research, there is an increasing understanding that health cannot be understood from a purely medical expert perspective. In some arts and humanities disciplines there has been significant experimentation with co-production, encouraged by the Connected Communities programme, funded by Research Councils UK. But progress has been uneven, with History, for example, falling short of the advances in co-production made in some other humanities disciplines. Historical research is still largely seen as an activity involving lone scholars working individually and directly with historical documents (whether they are in archives or elsewhere), and then publishing in forms that are reviewed by their peers. History has had limited intellectual engagement with methodologies being used in other disciplines, and many historians continue to view public engagement as an 'impact' activity, that is, linked to the Research Excellence Framework's demand that research is 'a process of investigation leading to new insights, *effectively shared*' (REF, 2011, pp 21–2) rather than a dialogue with those outside universities (but see Lloyd and Moore, 2015).

We are both interested in what happens when knowledge becomes, in some way, contested, and we are interested in how this has an impact on communities when we do research. Concepts such as 'exclusion' or 'division' can be differently perceived by different people. When I (Kate) worked in Rotherham, the concept of 'participation' was differently understood by different people. Concepts were contested as people's experiences varied and ideas of participation and inclusion were experienced in different ways. I could not rely on one definition of the concept of 'safe spaces for women and girls'. In our work, we worked with multiple definitions and recognised that working with diversity also involves the recognition of different perspectives in communities, drawing on the work of Chantal Mouffe (Miessen, 2010, pp 105–60). We began to see how difference could be productive, and in our joint working, we began to articulate ways in which we could hold different ideas and opinions in one shared space. The joint 'space' we created was a book proposal, 'Re-imagining contested communities', which attempted to tackle, from multiple perspectives, some of the challenges Rotherham was facing at the time of writing. Rotherham was experiencing a combination of far right marches and the collapse of centralised authority. The research we were doing focused on writing, on arts practice, history, culture and identity. It was generated and developed by community partners. The co-produced nature of the research was vital in that it became the space where questions of identity, culture and histories were discussed and presented (Shah, 2015). Zanib Rasool, co-author, in particular, became increasingly clear about the importance of collaborative research in creating a space for young people to articulate their sense of exclusion and division. As part of the 'Imagine' project she set up a girls poetry group that explored these issues. As one of the young people in this group wrote:

> Rotherham is my home and I like living here and every time the 'Army of Hate' visits us they leave our community feeling vulnerable, the police have enough to deal with, without this unnecessarily pressure added.
>
> The EDL's motto is 'Not racist, not violent, no longer silent.' Does anybody else see the irony in this? 'Not racist' EDL is a fascist group who are clearly Islamophobic; they are not silent when they are hurling racial abuse. Most Muslims in Rotherham respect the law and want to live peacefully, if EDL allow us. I write this sitting at home as EDL have disrupted another Saturday and created tension between communities long after they are gone, which hardly seems fair. (Aliya, aged 16)

In Huddersfield, where Paul works, a variety of minority ethnic community organisations consider that exclusion from local centres of power such as the local authority and the university disempower them, hindering their efforts at community development in the short term and obstructing the potential to recognise their historical contributions to the town, through the organisation of events such as Black History Month and the Huddersfield Carnival, as part of the real history of the town. They feel excluded from the dominant historical and cultural paradigms and held in the margins, with austerity and cuts in council funding hitting them particularly hard.

Here cultural framings from academics often feel partial and limited, particularly when the lived experience of the people we write about is not immediately accessible to us. We recognise that research itself is partial as a tool for inquiry (Law, 2004), and that it can contribute to exclusion if it privileges knowledge that is created and circulated only inside universities and academic networks.

Arts-based work in community contexts can tackle complex ideas in very different ways. In Kate's work in Rotherham, she collaborated with an artist, Zahir Rafiq, who explored the face of British Muslims today through a portraiture project. In this project, his aim was to capture the face of the 'everyday' Muslim person. Rather than focus on the images of British Muslims often represented in the press, Zahir's approach was more nuanced:

'I feel that we need to approach such studies from a different angle when it comes to exploring British Muslim identity; a balanced approach, which not only deals with history and diversity, but also complements the data with common social subjects, such as exploring themes of the everyday British Muslims, not just those who have set themselves up as the faces of the community.'

In his portrait 'Material knowledge' (see Figure 8.1), Zahir was able to capture the lived experience of his mother, who ran a material shop in Eastwood, from his perspective. The richness of the material shines out as being part of a much wider understanding of ways in which knowledge could be re-framed within community settings.

In Huddersfield, Kirklees Local TV, a social enterprise that seeks to 'document our local community', uses film to provide audiences 'with access to people and perspectives rarely seen or heard.' Its aim is 'to provide both an exciting and interactive experience by capturing and presenting the thoughts and memories of our local communities.' As with Zahir's portraits, it makes accessible the lived experience of communities in Kirklees, which includes the metropolitan areas of Huddersfield and Dewsbury, through a lens (literally) not available to academics. Its chief executive and black community activist, Milton Brown, explains:

'It's for people who don't have a voice. It's not about "black", it's not about white, it's about those who don't have a voice. Mothers, fathers, sisters brothers ... who are marginalised for any particular reason. I wanted to provide an alternative "news" for those kinds of people. It has been criticised that it's never going to make any money because of those social values, but I'm happy with that because I don't measure success, by money.' (Interview with Milton Brown, 26 February 2016)

Figure 8.1: 'Material knowledge' by Zahir Rafiq

Such community-based efforts to tackle exclusion provide new sources of knowledge with which academics can connect through long-term collaboration.

Concepts such as 'exclusion' signal the presence of discourses of otherness that many people who researched with us resisted. Alisha Berkoh, the black history coordinator at Kirklees Local TV, points out that "it's important to research black British history because it is just as much part of *our* culture as white British history" (interview with Alisha Berkoh, 26 February 2016). In this way people from minority ethnic groups are part of Kirklees, not 'other' to it. This re-situating of knowledge presents important challenges to ways in which we come to 'know' about communities, as Zanib Rasool, community researcher, points out, when discussing a project in which women brought their herbal remedies to share and then published them as a book:

Everybody holds the key to knowledge and it can be found in every community and every house in the land, although we put different value on that knowledge. For a long time community knowledge was seen as being far down the ladder from academic knowledge held by scholars; adults in our communities are not blank slates, they have life and cultural experiences and through that they acquire their own funds of knowledge and we should not disregard that when we work with communities. (Rasool, 2017, under review)

This leads to different understandings of what the issues are. When we open up our lens to differing perspectives, communities can look different. Social science-infused ways of knowing can also be challenged through ways of knowing that are influenced by historical, literary and artistic experiences. Rather than see communities as 'lacking', they become alive with possibilities and histories. These ways of seeing can de-stabilise settled assumptions about whose definitions count in what contexts.

In Huddersfield, organisations such as Building African Caribbean Communities (BACC) consider that history enables community development, but their idea of what constitutes 'history' crosses disciplinary boundaries without anxiety, destabilising how many in universities see the discipline. Explorations of the past, the town's space and places, carnival costumes, sound and sound systems readily merge in celebrations of local, regional, national and international achievement by members of the community, such as at the Black History Month Showcase, the Black Achievement Awards and Huddersfield Carnival. Knowledge is considered differently when its purpose is to build and celebrate communities rather than as an academic exercise. It enables knowledge to interact with townscapes and neighbourhoods that generate new ways of understanding, highlighting what Dolores Hayden (working in Los Angeles) explained as 'The Power of Place', in which 'combining research with community activism helped identify, interpret, and expand the intersections between everyday experience and the built environment, between the past and the present' (quoted in Meringolo, 2014, pp 419-20). In 2013, Let's Go Yorkshire initiated an arts and heritage project, led by Mandeep Samra, named 'Sound System Culture'. For many years in Huddersfield a thriving sound system scene existed out of proportion to the size of the town. The project documented the lives and experiences of those who were involved. It was a project in which the participants sought to understand sound systems through an emotional attachment and empathy with those who had gone before them, developing forms of cultural expression embedded in Britain's urban environment. Again, there were no disciplinary limits imposed. As well as oral histories, the project used photography, model-making, film and an interactive sound installation called Heritage HiFi built by Paul Huxtable of Axis Sound, which participated in African-Caribbean carnivals in northern England. It was able to understand the complexities of what reggae and sound system culture meant in ways that an academic project alone would have been unable to achieve.[2]

Perhaps, then, what we are saying is that one disciplinary approach does not hold all the answers and communities are often better able to see this than many people working in universities. In the 'Imagine' project we have drawn on a number of different ways of knowing. Angie Hart and colleagues in Brighton have used a Communities of Practice approach to challenge particular kinds of disciplinary knowledge that rest within hierarchies (Hart et al, 2013). We have learned from the work of Sarah Banks, one of our team, in Durham, who has developed ways of working that involve dialogic co-inquiry spaces (Banks and Armstong, 2014). Concepts such as dissensus and agonism, coming from arts practice (Miessen, 2010, pp 105–60), recognise the ways in which divergent ways of knowing have to be recognised within the community context. We have used methods such as walking, drawing, reading poetry, writing and listening to funds of knowledge within communities to surface divergent ways of thinking about where we live and the everyday conditions of our lives. Our work has engaged with musicians, artists, poets and community workers in different and layered ways. While we recognise that many of these projects could have happened without university academics, there is also the need to recognise what happens to academic research when it is co-constructed by or inspired by community partners as initiators of research. Some academics have pushed back at this and argued against the imposed regime of 'impact' and 'co-production'. Others have said that this is all part of the neoliberal conspiracy within universities driven by Conservative ideas about 'the big society' that privatises public services and subordinates knowledge to utility, reducing academic autonomy and freedom. But academia also offers difficulties – it remains unrepresentative of British society, continuing to present institutional obstacles to diversity. In such circumstances, shouldn't arts and humanities academics think about 'user-inspired research' responding to the needs of communities being savaged by ideology-driven austerity policies?

In response, on the 'Imagine' project we have worked with ideas of hope and 'utopia as method' (Levitas, 2013), focusing on systemic change within communities to show that it doesn't always have to be like it is now, but in our case, with a focus on the arts and humanities. Our theories of change have come from artistic methods, history and literary texts. Zanib's vision for the 'Imagine' project involved reading the poems from Urdu women poets of South Asia as a way of re-positioning ways in which women's voices were heard and perceived in contemporary Rotherham.

Proposals to improve conditions and outcomes

Our work has informed the Department for Communities and Local Government (DCLG) Integration Unit, that has recognised the efficacy of arts-based projects, led by women, who work across communities and do not rely on one particular model of community development or organisational structure. Women meeting at the school gates, or doing things like sewing, walking or making, might not look like activist organisations, but their power is great in making change happen.

We would like to see alternative forms of representation, such as film or theatre, or visual arts, credited within universities as ways of knowing in their own right (Pool and Pahl, 2015). And not just in performance or creative disciplines. Peer-reviewed, text-based journal articles and monographs are but one form of knowledge, not the only form, or even the best. We would also like to see ways in which children and young people could contribute to informing government about what they require for their communities, whether it is a place to meet, drama after school or more job opportunities (Pahl and Allen, 2011; Pahl and Pool, 2011). Working with groups outside the dominant paradigm of local authorities, large cultural institutions and 'community groups' lets in different kinds of knowledge. Re-positioning children and young people as 'agents' of their own lives, and providing ways in which they can develop arguments and articulate concerns is part of the process of creating spaces for things to happen in communities that push back against the trope of 'exclusion' (Pool and Pahl, 2015).

We draw inspiration from 'history from below' methodologies, such as those articulated by E.P. Thompson. Peter Gurney has explained how a

> ... sense of possibility sprang from the romantic and utopian coloration of Thompson's historical imagination; running through his oeuvre is the belief that a fully human existence was possible in the future, indeed sometimes could be almost palpable or immanent in the record of the past, and part of the historian's role was to help in the "education of desire" necessary to make such moments become lived reality. (2013, p 347)

We can search the past for expressions of hopeful future thinking. We can do this from within universities, but if we only do it from within, the potential for change is extremely limited, since universities continue to be exclusive places.

One of our key principles is the concept of emergence, uncertainty and mess in research. In history, we need to think about the enormous variety of interpretations possible when we work with others to explore the past. As Raphael Samuel argued, 'history is not the prerogative of the historian.... It is, rather, a social form of knowledge, the work, in any given instance, of a thousand different hands' (1994, p 8). We are in the research and our practice is connected to our lives and our enduring work together. Arts practice methodologies unsettle some of the settled determinisms of social science research in that things unfold through materially situated and embodied experience, creating spaces for things to happen that entangle knowing with feeling (Coessens et al, 2009; Ingold, 2011). The following vignette from Kate illustrates this experience.

Soundscapes in Eastwood, in Rotherham, one evening

I have a long history of working with youth worker Marcus Hurcombe. Our work draws on the imagination, on Marcus' work with young people, and on artistic ways of knowing. We made a film with young people that was shown to government, where they danced their rage away. As a youth worker in Rotherham, Marcus's inspired practice helped us see things on the ground, the exclusions and disconnections young people experienced, but also their hopes for the future. As part of the 'Imagine' project Marcus worked with a group of Roma heritage young men to re-imagine their futures through exploring their past heritage. We worked with artist Steve Pool, currently artist in residence on 'Imagine', who had made a number of films with the communities we worked with, on fishing, on representation and on hope.[3]

Steve was interested in the idea of a soundscape through the place where the young people lived, Eastwood in Rotherham. The community had been demonised through recent Channel 4 'Benefit Street'-type programmes. We recognised the need to support a vision of the area drawing on hopeful perspectives of artists who lived there. I co-wrote a bid, 'Threads of time', with Mariam Shah, community researcher on 'Imagine', on writing poetry with Roma and Pakistani heritage girls in in Eastwood together with Eastwood-based artist, Shaheen Shah.

Marcus, Steve and I saw Eastwood as a place of hope and possibility. In that spirit we met one cold but clear January to record the soundscape. We met outside the bicycle shop. Marcus knew someone in the bicycle shop and immediately, and slightly strangely, I thought I would really like to buy a bicycle. So I shot in and it was an amazing; Steve and Marcus meanwhile became surrounded by a group of young Roma heritage boys, who started to sing some of the songs they knew from home. We moved through the streets, and young people came and sang for us. At one point a couple turned up who had worked with Marcus. One of the young people was in further training and her partner wanted to be an electrician. They were full of praise for the area, and for the housing association that had found them a house.

'Playing out' is one of the glories of childhood. These young people were in the streets in the evening, singing, playing, being. We recognised that while for many young people the street is a liminal space (Mathews, 2003), it is also a place of possibility and hope. We recorded this in our soundscape.

I bought a bicycle instead and rode it down the Rochdale canal the following weekend.

Methodological challenges

One of the challenges of this sort of work is that it appears to be vague and messy and not as 'robust' as traditional social science. We work with a variety of community partners who have their own way of doing things, and this might not always be visible to academics, who might find these ways of knowing opaque. For example, on one of her projects, Kate worked with a group of young people who wanted to go fishing, together with the youth service and a group of experienced, older anglers. The project could have been framed as being about socially excluded young people and their need to be rescued by calm and quiet activities such as fishing. However, the reality of the project was that the young people knew quite a lot about fishing, from older members of their community, and were able to teach the research team (and the older anglers) how to fish. Knowledge was re-positioned in this project, and the nature of wisdom was considered from the position of lived experience, and the tacit and embodied skills we learned by the side of the pond.

Likewise, representation forms in community contexts might remain unrecognised within more formal channels of communication. A project by Steve Pool and Kate Pahl, involving a group of young people who made a film about how they felt disengaged from government, was made for the DCLG. However, we later found out that the civil servants we had made it for did not manage to watch the film, despite it containing key messages (Pool and Pahl, 2015). We realised that ways of knowing in communities are not always accessible to outsiders, and research with, not on, communities can remain within those spaces as we were not able to produce a traditional executive report or slide pack detailing our 'findings'.

Collaborative interdisciplinary research cannot be understood through the traditional prism of social science evaluation tools. Instead, divergence, openness, messiness, complexity and process models offer a different lens from which to look at research of this kind. Working in communities requires attention to particular ways of framing things and understanding local concerns. Milton Brown points out that this is a case of universities thinking closely about how their values as large corporate bodies can ride roughshod over people-led community organisations:

> 'There's a value-based issue with community groups in how they are structured when they are established as social enterprises, where their capital is people whereas universities where their capital is knowledge but often also economics. Somebody who is running that project in the university has got to have a depth of understanding to open themselves up to hear what the value base of that organisation is and needs for it to be successful and not leave a big void when it's finished.' (Interview with Milton Brown, 26 February 2016)

Residents in Rotherham, where Kate works, can be offended if their community is described as 'deprived' or 'at risk' or 'excluded', although these words are often used and can be a gateway to funding. Current media headlines do not help this process. Instead, working with, not on, communities can support new kinds of knowledge to emerge.

Conclusion

The role of universities is, ideally, to create and disseminate knowledge. Yet if universities, which remain socially restrictive institutions, get to define what constitutes knowledge, they will remain agents of exclusion. Anna Sheftel and Stacey Zembrzycki ask, 'How can we represent the people with whom we work, not just as collections of stories but also as human beings?' (Sheftel and Zembrzycki, 2010, p 209). Academics who want to make universities sites of hope for the future need to consider the methodologies that can be used to think about accommodating diverse opinions and ways of knowing that emerge from communities, to represent them as human beings. We hope that community research is being transformed by developments in social research methodology, particularly the development of collaborative methods and methodologies from the arts and humanities. We welcome the idea that this requires pluralistic tools that cross arts and humanities and social science, to access ways of knowing that are slippery, evasive, that are not linked to dominant paradigms, and enable communities to imagine different, better, futures and make them happen.

We would therefore like to pose the question: how does co-production alter what research we do, and for what purpose? How do these processes open up new ways of knowing that stretch and extend the kind of research academics want to do? What kinds of experiences are then let in? We also want to highlight that the effect of this kind of research is sometimes to surface tensions that do not always sit comfortably within academic domains of practice. Community concerns can be uncomfortable and the framing of research can become a challenge to academic-defined research. Whose voice counts and in what contexts is clearly a question for co-produced research. We think it is worth feeling uncomfortable to create spaces for this questioning process to happen. When universities and communities create knowledge together, we require new kinds of thinking tools, that embrace uncertainty, mess, disorientation, disagreement and emergence (Facer and Pahl, 2017). This enables a different kind of sense-making to happen, which itself can be about unknowing as much as knowing. However, we both think this process is worth doing and can lead to some more hard answers.

Notes

[1] See www.imaginecommunity.org.uk
[2] See http://soundsystemcultureblog.tumblr.com/
[3] See http://spsheff.wix.com/fishingaswisdom

References

Banks, S. and Armstrong, A., with Mark Booth, Greg Brown, Kathleen Carter, Maurice Clarkson, Lynne Corner, Audley Genus, Rose Gilroy, Tom Henfrey, Kate Hudson, Anna Jenner, Robert Moss, Dermot Roddy, and Andrew Russell (2014) 'Using co-inquiry to study co-inquiry: community-university perspectives on research', *Journal of Community Engagement and Scholarship*, vol 7, no 1, pp 37–47.

Coessens, K., Crispin, D. and Douglas, A. (2009) *The artistic turn: A manifesto*, Ghent: The Orpheus Institute.

Facer, K. and Enright, B. (2016) *Creating living knowledge: Community university partnerships and the participatory turn in the production of knowledge*, Bristol: University of Bristol/AHRC Connected Communities.

Facer, K. and Pahl, K. (eds) (2017) *Valuing collaborative interdisciplinary research: Beyond impact*, Bristol: Policy Press.

Goddard, J. and Vallance, P. (2013) *The university and the city*, London: Routledge.

Gurney, P. (2013) 'History and commitment: E.P. Thompson's legacy', *Labour History Review*, vol 78, no 3, pp 331-49.

Harding, S.G. (2015) *Objectivity and diversity: Another logic of scientific research*, Chicago, Il: University of Chicago Press.

Hart, A., Davies, C., Aumann, K., Wenger, E., Aranda, K., Heaver, B. and Wolff, D. (2013) 'Mobilising knowledge in community-university partnerships: What does a community of practice approach contribute?', *Contemporary Social Science: Journal of the Academy of Social Sciences,* vol 8, no 3, pp 278–91.

Ingold, T. (2011) *Being alive: Essays on movement, knowledge and description*, London: Routledge.

Jay, A. (2014) *Independent Inquiry into Child Sexual Exploitation in Rotherham (1997-2013)*, Rotherham: Rotherham Metropolitan Borough Council (www.rotherham.gov.uk/downloads/file/1407/independent_inquiry_cse_in_rotherham).

Law, J. (2004) *After method: Mess in social science research*, London: Taylor & Francis.

Levitas, R. (2013) *Utopia as method: The imaginary reconstitution of society*, Basingstoke: Palgrave Macmillan.

Lloyd, S. and Moore, J. (2015) 'Sedimented histories: Connections, collaborations and co-production in regional history', *History Workshop Journal*, no 80, pp 234-48.

Mathews, H. (2003) 'The street as liminal space: The barbed spaces of childhood', in P. Christensen and M. O'Brien (eds) *Children in the city: Home, neighbourhood and community*, London: Routledge, pp 101-17.

Meringolo, D. (2014) 'The place of the city: Collaborative learning, urban history, and transformations in higher education', *Journal of Urban History*, vol 40, no 3, pp 419-24.

Miessen, M. (2010) *The nightmare of participation (Crossbench praxis as a mode of criticality)*, Berlin: Sternberg.

Ostrom, E. (1990) *Governing the commons: The evolution of institutions for collective action*, Cambridge and New York: Cambridge University Press.

Pahl, K. (2017) 'The university as the imagined other: making sense of community co-produced literacy research', *Collaborative Anthropologies*, vol 7, no 4, forthcoming.

Pahl, K. and Allan C. (2011) 'I don't know what literacy is: Uncovering hidden literacies in a community library using ecological and participatory methodologies with children', *Journal of Early Childhood Literacy*, vol 11, no 2, pp 190-213.

Pahl, K. and Pool, S. (2011) 'Living your life because its the only life you've got: Participatory research as a site for discovery in a creative project in a primary school in Thurnscoe, UK', *Qualitative Research Journal*, vol 11, no 2, pp 17-37.

Pool, S. and Pahl, K. (2015) 'The work of art in the age of mechanical co-production', in D. O'Brien and P. Mathews (eds) *After urban regeneration: Communities policy and place*, Bristol: Policy Press, pp 79-94.

Rasool, Z. (2015) 'Emotions in Community Research', 'Imagine' Conference keynote, University of Huddersfield, September 2015.

Rasool, Z. (2017, under review).

Samuel, R. (1994) *Theatres of memory: Past and present in contemporary culture*, London: Verso.

Shah, M. (2015) Talk given at the ESRC-funded seminar series, 'Ways of knowing in neighbourhoods', October.

Sheftel, A. and Zembrzycki, S. (2010) 'Only human: A reflection on the ethical and methodological challenges of working with "difficult" stories', *Oral History Review*, vol 37, no 2, pp 191-241.

NINE

Putting 'the social' back into social policy

Steve Corbett and Alan Walker

As a result of the dominant neoliberal approach to economic and social policy in the UK over the last three-and-a-half decades British society is becoming increasingly fragmented, with, for the first time since the 1930s, a generation of people set to experience worse living standards than their parents. This includes a decline in social mobility within and across generations, a vast chasm emerging between the haves and have-nots, a long-term squeeze on wages and living standards, health crises relating to underfunding and running down of the NHS, and the move towards a rote learning-based secondary education system geared towards a low-wage, low-skill economy and a debt-fuelled higher education system that taxes aspiration and promotes the exclusion of less affluent students. This is supported by a political economy focused on the socialisation of financial sector risk, lax tax regimes for multinational corporations, and an economic model dependent on a housing bubble in London and debt-fuelled economic growth on the one hand, and, on the other, the individualisation of social, economic and environmental risks in terms of residual social protection, high levels of personal debt and unwillingness to prepare for, and adjust to, crises caused by increasing extreme weather events associated with climate change.

The individualisation of risk has been evidenced in the transformation of social policies and the welfare state, from 'social security' to 'welfare' (usually used in the derogatory sense to refer to a lack of self-reliance or 'cultures of dependency'). A two-track approach to social policy-making in practice has emerged focusing on 'good welfare' and 'bad welfare'. While 'good welfare' involves corporate subsidies and tax breaks for big business or 'wealth creators' (corporate welfare) and, to an extent, pensions and benefits for older people, 'bad welfare' involves the management of the deficient and deviant behaviour of individuals into whom personal responsibility and self-reliance must be instilled, for example, in punitive workfare programmes in which unemployed people must work for benefits and by the removal of social housing provision and disability support schemes. The visible world of the welfare state in the, overwhelmingly negative, mainstream political discourse over the last 35 years has usually focused on problems with the latter while ignoring the negative consequences of the former.

In this context it is essential to reassess the meaning and purpose of social policy and where it fits within the overall direction of contemporary British society. With the marginalisation of the collectivist and humanitarian aims of the post-war welfare settlement and promotion of a strongly individualistic culture and politics, it is necessary to reconsider what 'the social' means and why it is important for societal progress. First, this chapter considers what 'the social' has meant for social policy in the post-war welfare state period. Second, the chapter examines how 'the social' aspect of policy has been downgraded over the last three-and-a-half decades by the dominant neoliberal approach. This has been achieved by a combination of policy change, the biased mobilisations of public discourse, and increasing individualisation and disempowerment experienced by citizens. Third, an alternative 'social quality' approach is proposed, which seeks to put 'the social' back into both social and economic policy. This alternative model, which focuses on humans as social beings and collective solutions to social problems, provides an as yet incomplete but promising basis on which to oppose neoliberal policy and promote an alternative vision for social policy in the 21st century.

What is 'social' policy?

Two major strands of thought underpinned the social democratic post-war welfare state: democratic socialism and social liberalism. While the former position idealistically saw the welfare state as part of a parliamentary democratic route to a socialist society, the latter position placed a pragmatic and reformist emphasis on humanising the worst aspects of capitalism through the provision of welfare services without a requirement to overthrow it. Both strands of social democratic thought are intertwined in the development of social policy, formerly 'social administration', as an academic discipline. Social administration had origins in, among other places, the London School of Economics and Political Science (LSE), with Tawney's pre-Second World War work on equality and fellowship, and Titmuss as the first Professor of Social Administration at LSE in 1950. The social administration tradition paraded its multidisciplinarity in drawing from economics, politics, philosophy and sociology coupled with a very practical orientation towards addressing social problems, rather than abstract theoretical concerns and obscure academic debates. Instead, its great strengths were (and still remain) a fundamental belief in collective provision as an expression of humanitarian values and a pragmatic, problem-solving, approach to social welfare issues: the positive 'commitment to welfare', as argued by Titmuss. Social policy within this framework was simply equated with public policy in the realm of social welfare, policy directed at improving society. Marshall (quoted in Townsend, 1975, p 2) captured this perfectly:

> ... [t]he policy of governments with regard to action having a direct impact on the welfare of citizens, by providing them with services or income [the central core of which includes] social insurance, public (or national) assistance, housing policy, education and the treatment of crime.

Criticism of the two main planks of this tradition – the equation of the social with public services and the presumption that the welfare state always enhances welfare – was expressed famously by Titmuss in his seminal essay 'The social division of welfare'. From a critical sociological perspective Titmuss argued that 'social services' should be defined by their aims, rather than their technical methods of administration and institutional procedures. By distinguishing social (or public), fiscal and occupational welfare, he demonstrated that social policy might be implemented through a range of institutions rather than those conventionally labelled as 'social services'. And, as the broadcasting of *Cathy Come Home* to a shocked nation in 1966 showed, the welfare state was not always benign in its treatment of people. For those on the receiving end of it often felt like social control and disempowerment. Thus, in Titmuss's (1963, p 53) words, the 'welfare state' is a 'stereotype of welfare which represents only the more visible part of the real world of welfare'. While Titmuss's social division of welfare represented a paradigm shift in the analysis of social policy, it only implicitly addressed the meaning of 'the social'. That task was left to other sociologists, such as Donnison, and Townsend, who prioritised the distributional core of social policy:

> ... [s]ocial policy is best conceived as a kind of blueprint for the management of society towards *social ends*: it can be defined as the underlying as well as the professed rationale by which social institutions and groups are used or brought

into being to ensure social preservation or development. (Townsend, 1975, p 6; emphasis added)

Although the radical potential of social policy conceived in terms of rationale is clear, the above definition focuses mainly on the 'policy' side of the pairing. What is still lacking is an understanding of the 'social' side that goes beyond the organisational and institutional dimensions. Thus, fast-forwarding to contemporary work, we find 'social action' is substituted for 'governments' but, otherwise, the essence of the optimistic Marshallian definition remains intact: social policy is 'support for the well-being of citizens provided through social action' (Alcock, 2008, p 3).

This perspective on the potential of collectivist, democratic and humanitarian values, especially in the form of a broader 'welfare society' rather than the narrower 'welfare state', begins to capture the sense of 'the social' in social policy. This theme is taken up further below in the proposition for the social quality approach to develop this idea. However, in practical policy terms, the positive vision of the classic social policy thinkers was, aside from the huge strides made in the immediate post-war Attlee administration, reluctantly embraced by British politicians and policy-makers. Indeed, this led Esping-Andersen (1999) to consider Britain to have implemented a 'mutated' variant of social democracy. Despite some gains in areas of social welfare and collective organisation in the post-war years, classical free market liberalism and Victorian morality (institutional responses and policy interventions towards social problems that target only individual responsibilities and circumstances and not wider social structural causes, and moralising and degrading distinctions between 'idle' and 'deserving' poor) remained strong influences on political thinking in the post-war period. This legacy was explicitly revived in the late 1970s and contributed heavily to the downgrading of the idea of 'the social' in Britain.

The neoliberal project and the downgrading of 'the social' in policy

Neoliberalism, an economic and political ideology which prescribes that human wellbeing is best fulfilled by free markets, free trade and individual choice, has been the dominant policy paradigm, especially in the Anglo-American world, since the late 1970s (Harvey, 2005). The normative argument for the value of individual freedom in the face of bureaucracy and totalitarian state interference has a long legacy in right-wing libertarian and liberal thought, with Hayek's *The road to serfdom* being a key contribution. This perspective has particular salience in liberal societies, such as the UK. In practice, the dominance and 'scientific authority' of economic thinking over the last three-and-a-half decades has underpinned a global political and economic class project to reassert the concentration of extreme individual wealth and power in the hands of the few (Dorling, 2014). The consequences of this, apart from damage to the social fabric and the individual and social costs of increasing precarity and inequality, is to establish a new 'common sense' around individualism and individual 'projects of the self', and the exclusion of the values of democracy, collectivism and social integration. This transformation has provided the basis for the downgrading of 'the social' in both policy and everyday life.

In the 1980s, the Conservative governments were brazen in their promulgation of neoliberal economic doctrine and neglect of 'the social', with Margaret Thatcher famously denying the existence of society itself, and also arguing that 'economics are the method; the object is to change the heart and soul.' The intended change was to remove the values of collectivism and the socialisation of risk among citizens, in favour of a more individualistic, self-interested and competitive society. Successive British governments of both right and left have constructed different narratives to try to differentiate themselves from the toxic legacy of 1980s neoliberalism (examples are John Major's *Citizens' Charter*, Tony Blair's *Third Way* and David Cameron's *Big Society*), but despite often large differences in rhetoric and small differences in policy, the overall logic driving these governments has been largely the same. The consequences of this have been felt not just in policy terms and the effects on work and living standards, but also in the organisation of power and influence within society as transmitted and amplified in the mass media, and concurrently, in the everyday imagination and 'common-sense' language of people in Britain.

Economic versus social policy: from Thatcherism to 'austerity'

It has long been recognised that neoliberalism prioritises economic policy and marginalises the concerns of social policy. It is arguable that social policy has always ultimately been subordinate to economic policy in Britain (Walker, 1984). Successive governments since the 1980s, under the influence of the global neoliberal project, have further marginalised social policy in favour of a strongly economic and rational self-interest conception of human beings. This underpinning rationality remains present in the context of a shift of emphasis in political rhetoric, public discourse and policy from the public sector burden arguments utilised widely in the 1980s, to the public–private partnerships in public services, 'active' welfare and consumer choice that characterised the British *Third Way* vision, to the emphasis on 'austerity' and deficit reduction to further entrench neoliberalism that has superseded the Conservatives' apparent but fleeting rediscovery of 'the social' in the *Big Society* idea.

Central to the political success of Thatcher's hard brand of neoliberalism and its subsequent variants has been the remarkable adaptation, by a right-leaning political establishment in Britain, to the 'culture of individualism' that has been promoted more widely in post-industrial societies. This has transferred risk and culpability from collective society, in the form of the state, to the individual, and downplayed the role and potential of 'the social' in policy. As Jordan (2006, p 129) puts it:

> … [f]rom the perspective of the neoliberal governments of the 1980s, it was much better for people to borrow from banks than to pay taxes and receive benefits, because personal debt was chosen by the individual, whereas the tax-benefit system was imposed by the collective authority.

The first phase of neoliberalism established the regulatory framework in the 1970s and 1980s by liberalising financial markets and constraining the scope of the public sector and the welfare state through cutting social expenditure, subsidising marketisation, implementing mean tests and residualising state provision. The period from the 1990s onwards established a so-called 'social' variant of neoliberalism, which sought to adapt to the deep social shocks of these transformations by developing publicly funded, but harsher, policies oriented towards individual initiative and promoting self-help, with work as the solution to social problems such as poverty. This theme was central to the 1997–2010 New Labour governments' focus on 'rights and responsibilities' with the development of a more 'contractualist' welfare state. The welfare contractualism of *Third Way* politics in the late 1990s and early 2000s enacted this new 'social' variant of neoliberalism despite some relative gains such as increased funding for the NHS, minimum wages and childcare.

This is evidenced in Giddens' arguments for a 'positive welfare' approach that emphasises individual initiative in finding suitable paid employment and individual responsibilities in exchange for the social rights of citizenship. New Labour's New Deal for Young People is a case in point where state support was called on in the demand for all under-25s unemployed for a period of six months to be doing either subsidised employment, environmental work, volunteering, or in full-time education/training and no 'fifth option'. Ultimately, however, the aim of individual self-help solutions to collective problems of the quality and availability of work, social and economic inequalities, poverty and care issues is one of making markets socially acceptable, even a market in unemployed people themselves, fighting over whatever job vacancies are available. However, this contractualist *Third Way* approach conceded too much ground to the neoliberals, and has furthered an individualistic conception of policy issues that neglects 'the social' and, under the guise of consumerism, actually disempowers users of social services.

The political response to the financial crisis has helped to shape a further period of neoliberal marginalisation of 'the social'. Under the narrative of austerity, the intensification of an unbridled neoliberal policy agenda has forcefully promoted the idea of social policy as a burden and a luxury, unaffordable in the new austere landscape. This helped to make 'austerity' narratives palatable to people as common-sense rhetoric about public spending as economically wasteful, although arguably 'austerity' is just the latest phase of the neoliberal project (Mendoza, 2014). Public policy announcements have reflected the theme of contrasting 'skivers' and 'strivers', dismantling a supposed 'something for nothing culture', and even helping people 'trapped in the welfare system', under the guise of 'making work pay', including a system of repeated assessments of people with disabilities to see if they are fit to work (and therefore no longer eligible for state support). Investigations have revealed a harsh, stressful and anxiety-inducing regime of testing people with disabilities, with tens of thousands of successful appeals and over 2,000 deaths of people with disabilities, shortly after being found 'fit for work'.

In this context, policies aimed at the so-called 'empowerment' of individuals (including children) and communities boil down to governing the behaviour of 'autonomous' individuals through imposing individual responsibility for their freedom of choice. In Ryan's (2011) analysis of techniques of governing children, shifting the focus of policy from universal provision to targeted supports for people that do not conform to the ideal of autonomous self-governing individuals means that issues such as child poverty, homelessness, suicide and harmful behaviours (smoking and substance misuse) become framed in terms of their detrimental (individual) effects on future employability. However, another facet of this change is that compelling people to compete with each other on unequal terms exacerbates the social and personal problems that collective provision and social citizenship were previously intended to address.

Recent proposals by the Conservative government to redefine child poverty along more individualistic and moralistic lines focus on addiction, family breakdown and personal debt while removing some long-accepted and internationally valid measures of relative deprivation, which are likely to reduce the official levels of poverty in Britain. In other words, for the government, poverty should be a concern centred round 'bad' life choices and 'cultures of worklessness' rather than structural issues of power, participation in society, material inequality and access to labour markets.

Ultimately, neoliberal marketisation under the guise of increasing individual freedom does not promote a voice for citizens, and nor does it increase the quality of public services such as transport, healthcare, housing or basic utilities, functions of the welfare state, or, indeed, the quality of 'the social'. Instead, the market solution enables 'exit' options, primarily for those with the money and other resources, to take up privatised welfare, leaving residualised services for those unable to opt out. The emphasis on the option to exit from collective provision to enable 'freedom of choice' has negative consequences for those without the resources to exercise such options. It has long been argued that the neoliberal project

> ... suppresses any conception that for many people a decent life means a constant struggle against the 'impersonal' decisions of the market. However, the unemployed, single parents, the disabled, the elderly, ethnic minorities, women, are unlikely to be impressed by the news that their disadvantaged positions are sure signs of their freedom, and by the insistence that any attempt to organise collective assistance for them will rob them of their liberty. (Belsey, 1986, p 193)

Although not mentioned in the 'freedom of choice' narrative and not often felt in the bubble of privilege that neoliberal policies create, the division of society between the haves and have-nots diminishes everyone, including the former. For example, Wilkinson and Pickett (2009) estimate that if Britain had the same distribution of income and wealth as the four most equal countries in the world, mental health problems might be halved.

The prioritisation of economic policy and economic thinking under the guise of individual freedom and consumer choice has marginalised the collectivist, egalitarian, integrative and empowering possibilities of a genuinely 'social' policy. The outcome of this neoliberal project is vast increases in inequality, and the reduction of life chances for many, coupled with increases in consumer choice for the rich and residual provision for those left behind. The operational meaning of 'social policy' in this context, in contrast to private debt-fuelled consumption, is increasingly individualised, punitive, authoritarian and *de-socialised*. One of the key challenges for the early 21st century is therefore to draw on the legacy of the earlier social policy tradition and to put 'the social' back into social policy in order to work towards societal progress.

For 'social policy' we need social quality

The idea of social quality emerged in the 1990s in response to the neoliberal-inspired downgrading of 'the social' in policy in different European countries and within European Union (EU) policy-making (Beck et al, 1997). Two challenges were spotlighted: the dominance of economic thinking and the democratic deficit. As within several member states at that time (and more generally later), the development of the EU was constructed almost entirely as an economic project. The foremost example was Economic and Monetary Union (which preceded the single currency). This was undoubtedly a historically unique form of European political unification, but while it focused on economic integration, it ignored the social dimension of this process. The social dimension has recently been recognised in the 'going beyond GDP' discourse (Stiglitz et al, 2009). However, even in Stiglitz et al's report, 'the economic' is foregrounded in place of 'the social'. The democratic deficit was hotly debated at the time, and has remained a deep concern ever since. Social quality was developed specifically to address these challenges by providing a conceptual and empirical tool by which, on the one hand, to frame comprehensive policy approaches that valued both economic and social dimensions and, on the other, a measuring rod with which citizens could engage in political debates about the direction and pace of development. It is expressly against the processes of individualisation associated with neoliberalism and for 'social' policy.

Social quality is defined as 'the extent to which people are able to participate in the social and economic lives of their communities under conditions which enhance their well-being and potential' (Beck et al, 1997, p 9). The centrality of participation in the definition derives from the core assumption that humans are social beings and derive their identities, self-realisation and, to a large extent, wellbeing, from social recognition. The contrast with neoliberal and neoclassical utility-maximising 'economic men' is obvious. The emphasis on democracy and participation also seeks to develop a new direction for social policy to overcome the prior problems of the uncaring or disempowering forms of provision, even in the social democratic welfare state.

Within the social quality model the social world comprises two sets of tensions. On the one hand, there is the tension between societal and biographical development while, on the other, there is the tension between the worlds of systems and those of communicative structures. Across the field of the interplay between these tensions is enacted a constant process whereby people interact within diverse collectives which, in turn, provide the essential context for their self-realisation. Human social action and the wider framing structure of society must therefore both be taken into consideration in devising social policies.

Everyday life takes place in the context of these two sets of tensions, and individuals seek self-realisation in their interaction within various collectives (family, community, workplace and so on). Then, and this is the critical step with regard to practical applications, there are four specific conditional factors governing the realisation of social quality:

- *Socioeconomic security:* the extent of ownership of material resources and rights over time (including environmental security).
- *Social cohesion:* the extent to which social relations, based on identities, values and norms, are shared.
- *Social inclusion:* the extent to which people have access to and are integrated into the different institutions and relations that constitute everyday life.
- *Social empowerment:* the extent to which social structures enhance personal capabilities and the ability to participate in daily life.

Although these four conditional factors are placed in a separate part of the quadrangle formed by the two interacting tensions, they overlap in practice (Figure 9.1).

For measurement purposes each of the four conditional factors comprises between four and six domains including financial resources (socioeconomic security), trust (social cohesion), citizenship rights (social inclusion) and supportiveness of institutions (social empowerment). The concept has been used extensively in social science research in both Europe and the Asia-Pacific region. This does not mean, however, that it is a finished product. For one thing it requires a relatively parsimonious aggregate index in order to measure and compare social quality across different nations. For another,

Figure 9.1: Quadrangle of the conditional factors

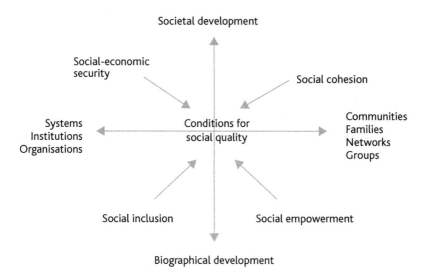

the complex task of developing and incorporating indicators of the impact (positive and negative) of environmental conditions on both objective and subjectively perceived security into the model needs to be undertaken. Sustainability is yet another dimension of social quality that requires attention in the face of increasing social and environmental catastrophes associated with climate change. Finally, there is the apparent paradox of a concept purporting to be 'social' yet being measured at the individual level. This is legitimate in methodological terms, however, first, because of the absence of comparative objective data for measurement purposes, second, because individual responses provide evidence of social context, and third, because these responses are aggregated. Despite its rough edges, social quality provides what myriad quality of life indices do not, which is an assessment of social relations and their impact. Moreover, it has the advantages over the rival concepts that it is far more comprehensive, oriented to society rather than interpersonal relations, and attempts to define and operationalise 'the social'.

With reference to social policy, social quality clearly goes beyond the conventional equation of the social with the state or with social welfare. Thus it offers an opportunity for social policy to connect, or re-connect, with the social and resist the widespread de-socialisation as a consequence of neoliberal policy choices outlined above. What would this mean in practice? It seems to us that the possibilities are legion. Here are just six for starters.

First, the application of social quality should awaken a debate about the essence of social policy and especially the 'social' part of the pairing. Second, it would provide a new focus for societal progress in the form of wellbeing-oriented participation for the many, instead of either economistic GDP growth or minimalistic welfarism protection from hunger and poverty. Third, it would provide new explicit and measurable social quality goals, such as maximising social cohesion and social empowerment in policy and theory. Fourth, the application of social quality would place social empowerment at the heart of social policy to replace, hopefully, the antisocial consumerist deception of individual choice, which too often masquerades as empowerment. Fifth, it would facilitate social policy as the focus for citizen participation and involvement, for example, by examining openly and democratically the social quality of different cities, communities or neighbourhoods, and participation in meaningful localised and democratic decision-making. And sixth, for social policy analysts there is the challenge to complement welfare regime analyses with an examination of social quality regimes. What configurations of institutional and policy paths, political priorities, normative values and structural relations (gender, race, age, class and so on) reproduce different outcomes in terms of social quality?

Conclusion: a defence of welfare or prosocial policy?

This chapter has considered the consequences of neoliberalism in policy terms and its connection to everyday understandings of the social, and suggested that in order to renew 'the social' in social policy, alternative approaches to the different variants of neoliberal policy prescriptions over the last three-and-a-half decades must be constructed. We began by bringing into focus the conceptualisation of social policy in post-war social administration perspectives, and the importance of 'the social' part of the concept. Evidence in the second part of the chapter highlighted the deeply corrosive consequences of centring neoliberal policy around individual freedom and consumer choice, which have, paradoxically, increased moralising techniques for social control and disempowerment while reducing individual freedom for many unable to advance through the market-based purchasing of welfare services. The prioritisation of an economic understanding of human motivation and downgrading of the social nature of human beings is cited as a key facet of this neoliberal reduction.

In order to overcome the problem of policy that focuses on correcting individual behaviours and 'enabling' individual projects of self-realisation we must consider what is entailed in putting 'the social' back into social policy. It was suggested in the third section that the social quality approach is a useful concept to seriously engage with a theory of the social and the political, policy and power implications of a prosocial policy. While social quality is subject to ongoing critical debate and development, socioeconomic security, social inclusion, social cohesion and social empowerment are recognised as legitimate conditional factors that a prosocial programme for government would need to engage with. But above all, the recognition that humans are social beings, rather than rational utility maximisers, would be a powerful starting point.

The social policy community, including academic, policy-making, practitioner and social activist dimensions, has, in recent years, been on the defensive, seeking to protect valued services and provisions from further neoliberal retrenchment. This is a valuable form of action, but what is also required is the momentum to develop a new direction for a prosocial policy that recognises the legacy of social policy traditions, but emphasises new forms of participation, empowerment and democracy in the service of collectivist and humanitarian societal progress. Hay and Payne (2015, p 3) have begun a debate on the parallel political economy dimension in the form of civic capitalism: 'the governance of the market, by the state, in the name of the people, to deliver collective public goods, equity and social justice.' These developments all emphasise the need to put 'the social' back into social policy, in the spirit of the optimistic and idealistic vision of the creators of the post-war welfare state, with the ultimate aims of combating inequality and promoting universal wellbeing.

References

Alcock, P. (2008) 'The subject of social policy', in P. Alcock, M. May and K. Rowlingson (eds) *The student's companion to social policy*, Oxford: Blackwell, pp 3-10.

Beck, W., van der Maesen, L. and Walker, A. (eds) (1997) *The social quality of Europe*, Bristol: Policy Press.

Belsey, A. (1986) 'The New Right, social order and civil liberties', in R. Levitas (ed) *The ideology of the New Right*, Cambridge: Polity Press, pp 169-97.

Dorling, D. (2014) *Inequality and the 1%*, London: Verso.

Esping-Andersen, G. (1999) *Social foundations of postindustrial economies*, Oxford: Oxford University Press.

Harvey, D. (2005) *A brief history of neoliberalism*, Oxford: Oxford University Press.

Hay, C. and Payne, A. (eds) (2015) *Civic capitalism*, Cambridge: Polity Press.

Hayek, F.A. (1994) *The road to serfdom*, London: Routledge & Kegan Paul.

Jordan, B. (2006) *Social policy for the 21st century*, Cambridge: Polity Press.

Mendoza, K.A. (2014) *Austerity: The demolition of the welfare state and the rise of the Zombie economy*, Oxford: New Internationalist Publications.

Ryan, K. (2011) 'Governing the future: Citizenship and technology, empowerment as technique', *Critical Sociology*, vol 37, no 6, pp 763-78.

Stiglitz, J., Sen, A. and Fitoussi, J.-P. (2009) *Mismeasuring our lives: Why GDP doesn't add up*, Report by the Commission on the Measurement of Economic Performance and Social Progress, New York: The New Press.

Titmuss, R.M. (1963) *Essays on 'the welfare state'*, London: Unwin.

Townsend, P. (1975) *Sociology and social policy*, Harmondsworth: Penguin.

Walker, A. (1984) *Social planning*, Oxford, Blackwell.

Wilkinson, R. and Pickett, K. (2010) *The spirit level: Why equality is better for everyone*, London: Penguin.

Part 3
Futures

TEN

Progress through protest

Samuel Burgum

If our aim is to open up imaginations and to re-think society, we must also ask why these activities are often considered to be impossible or naïve tasks. This kind of reaction has been explained by others in the current volume as the direct effect of a collective lack of imagination, in which the very idea of an alternative, more prosocial or better society has been undermined by a colonising market logic. Neoliberalism – a particular school of political and economic theory which argues that market competition, supported by the state, is the best way to organise the economy, government and society – has become so taken for granted that we no longer even perceive this model as one alternative among others, and instead as something closer to 'common sense'. Even the recent and great economic crash has not, so far, led to a serious questioning of this model, which instead appears to be continuing 'by default' (Winlow et al, 2015, p 2) as the 'least-worse option' (Badiou, 2002) where, to paraphrase Winston Churchill, most of us perhaps cynically agree we live in the worst possible society ... 'apart from all the others'. This lack of imagination, even in the face of the significant contradictions revealed by the crash, suggests many have lost the capacity to envisage alternative organising principles to society today.

While many may intuit that society today is in some way 'sick', it may also be the case that many of us are additionally unable to even imagine healthier forms of social organisation. Instead, many of us opt to address social and economic problems with palliatives – the sticking plasters of bailouts and quantitative easing, or minor surgery to national budgets. In this chapter I want to go further in order to find the root causes of *how* such a market-led social model has actually been maintained in the face of the crash itself and widespread protest against the system in the face of that crash which has, to date, failed to generate any kind of deep social change. One way of beginning to address such questions is to look at protests ostensibly aiming to bring about a better society in the post-crash context. Such activism helps to indicate many of the limits and challenges posed by re-thinking society, demonstrating how an apparent lack of imagination was reinforced despite a moment of crisis, as well as helping us to go some way towards an answer of whether progress through protest is possible.

I begin by outlining Occupy in London as a case study, based on research I conducted with the movement between 2012 and 2014, before elaborating the ways in which imagination and possibility have been effectively policed in post-crash London. I finish by outlining a number of purposefully naïve proposals that focus on how we might erode the constraints imposed on ideas fomented through recent forms of protest and occupation. By studying Occupy in London – and asking questions about the movement's potential (or lack of it) – my aim is to find the limits of social change, as well as the ways in which the very possibility of imagining an alternative society was prevented after the crash through appeals to common sense. Rather than relegating the movement to the past I argue that we can take a number of lessons from the Occupy movement regarding how protest might be able to contribute to social change in the future.

Occupy in London

While 'Occupy' became a common name adopted by a number of protests from 2011, the tactic of occupying city space can be traced back to many movements throughout history (to take a few well-known examples, the French and Russian revolutions; the Luddites, Chartists and Suffragettes of Industrial Britain; the 1960s Black civil rights marches and camps in Washington DC; the alter-globalisation movements in South and North American cities in the late 1990s; and the anti-Iraq war marches in 2003). Resistance, it seems, repeatedly finds itself being drawn to the streets, squares and buildings of the city, as a concrete and symbolic locus of power and therefore an appropriate stage for protest, and despite widespread championing of social media as being the new forum for 21st-century activism, it seems that urban occupation has remained a popular tactic of protest. Governments in Tunis and Cairo, Madrid and Athens have all experienced the power of occupation (leading to overthrows in the former two cities and the rise of new movements, on the right and left of the spectrum, in the latter), and it was from this recent resurgence of occupation that the 'Occupy' movement took its name. Coined by *Adbusters* magazine (a poster child of the alter-globalisation movement and self-nominated publication of urban resistance), Occupy quickly spread around the globe from the first site in New York, and has been attributed to 1,518 urban protest camps in 70 countries since September 2011.

As well as the name, each Occupy campsite shared grievances towards global socioeconomic inequality and democratic deficit after the financial crash, yet they also responded to different national and regional situations. In London, the Occupy movement began outside the London Stock Exchange and St Paul's Cathedral in the context of a post-crash, Conservative-led, coalition government that was reasserting a market-led model of society in two ways. On the one hand, market logic has been reasserted through appeals to common sense, positioning austerity measures and cuts to social services as the only rational options available in getting business back to 'normal', repeatedly arguing that 'we are all in this together', that 'we need to balance the books' and that we need to learn to 'live within our means' in order to restore economic order. On the other hand, such neoliberal common sense has also been maintained through the very concrete, steel and glass structures of the city. Architectural decisions on the layout and design of the city's space continue to impose a market-led idea of what counts as sensible or appropriate uses of urban space, and such a common-sense design has meant that despite the crash bringing attention to unprecedented social, economic and political inequalities, London has not moved in a more progressive social direction; instead, it continues to be developed into something resembling an 'alpha territory', where soaring house prices, gentrification and the urban aesthetic have created 'a city in thrall to capital' (Atkinson and Burrows, 2014).

The impacts of these changes can clearly be seen in London's domineering skyline. Deregulated under New Labour, the height of the city's skyscrapers have drastically changed the urban aesthetic through an 'arrogant verticality that introduces a phallic or more precisely a phallocentric element into the visual realm' of which 'the purpose of this display, of this need to impress, is to convey an impression of authority to each spectator ... verticality and great height have ever been spatial expressions of potentially violent power' (Lefebvre, 1991, p 98). Building upwards is justified as a cost-efficient use of city space, but it is also symbolic of an historical (post-colonial) economic and political power, accumulating capital into enormous piles that demonstrate the inevitable inequality of a market competition where the sky is (literally) the only limit. The Aviation Authority, it transpires, has had to set a maximum limit for London's skyscrapers so that planes won't have to slalom their way into land, restricting the aspirations of forthcoming plans for buildings like the somewhat Freudian '1 Undershaft' alongside plans for literally hundreds of skyscrapers across London (Wainwright, 2015). What these towers demonstrate, then, is that facilitating the market is considered to be the common-sense use of the city, casting long shadows across the urban space and offering an ever-present concrete reminder and assertion of the power of business and capital, both within and beyond London.

The infiltration of a market-led common sense into London's architecture is not only restricted to the skyline, but also filters through the entire city by designing out 'illegitimate' uses and users of London's space. This can be seen, for instance, in the use of defensive architectures like anti-homeless spikes (the often-overlooked studs and points installed outside shops, flats and under motorway bridges to deter rough sleeping) and 'bum'-proof benches (with high armrests and barrel-shaped seats to prevent not only rough sleeping, but also loitering and extended unproductive rest by consumers). Both the spikes and benches utilise design to subtly discourage certain uses of public space by certain people who reside in the city, deterring blockages in circulation and making the streets more consumer (market) friendly. Urban space is not being designed for everyone who lives in the city to access equally, and is instead made as a market-orientated location designed to encourage the turnover of consumers rather than facilitate social interactions. Worryingly, it seems such antisocial designs are now so much engrained into 'common sense' that they are even being incorporated into the planning stages of construction work, making it 'apparent that the question of "who do we want in this space, who do we not want" are being considered very early in the design' (Vallee, quoted in Quinn, 2014).

What both arrogant skyscrapers and defensive architecture suggest are a number of explicit and implicit decisions on what counts as a 'sensible' use of urban space, decisions that restrict and help to police what may (or may not) legitimately appear within the city. Returning to protest, we can see just such a policing in action when Occupy activists arrived at the home of the London Stock Exchange (Paternoster Square) in October 2011 and found that the entrance had been closed off by fencing. Located next to St Paul's Cathedral in the City of London, Paternoster Square is protected by a set of bars and chain restaurants that meet at an imposing Portland stone archway (a structure that once stood at Fleet Street, marking the boundary of the city's trade regulations, but which was relocated to Paternoster Square by the City of London corporation at a cost of £3 million when the space was redeveloped in 2004; City of London, 2016). Far from being designed for any social or political uses and appearances, the square's exclusive layout not only creates a defensive and enclosed space that permits only the circulation of workers and consumers (including tourists), but also *materially embodies* a wider post-crash context where the market and the stock exchange that caused the crash have remained exempt from any political challenge or intervention. What these institutions and their spaces represent, in other words, is the limit of any possibility of social change and alternative imagination set in stone, reinforced by the City of London that has reclassified the square as a 'city walkway' (enabling them to close of the space, as well as six adjoining lanes and alleyways, if they deem an 'imminent threat' or unforeseen events' to be likely; see Gander, 2014).

Subsequently, what Occupy in London confirms is that there are certain limitations on the 'sensible' use of the city's space for certain political and social appearances. Through protests like Occupy, we start to see a kind of aesthetic policing operating through a sense of what the city can legitimately be used for (such as skyscrapers and the unhindered accumulation of capital) and who should not appear there (the homeless, houseless and those deemed to be unproductive loiterers). Through this, the power of market logic after the crash was further reasserted via assumptions on what counts as a 'normal' use of the city and an 'abnormal' use of the city, having a knock-on effect in restricting our imaginations of radically alternative prosocial or political uses. To put this another way, the box we seem unable to think outside of after the crash is made more or less concrete by the design of the city itself.

The limitations and possibility of protest

After Occupy had established campsites in London – with the most well-known being at St Paul's Cathedral and Finsbury Square, Islington – there followed a string of attempts to dismiss their appearance as an illegitimate use of the city's space. One particularly notorious attempt by *The Daily Mail* (2011) was the use of heat-sensing equipment on the tents outside Paternoster Square to find that 90% were empty, leading journalists Damien Gayle and Tom Kelly to speculate from 'the damning images' that the 'vast majority of the demonstrators who gather around the cathedral to denounce capitalism during the day go home or to a hotel to stay warm at night.' The suggestion was that there was contradiction at play that meant their appearance was an illegitimate use of the city's space: the tents were empty and, therefore, there was nothing to see here. Similar attempts at dismissal also came from politicians such as former London Mayor Boris Johnson who designated the protestors as 'hemp-smoking fornicating hippies' (quoted by Parsons, 2011) and Louise Mensch MP who suggested that, because the activists had been buying coffee from Starbucks, this directly undermined the authenticity of their protest (YouTube, 2011).

We can go some way towards understanding the political significance of these dismissals of what was seen as the illegitimate appearance and use of London's post-crash space through the aesthetic theory of Jacques Rancière. Rancière sees the police as more than an arm of the state and the wider act of policing as a means of legitimating permitted activities while others are moved along or designated as something to be ignored:

> The police are … first of all, a reminder of the obviousness of what there is, or rather, of what there isn't: "Move along! There is nothing to see here!" The police say that there is nothing to see on a road, that there is nothing to do but move along. It asserts that the space of circulating is nothing other than the space of circulating. (Rancière, 2001, p 22)

For Rancière, such police commands are broader than any particular constabulary and are instead a shared common sense of the 'obviousness' that something can (or cannot) legitimately appear in the city. What's more, through the assertion of what is or is not a legitimate use of urban space, he suggests there is also a collective assumption that this is a space for speedy and efficient market flows, not for the slow and unproductive blockages of social or political interactions. In order to break from such policing and radically rethink society, therefore, Rancière argues that what is required is a politics that is not reducible to police common sense, and is instead 'an intervention in the visible and the sayable' (Rancière, 2001, p 21), which makes 'visible that which has no reason to be seen' (Rancière, 2001, p 24). In other words, he advocates a politics that:

> … consists in transforming this space of "moving-along" into a space for the appearance of a subject: ie the people, the workers, the citizens. It consists in refiguring the space, of what there is to do there, what is to be seen or named therein. (Rancière, 2001, p 22)

Against 'obvious' uses and designs of the city, which police appearances as sensible or non-sensible, Rancière puts forward an alternative politics that challenges these limits by making 'non-sense' appear against its policing as such. In contrast to restrictions that limit the appearance of contentious politics (such as at the gates of Paternoster Square) or which design out unproductive users of the city, this is a politics that directly challenges that very distribution of appearances. It is something that makes 'what was unseen visible' and 'what was audible as mere noise heard as speech' (Rancière, 2001, p 23) by stretching our imaginations to 'a possible world in which the argument could count as an argument' (Rancière, 2001, p 24). Applying these ideas we might suggest that the protest tactic of occupation has a radical potential. When compared to other methods – petitions, protest voting, marches, pickets and strikes – this is a particular form of activism that can radically contest taken-for-granted uses of urban space and therefore the taken-for-granted limits of what is considered to be sensible (or non-sensible). Occupying, in other words, has the potential to make the 'non-sense' idea of an alternative society appear in spite of its dismissal as impossible and naïve. It offers the potential to open up our imaginations and challenge the limits of common sense enshrined in urban design and policing, 're-qualifying these places, in getting them to be seen as the spaces of a community, of getting themselves to be seen or heard as speaking subjects' (Rancière, 2001, p 23).

Some naïve proposals

I now make a series of 'naïve' proposals on the use of occupation as a potential tool for protest that makes apparently impossible alternatives appear. I begin by outlining the potential benefits of occupation, before adding three caveats that stem from the lessons of Occupy in London as a movement that attempted to use this tactic as a form of protest in an environment that appeared to offer the basis for a radical rethink.

In the first instance, the occupation of urban space can be seen as having potential simply because it provides the groundwork from which 'non-sense' can intervene into the wider policing of appearances. By being *public*, occupying allows for a protest to directly perform a critique dismissed by others, as well as permitting interactions between a movement's vision for an alternative society and the sceptical 'common sense' of their audience. By being *semi-permanent*, such sites also offer a physical nucleus for a protest to gather around, allowing for a certain longevity of appearance in the face of those who would 'move them along' or dismiss them as 'nothing to see here'. And finally, by appearing within the *material-symbolic* context of the city – which physically embodies what they were protesting – activists can force the appearance of their particular 'non-sense' simply by juxtaposing themselves with the urban designs around them. For instance, the very positioning of Occupy tents in London, as well as their open and public meetings, stood in strong contrast with the city's domineering skyline and the enclosure of Paternoster Square, directly demonstrating how these are spaces in which 'only a specific type of public is welcome, and their activities are restricted to those of work and consumption … the camp itself was an intervention, a critique of the undemocratic design and control of the urban space that surrounded it' (Koksal, 2012, p 447).

On the one hand, therefore, the protest of Occupy in London suggested a certain potential, but on the other, the movement also highlighted significant limitations on this type of activism that also need to be reflected on. As such, I now suggest three naïve and perhaps easier-said-than-done reflections on using occupation as a protest tool, focusing on the problems that Occupy appeared to face in London.

1. The tactic of occupation – in order to force through a 'non-sensible' appearance – cannot be endlessly open and must be backed by a consistent identity

There is a temptation in social movements (particularly on the left) to try and protest hierarchical and undemocratic power by creating an endlessly inclusive and open-ended organisation, because this is thought to be a pre-requisite for any arguments for democracy and equality. As such, many movements (including Occupy in London) have attempted to establish themselves as having an undefined identity that is meant to allow for an un-restricted openness to different views, arguments and identities, allowing participants to exist alongside one another equally and without any preference for one political identity over another. Within the Occupy movement, this idea was embodied by the General Assembly model, where everyone and anyone (from within or without) was granted equal voice and appearance by using techniques that were intended to prevent inequalities from arising (such as ad hoc chairing in meetings or using hand gestures to prevent interruption but to allow interjection).

By definition, however, such an open organisational style creates an inconsistent appearance and consequently makes it easier for others to dismiss and police the movement by playing into their marginalisation as constituting a rather incoherent group. It is already difficult enough to make new ideas and alternatives appear as real possibilities if a group appears disorganised and inconsistent. In contrast, a common collective identity would allow others to recognise their appearance, allow the movement to identify itself and would create a necessary symbolic consistency. Perhaps Occupy's well-known slogan 'We are the 99%' carried the potential to do this (aligning 'we' with concerns around economic inequality and democratic deficit for the '99%'), but this identity became fractured by in-fighting and stubborn individuals unwilling to relent on their own personal views, yet who were given equal voice because of the movement's open and inclusive organisation.

Any proposal for collective identity is very much easier said than done because it raises concerns about what and who such an appearance might consist of: the worry being that more symbolic consistency would mean that traditionally privileged identities may come to dominate at the expense of others. However, it should be recognised that not only did such privileges persist within Occupy (despite their attempts at establishing an open and inclusive organisation), but also that any collective identity need not be permanent and might instead provide a space for negotiation. The line between who is included and who is not can always be altered, allowing for inclusion but without multiple conflicting views endlessly jostling for position, creating cliques and divisions that undermine an already fragile appearance. In order to allow this, however, my first caveat needs to be quickly followed by my second.

2. Activists must avoid the tendency of romanticising protest and instead adopt a position that allows for collective reflexive organisation

Next to the temptation for activists to construct movements as open-ended is a related tendency to romanticise their protest as authentic, uncorrupted and outside of the problems of wider society. While most do not go so far as to argue that their protest is completely pure, many nevertheless see it as an ideal to try and find a space that is as far outside from existing society as possible. In attempting to create an open inclusive space, for instance, activists often see their movement as itself enacting a future alternative society, prefiguring social change by taking seriously Ghandi's dictum to 'be the change you want to see in the world'.

The problem, however, is that this romantic idea that protest can find a space 'outside' of wider social structures prevents the kind of collective reflection needed to challenge subtle inequalities that continue to persist within movements. As Jo Freeman (2013) argues, such notions do not actually create flat and equal organisations, but instead a 'tyranny of structurelessness' where those who continue to exercise privilege become unaccountable to others (or, as one activist put this idea to me, "you can tell who the leaders are: they're the ones going around saying there are no leaders!"). In other words, by seeing their activism as untainted by wider social hierarchies – such as whiteness, patriarchy and class privilege – these inequalities, rather than being jettisoned, tend to be overlooked and persist largely unchallenged.

I argue that movements need to collectively recognise and reflect on their complicity with wider society, rather than presuming they can somehow find an unproblematic space outside. This means grappling with structures head on and recognising that that there is no space from which a completely 'authentic' protest can be launched, rather than over-celebrating activism as a unique microcosm of some future alternative society. As it stands, protestors play too easily into such ideas (for instance, by feeling guilty for their complicity when buying anything from Starbucks) and therefore allow their appearance to be dismissed as 'inauthentic'. Instead, in order for occupation to create an intervention, activists must simply accept their complicity and avoid the unwinnable position that they must adopt a moral high ground before making the argument for an alternative.

3. Protestors cannot continue to adopt cynical positions that attempt to root the legitimacy of their appearance in righteous indignation and powerlessness; they must instead become 'politically responsible'

Coupled with the tendencies for movements to aim for an open-ended organisation and to exist outside of wider society is the adoption of a cynical approach to resistance that searches for the legitimacy of protest in righteous indignation. Protestors often appear to try and find the authenticity of their actions as directly linked to their marginal status, suggesting a kind of underdog mentality that celebrates their powerlessness as 'an election and a distinction' (Nietzsche, 2008, p 31). This position is perhaps best illustrated by the way in which power is repeatedly described by activists as a conspiracy – all-encompassing, insurmountable and plotted in the unreachable dark halls of the 'powers that be' – and therefore that activism must be powerless, marginal and righteous in order to be authentic or legitimate.

However, adopting the status of the underdog does nothing to increase the legitimacy of an appearance, and instead reinforces the status of activists as marginal and powerless (making it easier to dismiss their protest as 'non-sense'). In contrast, protest must therefore stop being 'always morally correct, never politically responsible' (Dean, 2009, p 6) and instead embrace collective organisation while finding the courage to make arguments being dismissed as 'non-sense' with authority. What's more, once we frame power as something that is maintained through a policing of common sense and appearance, occupation can be recognised as a protest tactic that possesses authority and can disrupt policing, insofar as it is backed by a consistent identity, allows for collective reflection and is a politically responsible movement that *aims* to be powerful – that is, asserts its appearance and voice rather than wallowing in marginal righteousness. Currently, equations of authenticity and powerlessness only serve to further dismiss and sideline the possibility of imagining alternatives, and undermine the potential power of occupying.

Conclusion

So what does Occupy in London – as an attempt to make society better during the post-crash moment – actually teach us about the contemporary limits and the possible gains of protest? First, the movement demonstrates how any collective imagination of an alternative society is being policed, both through appeals to common sense and concrete urban design. London, despite the financial crisis, has been reaffirmed as a central node of finance and power via continuing 'common-sense' judgements on what may or may not legitimately appear within the city's space, which assert that this is a space for market circulation and not other (unproductive) activities. Second, following other movements in placing an emphasis on semi-permanent and public occupations as a protest tactic, Occupy also suggests the potential of such an approach in challenging common-sense policing by making 'non-sense' appear.

Rancière's ideas offer one approach to making an intervention into the policing of what is considered 'visible and the sayable', turning spaces (like the space outside Paternoster Square) into a platform for the appearance of 'non-sense' ideas that there could be an alternative type of society. In other words, against a collective lack of imagination that prevents us even considering that an alternative society might be possible, occupation can push cognitive and material boundaries by making the case for opening up our imaginations appear. However, as Occupy in London's apparent inability to capitalise on this potential of occupation demonstrates, there are perhaps a number of caveats in attempting to achieve such progress through protest (including the need for a consistent appearance, the need for reflection rather than romance and the need to avoid the trap of self-marginalising authenticity). Only if these 'easier-said-than-done' proposals are met, I suggest, can the possibility of progress through protest (and the very idea of an alternative society) be argued against wider social norms that otherwise sideline and lead to an ignoring of new formations by wider publics.

The way in which we decide to reflect back on movements like Occupy is important. Rather than taking part in a policing of the movement's appearance as a failure or over-celebrating and romanticising the movement without reflecting on its limitations, I advocate a constructive (genealogical) reflection that allows us to learn lessons from both the limitations and potential of occupation and protest. We can use such protest events in order to understand the challenges and limitations of making society better in a post-crash era that (instead of radical change) has so far only seen a strange continuation of our collective inability to imagine anything different.

References

Atkinson, R. and Burrows, R. (2014) 'A city in thrall to capital? London, money-power and elites', *Discover Societies*, 1 December (http://discoversociety.org/2014/12/01/a-city-in-thrall-to-capital-london-money-power-and-elites/).

Badiou, A. (2002) 'On evil: An interview with Alain Badiou', *Cabinet*, issue 5 (www.cabinetmagazine.org/issues/5/alainbadiou.php).

City of London (2016) 'Temple Bar' (www.cityoflondon.gov.uk/about-the-city/about-us/buildings-we-manage/Pages/temple-bar.aspx#).

Daily Mail (2011) 'The thermal images that prove 90% of tents in the Occupy camp in London are left EMPTY overnight' (www.dailymail.co.uk/news/article-2053463/Occupy-London-90-tents-St-Pauls-protest-camp-left-overnight.html).

Dean, J. (2009) *Democracy and other neoliberal fantasies: Communicative capitalism and Left politics*, London: Duke University Press.

Freeman, J. (2013) 'The tyranny of structurelessness', *WSQ: Women's Studies Quarterly*, vol 41, no 3 and 4, pp 231-46 [Also available at www.jofreeman.com/joreen/tyranny.htm].

Gander, K. (2014) 'Occupy London protests: Police to be allowed to clear Paternoster Square near St Paul's', *Independent*, 8 August (www.independent.co.uk/news/uk/home-news/occupy-london-protests-police-to-be-allowed-to-clear-paternoster-square-near-st-pauls-9657491.html).

Koksal, I. (2012) 'Walking in the City of London', *Social Movement Studies*, vol 11, no 3-4, pp 446-52.

Lefebvre, H. (1991) 'Production of space (extracts)' (http://isites.harvard.edu/fs/docs/icb.topic1412058.files/Week%203/Lefebvre.pdf).

Nietzsche, F. (2008) *On the genealogy of morals*, Oxford: Oxford University Press [also available at www.inp.uw.edu.pl/mdsie/ Political_Thought/GeneologyofMorals.pdf].

Parsons, R. (2011) 'Boris can't see big picture, say St Paul's "hippies"', *Evening Standard*, 28 November (www.standard.co.uk/news/boris-cant-see-big-picture-say-st-pauls-hippies-6372713.html).

Quinn, B. (2014) 'Anti-homeless spikes are part of a wider phenomenon of "hostile architecture"', *The Guardian*, 13 June (www. theguardian.com/artanddesign/2014/jun/13/anti-homeless-spikes-hostile-architecture).

Rancière, J. (2001) 'Ten theses on politics' (www.after1968.org/app/ webroot/uploads/RanciereTHESESONPOLITICS.pdf).

Wainwright, O. (2015) '1 Undershaft, the tallest skyscraper in the City of London revealed', *The Guardian*, 7 December (www.theguardian. com/artanddesign/architecture-design-blog/2015/dec/07/1-undershaft-tallest-skyscraper-city-of-london-eric-parry).

Winlow, S., Hall, S., Treadwell, J. and Briggs, D. (2015) *Riots and political protest*, London: Routledge.

YouTube (2011) 'Louise Mensch on Occupy London – LSX (HIGNFY)' (www.youtube.com/watch?v=3252FSW7OC4).

ELEVEN

Cities, crises and the future

Sophie Body-Gendrot

Our world is simultaneously disarticulated and re-articulated under the multiple impacts of terrorism, globalisation, migrations, inequalities, populism, xenophobia, intellectual upheaval and institutional shortcomings regarding global warming, among other key challenges of our time. In this context, the city has become unstable as an object of thought and action. In this chapter, I first intend to show how, in the 1960s, in the US as in France, state planners and public technocrats' neglect for democratic public space contributed to social and racial problems in inner-city areas, while also allowing private developers and landowners to grab public space for profit, thus further strangling the social possibilities of the city. There was, however, little denunciation of such trends due to a form of hegemony inspired by neoliberalism stifling dissent. Even when massive discontent, protests, strikes and demonstrations by the dispossessed were given visibility, there was no reverse to the free market ideology and policies of laissez faire. Second, I focus on public space as a lens for understanding larger processes in the city, and as a kind of laboratory for claims, protests and cultural insubordination. Forms of resistance in these sites are currently boosted by the use of social media, but space remains determinant as public spaces may be perceived as contributing to a focus on urban problems. Third, although I reflect on notions of order and disorder that often feed one another, I want to suggest here that disorder is not just a nuisance and an expression of opposition; it may also be a signal that change is possible, or at least it may stimulate the imagination of alternative aspirations.

Reflecting on cities and crises in the 1960s

In the US

The growth of inequalities in US cities and the persistence of a discriminatory society were usually generally ignored in the 1950s by the social sciences, heavily influenced by a search for consensus and by the pluralism of Robert A. Dahl, who optimistically claimed that, 'in a pluralist, open system, any group could be heard at a crucial point in the decision-process' (1956, p 145). Few scholars took a critical stand to this position, despite some famous exceptions. There was little urban theory questioning the outcomes of liberal democracy and its philosophy of deregulation and open competition. The potential of cities to produce widespread revolts and protest was often not addressed. At the same time many policies of urban renewal destroyed the social fabric of numerous urban neighbourhoods and working-class communities. Urban protests and race riots in the 1960s denounced the fate of minorities segregated in inner-city public housing estates with few public services. The pluralist vision, influenced by the 'market model', missed the dynamics of revolt in US cities, posing a political crisis for rulers who 'perceived that the myth and reality of their authority were then under threat' (Katznelson, 1973, p 467). The 1960s can then be seen as a time of negotiations through which old and stubborn problems of racial discrimination, social exclusion and fear in cities were seen to have been addressed. Serious problems, particularly concentrated in inner cities, were not alleviated due to the lack of more prosocial governmental interventions. At the same time weak or ill-adapted laws regarding the wide circulation of guns, drugs, domestic violence, the decarceration of those with mental ill health (often with little or no community support systems), along with cuts in all kinds of public services as well as states and local governments' choices in favour of profitable privatisation all compounded the socially regressive impact of these changes.

As unrest and urban violence grew, action had to be taken by the Democrats then in power and depending on urban votes – 'Each riot costs me 90,000 votes', President Johnson was heard to say. However, progressive measures in favour of the poor and racial minorities in the 1960s out of a background of summer riots in the inner cities of large and middle-size cities created a backlash, alongside compassion fatigue among the majority of white voters and their elected representatives who were hostile to forms of redistribution and affirmative action that might affect the merit principle. Due to the political instrumentalisation of fear in Americans' lives by conservative politicians, US cities in the last quarter of the 20th century became less democratic, more racially polarised and more uncertain. Gradually, the optimism that had marked the beginning of the 1960s, when a man could reach the moon and poverty was often seen as an 'anomaly' in the US, was replaced by the 'twilight of common dreams' (Gitlin, 1995).

Did the Democrats make a mistake in enforcing a prosocial vision? Rhetorically, mistakes were made, such as launching a War on Poverty that could never be won, or asking poor residents to produce ideal neighbourhoods when they lacked the resources, skills or willingness to do so, or deciding from Washington that states and local authorities would cooperate with progressive policies. It could not work this way. The war in Vietnam also took its toll, and the social policies – under the mantle of a War on Poverty – were never given enough funding, continuity and popular support to make a lasting difference to the concerned neighbourhoods and recipients.

Another critique should also be seriously considered. Saul Alinsky, a community organiser in Chicago after the Second World War, criticised the anti-poverty programmes of the Great Society as a top-down process, not allocating political power to the involved poor. Receiving subsidies and power from above was a poisonous gift, 'political pornography', he said (quoted by Sanders, 1965). (This expression became the title of a chapter of Hilary Clinton's doctoral dissertation on Alinsky [Clinton, 1969].) Empowerment, a learning experience, could be earned only via strikes, protests, intimidation, conflicts and confrontations in the public space, even temporarily. Without a learning process for snatching power, there was no collective capacity for teaching people how to decide for the best of their interests after solving their conflicts. 'Whose city was this?', Ray Pahl asked (1970). Certainly the mobilisations modelled after Saul Alinsky's responded 'Ours', as we, the people, fought for it. In this vision, the city belonged to all – we have as much a right to the city as mighty universities, financial institutions, real estate owners, city hall or the affluent population. Alinsky was aware, however, that such micro-victories did not fundamentally change existing power structures.

To be fair, the Great Society's programmes, the Model Cities, Head Start, Medicare, Medicaid and 1,100 community action programmes in 1967, did make a difference. Poverty rates fell in the 1970s, as more welfare was provided to dependent households. Also interestingly, through federal initiatives, discrete institutional structures were created outside of the usual political arrangements, involving minority militants as Model Cities directors or community action programme leaders. Later, these 'parallel political institutions for the discontented' (Katznelson, 1973, p 478) became trampolines that often temporarily enabled full position and patronage within the urban political system. A lot of these former militants are currently still in positions of power in cities, states or nationally.

However, the end of the 20th century in US cities is marked by an ongoing gradual loss of democratic public space. The consolidation of a post-war affluent society with more consumers' goods left without surveillance during work hours triggered a rise in thefts and burglaries. A 'culture of control' translated in to more surveillance, more punitiveness and more 'defensible' spaces endorsed by numerous local governments. Jane Jacobs (1970) denounced the triumph of a sterile urbanism and of sanitised spaces, with the disappearance of streets and democratic common grounds. Robert Putnam (1996) deplored the loss of civic capital associated with the war generation that was used to discuss community issues with neighbours over a cup of coffee. 'Public space is increasingly empty of public issues. It fails to perform its past role of a meeting-and-dialogue place for private troubles and public issues', Bauman regretted (2000, p 40). While the rise of the internet and of mediated connections has been interpreted as an escape from emptied-out space, recreating virtual communities, one can add that elites' 'fear of crowds' and their tendency to criminalise public gatherings also contributed to the destruction of a vibrant democratic space.

In France

A similar evolution of space and social decline could be observed for France, starting in the 1950s and 1960s when large-scale and high-rise public housing estates were hastily built to provide homes to workers recruited by large industrial firms. State technocrats never bothered to survey the wishes of the French used to a formerly rural society, aspiring to become small homeowners with possibly a patch of green space. Actually, according to the state rhetoric, these inhospitable architectural forms were a form of progress compared with working-class slums in city centres. This perception was partly true, yet it often failed to recognise the break-up of what were, in many cases, happy communities. At the end of the 1970s, a law provided an opportunity for access to homeownership. Many former working-class white tenants who had improved their socioeconomic status had by then moved out and were replaced by poorer immigrant households with large families.

Subsequently, French researchers found that space is produced; it doesn't just appear or develop 'naturally'. Because it is a social product that requires specific laws such as zoning and serious financial subsidies from the state, and as it has 'the potential to move people around against their will, the production of space always represents forces of capital, always implicates political elites, and sometimes also provokes collective resistance' (Zukin, 2012, p 10). At the beginning of the 1980s, the boredom of life in those housing estates began to be documented, but there was no general awareness that they could be potential sources of trouble as social conditions became more strained. Neither had state technocrats anticipated the social pathologies that were to follow, namely, ongoing 'riots' from French immigrant youths clashing with the national police accused of racism. The prevailing idea in French society then was that immigrant workers were 'guest workers' who were not meant to stay, so the issue of social 'integration' was meaningless. As early as 1979, the President of France, Valéry Giscard d'Estaing, had secretly decided to send back 500,000 migrant workers to North Africa over five years, although it proved legally impossible to implement such a plan. As successive oil shocks hitting France in the 1970s also had an impact on state finances, the urban sites concentrating and isolating the working classes of French and immigrant origin from mainstream society never received the kind of amenities necessary to make urban life acceptable: decent schools, parks and playgrounds, appropriate transportation to workplaces, leisure and city centres, trained public employees, services and cultural mediators. Some protests, hunger strikes and demonstrations took place at the end of the 1970s in the streets of the concerned localities, but for lack of rights and of unity between the activists and the victims of urban neglect, the 'discontented' did not join with the 'dispossessed' (Marcuse, 2012). Poor foreign migrants were not legally given the right to organise until 1981, and they remained in inhospitable dwellings until then, after which they gradually moved into public housing units.

Thirty years later, significant disenchantment is now associated with the *politique de la ville* launched in 1981 as a form of territorial affirmative action. Despite its utopian design, minor tools were used to address the major trauma caused by macro-economic changes, the growth of neoliberalisation and deep cultural transformations brought by individualisation and immigration from the former French colonies. To be fair, this form of preventative action was not entirely negative. It is difficult to estimate the number of crimes, suicides, divorces and disruptions that have been avoided with various forms of state and bureaucratic support. In 2004, an urban renewal policy started massive public housing destruction and reconstruction. This was seen as a tool for the transformation of public space intended to upgrade the residents' status, while making them feel more secure at the same time. CCTV cameras, electronic access control and better lighting contributed to an approach of crime prevention, avoiding acknowledging the failure of former social prevention schemes in a story heavily reminiscent of public interventions in other European countries like the UK. Yet what is frequently overlooked is that such 'state welfarism' also acted as a device that generated significant mobility and change, both positive and negative. Over 10 years, half the population of the urban zones labelled as *politique de la ville* would move out. Some families settled in detached homes, in nearby areas, while other households moved into the renewed buildings of these estates. In older public housing estates, the households that had left were immediately replaced by poorer immigrant newcomers. Consequently, due to continuous immigration flows and despite important social and urban transformations, the image of such zones was not transformed. Macro-social trends remained similar to those in other Western societies. The outcome of more individualisation, more pervasive social control, more fear of 'Others' fuelled by political ideologues all combined to reduce democratic participation.

To compare and contrast the meaning of 'whose city?' then and now leads to a critical reflection not only on the changes neoliberalisation has wrought on urban landscapes and on other issues, but also on changes in public spaces relative to these transformation processes.

Public spaces and the current urban crisis

'City-centers represent possibly the last significant concentrations of universally accessible urban public space' where people of different classes, races and cultures can meet (Tiesdell and Oc, 1998, p 639). Not all cities, however, provide shared open spaces, and, as has been stated above, numerous US cities, for instance, have replaced their public spaces with pseudo open spaces in commercial shopping malls set under heavy CCTV surveillance. In those malls and what is left of public spaces, marginalised categories of people may be aggressively policed, rejected and robbed of opportunities to voice their needs. If we consider that large cities concentrate a growing share of disadvantaged populations, it becomes obvious that 'cities have become a strategic terrain for a whole series of conflicts and contradictions' (Sassen, 1999, p 105).

Ideally, in a metropolis, anonymous people using public spaces should feel included, regardless of their differences. Anonymity and impersonality provide a milieu for more individual development. The resources that public spaces provide symbolise a collective feeling of belonging to a larger political entity. It has been observed that a common foundation of convictions, cultural evidences and mutual expectations, by sedimentation, forms the public space' (Sennett, 1970). Public space favours random encounters, for instance, during demonstrations and diverse assemblies. With the use of the new media, they may lead to the elaboration of common projects and their organisation. A large city is 'so full of unexpected interactions and so continuously in movement that all kinds of small and large spatialities continue to provide resources for political invention as they generate new improvisations and force new forms of ingenuity' (Amin and Thrift, 2002, p 157).

People can hopefully be educated to become socially mature and to overcome their ambivalences in joining others. As Bauman suggests, 'Mature people need the unknown and would feel incomplete without a certain anarchy in their lives and without the love of the Otherness among them' (1998, pp 46-7). But that is a difficult art. How, then, can public spaces support social inclusion, mutual trust and civic involvement? Two illustrations are now given.

Let us begin with urban parks. Numerous visions of parks or 'high lines' allowing a diversity of people to walk and enjoy selective moments are currently being developed in cities in the North and South. The goal of park designers is to coalesce a great variety of people together at the same time and in the same space. They have opted for a social vision transcending class divisions and bet on universal needs for public tranquillity, entertainment and recreation. Chapultepec Park in Mexico City represents one such success story. Its renovation was partly financed by the million-plus residents, each giving one peso for this large public space. Every weekend, 17,000 users mix and mingle in the park where signals of quietness abound. Micro-control systems are at work: acting invisibly, security guards help to ensure that interaction is respectful and safe, representing an alternative to CCTV and high-end surveillance technologies. The same could be said of cultural events attracting diverse crowds in low-income neighbourhoods of the city. Such actions are based on public trust and on the local organisers' savoir faire (Body-Gendrot, 2012, p 173). All of this is a question of dosage, timing, place and subjectivity that is not easily reduced to a simple recipe and yet, when it can be identified, the chemistry works wonders in particular localities.

A second illustration is provided by the political use of public spaces. For less affluent residents in cities, public spaces are a political resource for all kinds of grievances that are given visibility via the media and social networks. As revolutions have shown, protest is often linked to rites and key symbols; it is about belonging and sharing an experience in a symbolic site such as the Bastille in 1789, the Sorbonne in May

1968, Tahrir Square in Cairo or the Puerta del Sol in Madrid, both in 2011. Supported by internet networks, the new mobilisations are a novel form of mobility forming a connection between the global and the local. Aggregated by social media, mobilisations reinterpret public space and organise a drama in a context of marked and contentious territories (Body-Gendrot, 2017, forthcoming). Theoretically, they can be perceived as a 'voice' or a least 'a cry', a signal that disjunctive democracies are going too far in the excesses they allow among financial and social elites. In the Occupy movement (see Body-Gendrot, 2017. ch 3), the slogan 'We are the 99%' was expressed, and the public space of Zuccotti Park in New York provided a cementing ethos to masses of heterogeneous people connected and 'empowered' by the overlay of social media onto and through these spaces of congregation.

Diverse groups tend indeed to perceive the state as inefficient at alleviating their fears and concerns; they do not believe in the possibility of protection by elected representatives. Many now complain that national governments and institutions are too distant from societies' key changing nature, and that they are unable to make adequate, tailor-made decisions that would be beneficial. States are often seen as being on the other side, with an increasing stake in the kinds of runaway financialisation that now so clearly influence political decision-making and privilege corporate and wealthy key actors.

In 2011, indignant movements sprang in numerous places, after the Arab Spring awakening, from Madrid to Tel Aviv, Frankfurt, London, New York, Hong Kong and hundreds of cities, although the motivations of protesters in each city were in many ways unique and locally grounded. They nevertheless expressed the strength and near universality of public discontent that took political elites by surprise. They displayed an outrage at glaring inequalities, and at 'accumulation by dispossession' occurring through household evictions and displacement (Mayer, 2016). The communication revolution, ranging from satellite television to Twitter to camera telephones, made it easier to organise these protests, to keep them going while giving visibility to people occupying space or taking to the streets. Yet the political power of physical space is too frequently ignored, perhaps particularly so in an information age when so much is relegated to the ephemeral zone of social media. The 'sense of place empowers protests' (Kimmelman, 2011). It is important to think about how public space, buildings, monuments and bridges mobilise both memories of the past decades (or in Europe, of the past centuries), and the power of place to offer a site of dissent and expressivity. These spaces help create a political stimulus so that people may feel they can exercise a right to 'peaceably assemble, occupy public space, create a process to address problems', and hopefully in doing so, generate tiny solutions (Body-Gendrot, 2017, forthcoming).

So are massive occupations of space useful? Cities' power of redistribution is limited but not insignificant. They cannot bypass states or upper levels such as the European Community or the United Nations. In 2014, the case of Occupy Central in Hong Kong was particularly fascinating. The Hong Kong occupiers were challenging China's power of intimidation and its will to exert its domination on this semi-autonomous enclave after 150 years of British rule. China's use of violence against demonstrators via the triads eventually eroded the strength of the movement. However, despite its physical disappearance, the Umbrella mobilisation keeps haunting people's imaginary, and recent votes of the Hong Kong legislature show that the protest movement was not useless. Such events appear to reveal something of the kind of leverage some groups have managed to achieve over their own governance institutions, at least temporarily.

Likewise, in France, in 2005, the young 'rioters' were accused – mainly by the May 1968 generation – of being 'silent' and more or less absent of political expression. They were often depicted as leaderless and unorganised, almost nihilistic. But another interpretation is possible. To a certain extent, the silent disorders may appear as a healthy form of post-political empowerment by opposition to social alienation. *Post* means that 'rioters' did not need words for expression since they did not negotiate with power-holders from whom they expected nothing. Political? Imposing their massive presence in the public space via their movements, destructions and confrontations and suspending public order was the youths' weapon, a weapon of the weak. What is new is that public disorder affecting urban spaces as well as new modes of communication made highly visible precisely what is ignored in the elites' rhetoric: injustice and emotion. Disorder thus resonates with public emotions – urban sites of protest embody globalisation's social failures, they give it its confrontational dimension without immediately generating political claims. They then have some possibility of influence, and such disruptions cannot so easily be ignored. To prevent more polarisation, elites often feel the need to respond with concessions or repression.

Order and disorder in cities

A new radical generation involved in creating disorder has sometimes been called the Twitter or Facebook generation. After the Web 2.0

revolution, virtual communities have indeed emerged, yet the power of information and communication technologies has not been much help in understanding *how* exactly the use of these media reshapes the repertoire of contemporary movements and has an impact on the experience of participants. Social networks allow them to link globally, beyond national borders. They enable them to create visibility for a cause and get organised. But what has often been neglected is the power of space. The study of the intricate interaction between online communication and on-the-ground organising is challenging. Popular embryonic movements, such as Occupy Wall Street, Occupy Hong Kong and the Arab Spring (which, perhaps, in retrospect, was more like a winter) appeal to a diverse constituency encompassing many people concerned by social justice. What they have in common is to take hold of public spaces, a hold sometimes evolving into an occupation. Attention to disorder has been captured by the visibility of confrontations displaying the rituals of protestors as well as those of police forces, as much as by the use of social media. Disorder may be produced by a handful of actors who import their global views on the local space in order to cause a massive upheaval, as shown by the terrorist attacks in France in 2015. Here cyber-connections and networks of a handful of young men helped them to organise and create massive disorder in the city. It may also be that disorder comes from law enforcers themselves when their responses, their heavy-handed approach, their long chain of command raise outrage, or when they are unable to protect peaceful protesters who are exercising a right to assemble. For the police, striking the right balance between competing rights and interests in the public space, while protecting people and property from the threat or harm of injury that protesters raise, is a heavy challenge in relation to the policing of such protest.

Urban disorder is an important issue that cannot be understood without reference to the symmetrical notion of order. Order is a tacitly understood notion, a political matter that becomes problematic only when some 'disorder' becomes visible (Body-Gendrot, 2017, forthcoming). Order for whom and by whom? Both notions cannot be dissociated: order combats disorder, but disorder gets its meaning by denouncing order. In any society, some kind of necessary order is seen as a fundamental value, allowing an escape from some kind of chaos, founding social cohesion and elaborating normative markers. It also lets people function efficiently via shared norms, social values and customs, and to reach forms of public tranquillity, as shown by the example of the park. Conversely, disorder is routinely perceived as a disturbing and a destructive phenomenon, shaking collective norms and threatening the functioning of society in order to produce some change or to simply release emotions. It is a form of uncertainty that cannot be predicted and controlled. At the same time, public disorder is not meant to last, and it calls for elements of treatment that can generate new forms of order. It is likely that episodes of disorder represent the necessary steps in the adjustment of former situations to new ones: 'The future order is inside the transitory disorder which acts as its envelop. Consequently, the opposition of order and disorder has to be bypassed. Order cannot be dissociated from disorder and it needs it for its regeneration, adjustment and survival' (Chevalier, quoted in Body-Gendrot, 2017). In the history of societies, there were always non-conformist collective behaviours, transgressions, denunciations of collective values and norms and refusals to abide by accepted norms. This dissent should be welcome.

Conclusion

Contrary to what Dahl asserted, however, in a pluralist open system, it is not the case that any group can simply be heard at crucial points in the decision-making process. As disenchantment and anger towards representative democracy prevails, especially among the younger generation deprived of channels of participation, now and then masses of people resort to the streets, and/or among diverse channels of expression, voice their dissent via social media. In that respect, current mobilisations differ from those that took place in US and French cities in the 1960s, when denouncing how the massive neglect displayed by state technocrats towards the disadvantaged gradually shaped the control of their lives. For several decades thenceforth, a binary vision in favour of the corporate world and of the established pushed the outsiders who were losing their 'right to the city ... like a cry and a demand' to the margins (Lefebvre, 1967, p 158). Neoliberalism was not being destabilised, however, by the denunciations of 'the dispossessed' unable to join with 'the discontented'. More fragmentation, more individualisation, more displacements and evictions worked against a successfully unified opposition to global neoliberal processes.

Currently, the power of the Facebook and Twitter generation should not be dismissed (and the worrying rise of far-right groups in Western democracies may be one of its outcomes). The embryos of progressive movements do exist; the impossible may happen. Power-holders and dominant classes who perceive disorder as a threat to the functioning of societies and to their own status should anticipate a backlash, all the more violent as the constraint they exert is stronger. They are confident that public institutions can act repressively with no delay to restore common order. But even police forces, the army and judges, which should supposedly remain silent institutions, express their dissent when liberty is jeopardised to the benefit of politics. In a democracy, order needs to be contested when it is perceived as arbitrary and the product of a domination.

In our interconnected world, the ubiquitous power of information and communication should be used less for silently sharing outrage and despair when facing a screen than for inviting people to circulate ideas, experiments, successful changes related to the spaces where they live and for boosting their capacities for innovation, pressure, vetos and sanctions via the convergences that cities allow.

New actors may then combine the use of the internet with the empowerment given by space mobilisations and occupations. The spontaneous mobilisations of millions of French people in cities' symbolic spaces after the terrorist attacks of January 2015 and their visible presence in the streets, cafes and squares after the second round of attacks in November 2015 revealed unexpected forms of resilience and a watchful presence to be reckoned with. In such cases, public space reveals city users' social competence and their capacity for adaptation, mobilisation and resistance. It is perhaps hard to deny that such emotions and actions are temporary and will not bring a revolutionary change. They do, however, force power-holders to pay attention, and they may become increasingly recognised over time.

References

Amin, A. and Thrift, N. (2002) *Cities: Reimagining the urban*, Cambridge: Polity Press.

Bauman, Z. (1998) *Globalization: The human consequences*, Cambridge: Polity Press.

Body-Gendrot, S. (2012) *Globalization, fear and insecurity. The challenges for cities, North and South*, Basingstoke: Palgrave Macmillan.

Body-Gendrot, S. (2016) 'Making sense of French urbandisorders in 2005', *European Journal of Criminology*, vol 13, no 5, pp 556–72.

Body-Gendrot, S. (2017) *Public disorder and globalization*, London: Routledge.

Clinton, H. (1969) *There is only the fight: An analysis of the Alinsky Model* (http://www.gopublius.com/HCT/HillaryClintonThesis.pdf).

Dahl, R. (1956) *A preface to democratic theory*, Chicago, IL: University of Chicago Press.

Gitlin, T. (1995) *The twilight of common dreams*, New York: Metropolitan Books.

Jacobs, J. (1961) *The life and death of American cities*, Harmondsworth: Penguin.

Katznelson, I. (1973) 'Participation and political buffers in urban America', *Race*, vol 14, pp 465-80.

Kimmelman, M. (2011) 'Sense of place empowers protest', *International Herald Tribune*, 17 October.

Lefebvre, H. (1967) 'The right to the city', in E. Kofman and E. Lebas (eds) *Writings on cities*, London, Blackwell, pp 63-184.

Marcuse, P. (2012) 'Whose right(s) to what city?', in N. Brenner, P. Marcuse and M Mayer (eds) *Cities for the people, not for profit. Critical urban theory and the right to the city*, New York: Routledge, pp 22-41.

Mayer, M. (2016) 'Whose city? From Ray Pahl's critique of the Keynesian city to the contestations around neoliberal urbanism', *The Sociological Review*, DOI: 10.1111/1467-954X.12414.

Pahl, R. (1970) *Whose city?*, London: Longman.

Putnam, R.(1996) 'The strange disappearance of Civic America', *The American Prospect*, Winter, pp 34-48.

Sanders, M.K. (1970) *The professional radical*, New York: Vintage.

Sassen, S. (1999) 'Whose city is it? Globalization and the formation of new claims', in S. Body-Gendrot and R. Beauregard (eds) *The urban moment*, London, Sage Publications, pp 99-118.

Sennett, R. (1970) *The uses of disorder: Personal identity and city life*, New York: Knoft.

Tiesdell, S. and Oc, T. (1998) 'Beyond "fortress" and "panoptic" cities – towards a safer urban public realm', *Environment and Planning B: Planning and Design*, vol 25, no 5, pp 639-55.

Zukin, S. (2011) 'Is there an urban sociology? Questions on a field and a vision?', *Rivisteweb, Il Mulino,*. vol 3, December, DOI: 2383/36415.

TWELVE

Policy steps towards a better social future

Michael Orton

This chapter reflects on a possible vision of a more progressive future, doing so by focusing on a widely acknowledged contemporary problem – socioeconomic insecurity – and concrete, practical policy steps to seek its redress. Put more positively, it is about building a social and economic framework grounded in security, and it is from that starting point that a better future can be imagined.

The chapter is in four parts. First, the extent and effects of insecurity are considered, both in terms of insecurity as a tangible experience in relation to issues such as employment, household finances and housing, but also speaking to worry, anxiety and the sense that things are just not right. Second, the approach to identifying solutions to insecurity is discussed, with particular emphasis on pragmatism and drawing on ideas from across the political spectrum. Third, policy steps for redressing insecurity are presented under three headings: housing, children and income. Fourth, the concluding discussion reflects on a vision of a more progressive future that flows from the redress of insecurity.

The extent and effects of insecurity

Insecurity[1] is a hallmark of our times. For example, being in paid employment and on an average income is no longer a guarantee of being financially secure – three-quarters of middle and lower-income families are unable to afford the mortgage on a local three-bedroom home; stress and anxiety have become a cultural condition with mental health problems costing the economy a staggering £105 billion per year; and zero hours contracts are the tip of the insecure employment iceberg, with middle-class employment becoming more like that long endured by the working class. The recession may perhaps be over, but we are experiencing what *The Economist* calls a 'joyless recovery'; despite improvements in economic indicators, the benefits of growth are only being enjoyed by some, not all. The UK has been described as a 5–75–20 society – a 5 per cent elite, 75 per cent who are the new insecure, and 20 per cent who are poor and marginalised.

The causes of insecurity lie within neoliberalism which, as has been discussed in previous chapters, has been the dominant political economy of the last 30 to 40 years. The UK's post-war settlement had socioeconomic security at its heart, promising protection 'from cradle to grave'. But neoliberalism rejects that approach, instead being based on an absolute belief in market principles and involving ongoing policies of privatisation, marketisation and cutting public provision. Zygmunt Bauman (1994) was highly prescient when he warned that the superficial attractions of a consumption-based privatised existence deny the basic human need for belonging and create uncertainty, loneliness and the future as the site of fear, not hope. Fragmentation and discontinuity create a sense of flux rather than solidity, and our lives become disjointed and inconsequential rather than flourishing and fulfilled. We are left as individual pieces of flotsam in a shifting world, and when misfortune strikes, for example, redundancy, ill health, disability or relationship breakdown, we are very much on our own, as collective responsibility for shared fates is lost and insecurity dominates.

Concern about insecurity is widespread. For example, Labour MP Chuka Umunna has talked of how large numbers of people "simply don't know what next week will hold, or where [their] life is heading. And the unknown is uncertain – and uncertainty breeds insecurity … [their] vision of the future is one of stress and worry." In the 2015 general election campaign, the very title of the Conservative Party manifesto was *A brighter, more secure future*, and the July 2015 budget began with the then Chancellor George Osborne stating, "This is a budget that puts security first."

With insecurity such a major problem and so widely recognised, the obvious question to ask is, 'What are the solutions?' The glib answer is to say we need an alternative political economy to neoliberalism. But designing an entirely new socioeconomic nexus is a daunting task. This chapter therefore draws on a project that took a rather different approach to identifying solutions to insecurity – but which also, even if implicitly rather than explicitly, points to a future very different to that offered by neoliberalism.

Identifying ideas to redress insecurity[2]

The project on which this chapter draws intentionally rejected an ideological approach and instead posed the question, 'What practical, concrete steps can be taken to redress insecurity?' There were three key starting points, as follows.

First, the project methodology was based on engagement with civil society. This is because attention being given to in/security by government is not necessarily providing solutions, whereas within civil society many detailed plans already exist. Civil society is defined broadly as including third sector organisations, charities, think tanks, unions, media, academia and so on. The project began with a conversation with a purposive methodology, seeking the views of a range of social actors. The conversations allowed key issues and broad areas of potential agreement to be identified. They were critical in shaping the approach taken, and helped greatly in drawing together a very broad range of published material, on which the second project drew.

Second was the strong emphasis on pragmatism. An ideological approach would take an either/or starting point; for example, *either* security is best offered by free markets and a small state *or* capitalism is the cause of insecurity and security can only be achieved by its overthrow. A pragmatic approach dispenses with such binaries, and instead recognises a role for the public *and* the private, the collective *and* the individual, the financial *and* the relational, the state *and* civil society, and communities *and* families.

Reflecting this pragmatic approach, engagement with civil society encompassed a broad spectrum of organisations and individuals. These ranged from the Centre for Social Justice to the Fabian Society, Bright Blue to Friends of the Earth and The Good Right to the Trades Union Congress. The ideas that have been identified offer the possibility of consensual support because they are not based on any one political tradition.

Third, social actors expressed a strong preference for ideas that are realistically achievable within current circumstances. This means that while there are enthusiastic advocates of more radical approaches – from even greater pursuit of market principles to an unconditional citizen's income, new forms of taxation and greatly reduced working hours – the emphasis here is on ideas that are affordable, feasible, gradualist and sustainable. In terms of affordability, the adopted approach is based on the argument that it is far better to focus spending and investment on proactive upstream measures that create security and prevent difficulties arising rather than finances going on reactive downstream policies that deal with symptoms and consequences of problems. The points discussed here in effect formed the criteria against which ideas were assessed.

Ideas to redress insecurity, and to build a more secure future

The project identified a number of detailed core ideas, but the focus here is on three themes – housing, children and income – which illustrate the kind of practical policy steps that would redress insecurity.

Housing

Shelter is a fundamental human need, but housing in the UK is currently a highly problematic issue. It is widely acknowledged that there is an affordability crisis, both with regards to buying a home and renting – for example, for many years rents have risen much faster than the rate of inflation. The rapidly growing private rented sector is notoriously unstable and insecure. There is particular concern about a generational impact, with young people increasingly squeezed out of the housing market.

So how might housing insecurity be redressed? A rather self-evident idea is that if insecurity (for renters) is caused by short tenancies, then lengthen them, and if rapidly rising rents adds to insecurity, then use measures to rein in those increases. Before the Housing Act 1988 local authorities had some control over rents. In France, Spain and Germany rents are still regulated. There is a case for introducing fair rents for all private rented accommodation, which reflects a landlord's need for a reasonable return (on what is a very safe investment), but which curtails excessive profit. Similarly, in the UK the minimum security of tenure in renting is just six months, whereas in France it is three years, in Spain it is five years and in Germany it is indefinite – the UK has the worst level of tenant security of tenure in the OECD. Shelter has called for the introduction of five-year contracts, below the OECD average, but which would still provide greater security than is currently the case. Bentley (2015, p 3) advocates measures that would best provide greater security, summarised succinctly as:

> A new regulatory framework should be considered that would curb future rent growth and improve security for tenants. This should include indefinite tenancies within which rents (freely negotiated at the outset between landlord and tenant) would only be allowed to rise in line with a measure of inflation.

A second idea is an example of a very straightforward proposal that would provide hugely greater security for home buyers. As things stand, the prospects for people who find themselves unable to meet their monthly mortgage payments – invariably due to a change of circumstances such as job loss or relationship breakdown – are bleak. Forced eviction and homelessness is a real possibility. At best, a person might be able to sell their home and repay their mortgage, but they still face the difficulties of moving, with consequences for access to employment, schooling and so on. Danny Dorling has suggested the introduction of a right to sell and stay, so that anyone who can no longer meet mortgage repayments can sell their property to a registered social landlord, but remain as a tenant paying fair rent (Friends of the Earth, 2014). This draws on the now discontinued Mortgage Rescue Scheme as a potential model. A right to sell and stay would immediately redress such chronic insecurity, as anyone faced with mortgage problems would have a fallback of being able to sell to a registered social landlord and the knowledge they could stay on in their home as a tenant.

The third housing-related idea is that there is a fundamental lack of supply that needs to be redressed by a government-led mass housebuilding programme, tied to increased home energy efficiency. This idea is shared by many civil society groups across the political spectrum, and with several setting out detailed plans for different elements. Shelter and KPMG (2014) set out a particularly detailed plan for increasing housebuilding, while Friends of the Earth do the same in relation to improving home energy efficiency. There are, of course, some points of difference. For example, Shelter and KPMG and The Good Right emphasise building new garden cities, whereas Friends of the Earth give greater prominence to well-designed, compact towns and cities. But all share a common theme of the need to increase dramatically the level of housebuilding, with the core idea summarised well by The Good Right as: 'A Harold Macmillan-sized, state-supported housebuilding programme ... designed to the highest environmental standards'.[3]

Children

The idea regarding children is based on growing recognition that the very earliest stages of childhood are critical to future life chances; security here is not in the direct cause-effect sense as with housing above, but in providing the very best foundations for the early stages of childhood, with there also being major implications regarding parents and employment. Consideration of the issue is therefore required in building a more secure future, especially one based on an upstream approach.

Currently, only a minority of children receive early education of the standard needed to improve developmental outcomes. Focus is on childcare rather than a more rounded concept of early years education and care. Even with childcare, the system of support with costs is excessively complex and does not provide adequate help to many parents. In fact it creates financial risk for parents, is poorly suited to fluctuating childcare costs, and fails properly to address basic affordability challenges such as deposits and up-front fees.

An idea on which many organisations within civil society agree is to make early childhood education and care (ECEC) a specific and distinct element of the universal care and education system, free at the point of delivery. Within civil society there are detailed plans in place regarding ECEC. These include the Centre Forum's Early Years, Transforming Childcare; Changing Lives by the Centre for Social Justice; the Institute for Public Policy Research's Early Developments and No More Baby Steps; Compass's Big Education; and the Family and Childcare Trust's Building Blocks.

As with housing, there are points of difference, but key shared themes include moving to a fully qualified, graduate-led workforce; increasing pay among early years staff to support professionalisation; strengthening requirements within quality frameworks that have an impact on children's development; creating links between childcare provision and children's centres in order to strengthen the early intervention framework; and introducing age-appropriate developmental assessments for children on entry and exit from early education, to support development.

The ECEC approach also has major (positive) implications for parental choices around employment. This has potential beneficial effects on household income and better work–life balance – two key elements of in/security. It is estimated that there would be £37 billion in annual savings to the Exchequer if parental employment in the UK matched the highest international performers (Butler and Rutter, 2016).

Income

In a market economy money matters. However, even being in paid employment is no longer a guarantee of a decent basic standard of living. Well-known problems include low pay, a high cost of living, high levels of child poverty and so on.

Given that discussion of incomes involves a wide range of issues, many of which are highly contentious, for example, wages, welfare benefits and taxation, it is perhaps unsurprising that this is a topic on which there is little agreement about ways forward, and no detailed plans exist within civil society, unlike for issues discussed above. Indeed, current discussions in this field have been described by Julia Unwin as consisting of 'angry and fruitless debates' (Unwin, 2013). However, three potential ideas were identified that would help redress income insecurity. The first relates to low wages. Confusion has been caused by the National Minimum Wage (NMW) having misleadingly been renamed the National Living Wage (NLW) – it is a misnomer because living wages and minimum wages are very different, and the NLW is really a minimum wage premium for people aged 25 and over (Kelly, 2015). But whether relating to the former NMW or the new NLW, disagreement continues over the level at which the minimum wage level should be set. A way to cut through this would be that 'Above inflation increases [in the national minimum wage level] should become the norm in periods of economic growth until there is an indication of a negative impact on employment' (Skelton, 2015, p 7). The attraction of this idea, which is proposed by both the Centre for Social Justice and The Good Right, is that it cuts to the heart of the matter – security requires decent wages. A significant factor in setting a minimum wage level is fear of the possible impact on job growth. The idea identified here switches the emphasis in this thinking. The minimum wage level should be increased at above the rate of inflation until there is actual evidence of harm being caused. Rather than the current confusion, achieving decent wages becomes centre-stage.

Second is a growing case for putting Child Benefit at the heart of a re-envisaged system of social security. This runs contrary to the government's current position, but that position is being challenged. Wages are paid for individual labour, not for children, and it is in the interests of all that there is support for the very high costs of raising children. A child tax allowance was first introduced over 200 years ago, in 1798. In the UK today, Child Benefit is a means of putting money into the pockets of families, directly redressing income insecurity. The Fabian Society (Harrop and Reed, 2015, p 3) has called for 'significant real increases to child benefit', as did Sir Tony Atkinson (2015). Allied to the emphasis being placed on the NLW, an enhanced level of Child Benefit would act as a key element in the provision of income security.

Third is the recognition that building a new consensus on incomes is critical. Seeking to redress insecurity is a way of doing so, helping to provide an analytical and policy development framework that steps away from cul-de-sac arguments about welfare, benefits and recipient others, to how we build a comprehensive system across tax, employment and other policy domains, which builds upstream preventative social security for us all. Again, drawing on The Good Right:

> It is not enough for the very poor to be lifted out of absolute poverty as Adam Smith himself understood. A generous rather than minimalistic safety-net for those who can't help themselves should never be an after thought.... It must be a prized duty.

This final point is not a policy in itself, but given the current state of debate, agreement to seek a new consensus around social security as a 'prized duty' would represent a major step forward.

Discussion and conclusion: building security and imagining a better future

The ideas discussed above offer practical steps to redress the problem of socioeconomic insecurity, eschewing ideology and focusing on the practical and pragmatic – but implicitly, if not explicitly, the ideas also point to an approach different to current neoliberal orthodoxies. A specific vision of a better future is not posited and the ideas do not suggest rejection of capitalism or markets. But they self-evidently run counter to neoliberalism's absolute belief in markets as the best form of social and economic organisation to the exclusion of all else. The ideas see a role for markets and the state. They view income security as a prized duty, not a burden. Housing is about much more than profit. Consensus is offered rather than the hegemonic intent of neoliberalism.

It is a sign of how dominant neoliberalism has become and the certainty of the trajectory in which we remain headed that what are not necessarily very radical ideas are so far distant from current orthodoxies. As noted above, however, trying to formulate an entire ideological alternative to neoliberalism is a daunting task. The approach adopted here – of identifying solutions to a specific problem, that is, insecurity – provides some starting points for imagining a different, more progressive future. It suggests a future in which security is key and basic human needs are met. From there we can imagine a future where people have freedom to choose how to lead their lives, developing materially, emotionally and creatively. We can imagine a future dominated not solely by market principles, but in which people can choose what constitutes for them a flourishing life, participating and contributing in diverse ways not solely as autonomous economic agents. A vision emerges of neoliberalism's single measure of success as monetary, withering away to be replaced by a rounded sense of human wellbeing and a goal of building a fair and sustainable future for the next generations.

To emphasise these points by way of imagery, we could perhaps think of neoliberalism's relentless promotion of markets as being like a boulder steadily rolling down a hill, destroying the social and leaving in its wake insecurity and a host of other problems. Under the pressure of the boulder, and perhaps preoccupied by defence and protection of social elements that still stand in the boulder's path, it becomes hard to imagine a better future or even find space for such reflection. Rediscovering a more progressive future means first stopping the boulder and then pushing it back up the hill. To start that process requires small steps – as suggested in this chapter – but if the neoliberal boulder can successfully be pushed back to the top of the hill, who knows what vistas, possibilities and utopias will unfold.

Notes

[1] This section draws on Orton (2015), which contains detailed referencing of sources.
[2] This section draws on Orton (2016), which contains detailed referencing of sources.
[3] The source for all references to The Good Right is http://immersive.sh/thegoodright

References

Atkinson, A. (2015) *Inequality: What can be done?*, Cambridge, MA: Harvard University Press.

Bauman, Z. (1994) *Alone again: Ethics after certainty*, London: Demos.

Bentley, D. (2015) *The future of private renting: Shaping a fairer market for tenants and taxpayers*, London: Civitas.

Butler, A. and Rutter, J. (2016) *Creating an anti-poverty childcare system*, York: Joseph Rowntee Foundation.

Friends of the Earth (2014) *An environmental and socially just agenda for housing*, London: Friends of the Earth.

Harrop, A. and Reed, H. (2015) *Inequality 2030: Britain's choice for living standards and poverty*, London: Fabian Society.

Kelly, G. (2015) 'Raising low pay is welcome. But we should still fear the forces hurting family incomes', Resolution Foundation blog, 12 July (www.resolutionfoundation.org/media/blog/raising-low-pay-is-welcome-but-we-should-still-fear-the-forces-hurting-family-incomes/).

Orton, M. (2015) *Something's not right: Insecurity and an anxious nation*, London: Compass.

Orton, M. (2016) *Secure and free: 5+ steps to make the desirable feasible*, London: Compass.

Shelter and KPMG (2014) *Building the homes we need: A programme for the 2015 government*, London: Shelter.

Skelton, D. (2015) *Tackling low pay*, London: Centre for Social Justice.

Unwin, J. (2013) *Why fight poverty?*, London: London Publishing Company.

THIRTEEN

The (in)visibility of riches, urban life and exclusion

Rowland Atkinson

On a quiet street in Notting Hill it is possible to find what used to be a defunct pub that now houses a hedge fund office. Outside hangs a repainted sign on which the legend reads 'Live to live' as though in response to a request for a fictional coat of arms and motto from the *Financial Times* magazine. This inscription suggests a celebration of life and all its potential prospects. An alternative interpretation might be that growth, accomplishment and autonomy are potentially limitless for those working inside high finance. Such possibilities belie the ways in which social structures or bad luck restrain the achievements of many (Atkinson, 2015). Yet the grip of the story of personal success and achievement, shorn of its social context, helps to facilitate a zero sum game of 'if I can win, you will lose' that is the reality of our business culture and, increasingly, that of political and social life more generally. A key argument of the many contributions in this volume has been that there isa need to celebrate and nurture institutions and support for the shared spaces, infrastructures and services that protect and propel private individuals in publicly oriented societies – yet what we find in many cases is an erosion of these supports. So far so well understood; assessments of austerity, capitalism, crisis and inequality all tells us what we need to know. What we more rarely question is the position and relative legitimacy of the rich and the institutions that support them (di Muzio, 2015). How have the wealthy and a compliant butler class of politicians enabled these inequalities and the spectacular growth of the wealthy?

One way to approach these questions is to consider the position of the wealthy and their relationship to society at large. As the sociologist Richard Sennett once argued, withdrawing from society encourages callousness and a less empathic attitude to others (Sennett, 1992). This chapter focuses on the question of the relative invisibility of the rich, and a related problem – how might we begin to connect the wealthy to the kinds of social problems that are so evident to those of us who live less secluded lives? These themes have a long history in the social sciences. Social research has long observed and analysed those at the social bottom – endless studies of poverty, crime, segregation and what some have seen as exotic portrayals of the excluded and marginal. From the 1960s onwards this singular viewpoint generated increasing concerns that sociology and related disciplines were, in effect, acting as a wing of the state and corporate funders who wished to understand, discipline and contain problem groups and problem people. In the 1968 presidential address to the American Sociological Association, Martin Nicolaus described a 'fat cat sociology' that was funded by the state, whose writings were inaccessible to the wider population, and which supported an essentially conservative state apparatus that continued to preside over rampant inequality. Nicolaus' challenge was to ask what would happen if this:

> … machinery were reversed? What if the habits, problems, secrets, and unconscious motivations of the wealthy and powerful were daily scrutinized by a thousand systematic researchers, were hourly pried into, analyzed and cross-referenced; were tabulated and published in a hundred inexpensive mass-circulation journals and written so that even the fifteen-year-old high-school drop-out could understand them and predict the actions of his landlord to manipulate and control him?[1]

Changes and continuities exist with our own time, but the deeper question, of whether and how social science can be used to survey and help society at large to understand those conventionally absent from its studies, the rich and powerful, is an important one. More than this it also begs the question of the extent to which, under current conditions, the wealthy not only are relatively invisible to sociology, but that they also actively avoid societal membership through their pursuit of inaccessibility. Can the rich be considered members of society at all given their various escape attempts via forms of money laundering and tax evasion, retreats to gated communities and fortress homes? As Andrew Sayer (2015) has argued, can we afford to support such groups given their monopolisation of the political system, their persistent fight against the need for public support for public services paid for by common taxation, and their damaging pursuit of hyper-mobile lives and ecologically unsustainable materialism?

The rich – a brief profile

A scan of the few sources I have referred to so far in this chapter tells us something about a new groundswell of activity that appears to respond to the call of Nicolaus and others to turn our eyes upwards and study the wealthy and powerful. Alongside Thomas Piketty's (2014) meticulous study of the increasing global fortunes of the already wealthy there has been a sudden surge in interest in, and surveys of, the global wealthy and what they mean for society more broadly.

The extent of wealth and gains to those at the top are now so massive as to stretch credulity. These financial wizards conjure and play with systems that bring enormous wealth. This wealth is seen as hard-won and perhaps also generated by some degree of skill and luck, a roulette wheel that can be partially mastered if its complex inner mechanism can be understood and learned. Two questions emerge from this context. First, to what extent does the wider city, society and indeed global society win or benefit from this feverish activity? Second, and flowing from the first, what is the relationship of wealth generators and the wealthy to the wider citizenry and populace of which they are ostensibly a part? We know that London is now home to around 80 billionaires (the most either in raw numbers or per capita of any city globally), but it also accommodates around 4,000 UHNWIs (ultra high net worth individuals) and 377,000 HNWIs (high net worth individuals).[2]

Over the past two to three decades a tacitly understood rule has emerged dictating that even if greed itself isn't good, the greedy themselves are to be courted and invited to reside and invest in the city, that London needs those who have done well either through hard work, massive rewards to corporate chieftains or gains from theft and financialised criminality (such as oligarchs, currency manipulators and launderers). As finance has become the mainstay of the city and nation's economy, attracting footloose capital and investors has become important for fear of losing out to other cities globally. This is a pernicious game, not least because many apparent gains are ephemeral or subject to the vagaries of markets. More broadly, they impact on the life of the city for those not employed or linked to the high finance economy. This asymmetry in the basis of the economy and city life becomes, in effect, a kind of curse for the broader population (Shaxson, 2012). It plays an important role in dictating what gets built and by whom, what decisions are made about infrastructure and, crucially, how we should view and support the poor and excluded who are increasingly viewed as marginal to the needs of society and an economy built on finance and flows of money and property. What is worse, such groups are viewed by many politicians and citizens as scroungers and idlers (Meek, 2016).

Hiding from society – the places of the rich

On the back of this initial sketch let us consider in more detail the places of the wealthy and how such places enable the rich to more or less hide. How might the places of the wealthy affect the moral frameworks and politics of those who have risen so emphatically to the top in recent years? The discreet offices of the hedge funds mirror the way that wealth, despite its conspicuous presence in London, tends to occupy hidden spaces. The homes of the wealthy form an archipelago of retreats that hide behind exclusive and excluding facades and gates. These fortress homes are located in leafy streets and distant suburbs in which hyper-consuming households can live untroubled by the social anger regarding austerity measures or the potential risks of violence, disorder and street crime. Such districts also lie untroubled by society at large, because existing social norms enable gross material inequality to be viewed as legitimate, to the extent that we tend to believe that there is some possibility that anyone can win out in such a system. This lottery vision of excess and participation can, of course, be linked to the popularity, fuelled by desperation, of gambling and a celebrity culture that drives many more people to throw themselves at potential 'get rich quick' scams and potential opportunities.

London's new mayor, Sadiq Khan, has described[3] his rise from an overcrowded council flat in Tooting to Lord Mayor as being 'the best of London', an almost Dick Whittington-esque story of the outsider who makes good. There is much to laud in this personal triumph, yet the story of the lowly but diligent individual overcoming adversity does much to mask the widespread and countervailing forces, repertoires of discrimination and inequality, that hold so many others back. For it is in this same city that educational opportunity and work remain challenging for many, a city where pockets of extreme poverty stubbornly remain and many of the poor are exiled to remote towns and cities as a result of benefit cuts and housing re-allocations in a city that Khan wishes to be open for all. Here the message is, perhaps, that we must take the city back from the rich and return it to the whole population. However, to do this we will have to work hard to ensure that the city continues to pick up the golden eggs laid by the global finance community while at the same time tackling an over-inflated housing market and its multifaceted effects on the city and its populous.

Can we reconcile the reformist ambitions of the mayor and so many citizens clamouring for space in an over-heated, over-crowded and over-priced housing market with the demands of capital for yet further rounds of asset price growth and a search for new up-and-coming neighbourhoods full of soon-to-be-displaced 'creatives'?

In this context how can the wealthy know, understand and empathise with those facing deepening challenges? We have a problem here because from an increasing number of research forays into the territories of the wealthy we know that many within its burgeoning ranks operate within a belief system in which a life lived without reciprocity or mutual obligation to those around us is not only possible, but also desirable, principally because of the sense of freedom and autonomy that it offers. We should probably be fairly pessimistic about the degree to which these districts and the values that predominate within them can be challenged or re-connected to some kind of social project that stresses common interests and shared fate.

How do we make cities less unequal and less generative of the kinds of conditions that create such worrisome and unjust social problems? One way of responding to this challenge is to see cities as systems that produce harm while insulating policy-makers and other elites from the consequences of the programmes they have unleashed. The response of our political elite in the wake of London's 2011 riots was instructive because it gave an insight into the ways in which a remote class spoke only with outrage about the actions of rioters, and ignored the social conditions and inequalities that made such an explosive reaction a possibility. Their explanations have done little to make future eruptions less likely, but remain compatible with the view that our elites act more to shore up the interests of the wealthy, homeowners and landlords than they do the excluded.

In cities like London, and many others globally, we find a wide range of deep social problems while at the same time, the wealthy and its political class appear untroubled by declining social cohesion, massive inequality and a lack of adequate housing. In years gone by analysts like J.K. Galbraith made the argument that inequality generated problems that exposed the wealthy as much as the weak, thus offering an inducement to reform – if we didn't want to be exposed to a lousy public realm, the risk of public violence and declining essential services, the rationale for tax and public investment was clear. Now these relationships are much less clear – staggering wealth combined with new technologies and mobilities allow the wealthy to make housing choices and decisions about how they move around the city that enable these problems to be circumvented or for secluded spaces (key buildings like the Shard, One Hyde Park, The Lancasters, The Chilterns and many others), residence of which grants the ability to essentially offshore risks and social problems. This possibility raises the question of how the city and its spaces affects the mentalities and dispositions of those in power and their relationship to social problems.

One way of thinking about the nature of this social and physical environment is to use Robert Sack's (2003) arguments about the relationship between place and understandings of social reality. This is useful because Sack invokes the idea that places can be considered to be more or less good or bad, moral or immoral, depending on the degree to which they allow us to see and be connected to the communities and life of the world of which we are a part. Cities like London have become difference machines that sort wealth and illicit gains from poverty and exclusion, offering both segregated and insulated spaces. Going back to the riots, it is important to try and understand how bad places celebrate a form of urban culture and space that permits disregard, aloofness and disinterest in the casualties of the urban and national economy and its withering welfare system. The perverse triumph of such a city is to cleave away the socially marginal and to neutralise any externalities or risks that they might generate for the affluent; indeed, to remove them from view by virtue of the way that the wealthy flow through the city and engage with public spaces and the city's population. As we see in this vignette from research with the super-rich in London, the city becomes a place of unremarkable encounters and is denuded of contact with social distress:

> 'I think there are inequalities but nowhere near as extreme as in other global cities I've travelled and visited. I think inequality's just one of the sad facts of the way the world is. Although London has it I think there is a good welfare system, a good support system and generally if people are willing to work there are jobs around right so it's rare that you really see poverty, people really struggling.' (KJ, senior investment banker)

Neighbourhoods that cocoon and protect the wealthy also help to create an insulated worldview that may enable denial and disconnection from the wider problems of the city itself (hit by widespread gentrification and displacement, public housing demolitions and welfare reforms) and the woes of the globe more broadly. Sack would call these immoral places since their daily life and physical seclusion enables a kind of distancing from the reality of the world, an analysis perhaps particularly well suited to gated communities. London, and other cities like it, have become what Davis and Monk (2011) describe as a kind of evil paradise – appearing to offer all that is desired while concealing the presence of low-paid labour, high housing costs and social exclusion that are essentially required in order to help the rest of the city function.

Recent revelations about tax avoidance by the wealthy have highlighted an important yet neglected aspect of daily life – the role of space or, more specifically, the non-spaces of jurisdictions deemed to be 'offshore' that are a key element of the financial system. As sociologists and economists have long pointed out, the global economy is a space of flows and finance that is generative of a range of risks and interconnections that challenge the ability of individual countries to set rules that might otherwise prevent or draw benefits from these flows. Tax avoidance and evasion highlight one such risk and represent the search by those with money (both individuals and corporations) to get preferential investment returns by moving money to places where taxes are lower or from which they can conduct business anonymously. Yet these anonymous and illicit flows have only tended to be challenged where governments sense that their own coffers are being cheated. The revelations in the so-called Panama Papers that the former UK Prime Minister and many others had used such methods to protect their personal fortunes was seen to speak volumes about an elite with one toe planted outside their own jurisdiction. Space matters to money since being offshore has a number of benefits that those with stronger morals or smaller purses are unlikely to want, or be able, to pursue. If taxes are the sign of a civilised society, what does it say that those governing it are happy to play with the rules under which these essential revenues are generated?

In all of this debate there is plenty to be angry about. Money laundering by global criminal enterprises, the glacial pace of moves towards naming and prosecuting tax avoiders, the extent to which finance is held in thrall by political life and the disconnection of finance from the essential role of being in service to society and its economy are just a few such reasons for resentment. But something is missing here, and to find out what it is we should turn our attention a little closer to home. We should begin to shine a light on the hidden yet very much 'onshore havens' of the neighbourhoods, enclaves and gated communities of the elites themselves. Here the picture is not only one of profound economic vitality but of affluent lives unimpinged by the sight of social distress, scarcity or competition for life's fundamentals. London's commuter belt – and those of Manchester, Sheffield and Birmingham among others – offers an archipelago of electronic cottages, barriered homes, modern bunkers and Goldfinger-like lairs that protect the lives of those avidly looking after their fortunes while they very patiently explain how important it is that property and corporate taxation should remain as low as possible in order to retain the footloose wealthy and other investors. In this context we need to formulate careful arguments and mechanisms for reconnecting these social escapees, from their homes, pretty towns and like-minded social networks to the lives of the damaged and excluded, not least because their fortunes are so clearly interconnected with a vocal call for an assault on public spending that has so often been justified by a lack of public resources.

In the projects of secretion and evasion pursued by many of the wealthy we can see that the relative immorality and corrupting of upper middle class and elite life is in part influenced by the kinds of places and spaces where they retreat behind gates and high walls. Sociologists have long been concerned with the proposition that the sense of reality we have is deeply influenced by the social groups we are part of. Who we associate with, the peers and networks that form our daily social life, shape our values, our impression of the structure of social life (for example, whether we think social mobility is an open and fluid process or one shaped by significant inequality and a rigged system) and its relative rules. Can such arguments be applied to the super-rich and the spaces they inhabit? Does working within particular institutional settings or being faced with the pressures and routines of life in, say, the corporate banking industry, in leafy suburbs or among the rich themselves foment a worldview that is at once mercenary and immune to questions of inequality and social distress because of the physical, as well as social, distance between them and others? How can social problems form any real meaning within the social lives of such individuals operating in these groups and spaces? But we can perhaps go further. If class and segregated wealth enclaves enable the disregard for those who experience considerable hardships within the same society, if, indeed, wealthy places permit the *reproduction* of such benign yet callous dispositions, can we not say that they are essentially immoral? Yet, of course, the same form of argument is often applied when it relates to planning applications for public housing (too much in one place, in fact, even a little, is considered to be problematic) – could not similar principles be applied to more wealthy areas? Perhaps social diversity is something that lesser folk appear to have to endure, despite pronouncements from on high asking us all to do our bit.

In this kind of society it is not the rich who are the robbers but the poor, the excluded and immigrants who are viewed as criminals or scroungers, while tax evasion and financial secrecy that enables criminal activity and personal gain at the expense of others is seen as a pragmatic path to getting ahead in life (see Chapter Fourteen for more on these belief systems). Here it is important to understand that social norms about what is acceptable are shaped in part by the spaces and groups we live in and which help to produce the kind of uncaring and self-serving ideas of the wealthiest that have generated straitening programmes towards the poor and the marginal. Those with money want to keep a larger share of it while helping others elsewhere to be seen as a threat to economic prudence and flourishing. The depths of the revelations about how elites have worked to circumvent the rules of their 'local' tax offices have ultimately helped to rebalance the distribution of information between the have-nots and have-lots, but who wish to hide these facts. If thinking about a simple binary division between the 99% and 1% has, for all its undoubted simplicity, helped many to understand the extent of wealth concentration at a time of hand-wringing austerity, then the debacle around the use of tax havens, evasion and money laundering has also highlighted how a rigged system was not only invested in by political leaders who spoke of 'being in this together', but also show little interest in doing something about offshore investments and laundering.

Grounding affluence – where do we begin?

Despite the rather depressing context outlined so far in this chapter, it is clear that there is a profound public hunger to identify potential methods of thinking and acting on the question of inequality and, related to this, what are perceived to be excessive rewards to those at the top. One of the key reasons for much of this dissatisfaction relates to the excesses at the top, at a global as well as national scale, but it is also clear that the unfairness of a system in which rewards go to those who are electing to play a different game is being better understood by many. Yet the spluttering headline-reader of the right of centre tabloid has much in common with the similarly angry reader of the leftist broadsheet. Both can understand the unfairness that lies at the heart of how and who business and finance works for. It also seems likely that they would have much to agree on in terms of the methods that might be used to address these issues, but this is also where things get complicated, and difficult.

The first step to address material inequality is fairly straightforward yet filled with problems and conflicts. Essentially this relates to how the extreme levels of wealth inequality that have re-formed in the past half-century can be challenged. This is a political statement, necessarily so since questions of resources and distribution cannot be disconnected from the kinds of material excess and social distress we see around us. This is not the place for long deliberations on tax, wealth redistribution, financial reform and economic strategies devoted to challenging regional inequality and urban decline. Rather, it is the place to acknowledge that these are the necessary preconditions for a fairer society that would form the basis on which a wide range of social problems would either be nullified or dramatically softened. Of course, the critical reading here is Wilkinson and Pickett's *The spirit level* (2009), which makes the point that societies with unequal outcomes damage the middle classes as well as those who don't do well.

There are significant social movements and an underlying sense of anger at the way that the world economy works and its creation of super-rich groups. In fact, a wide range of ideas about 'de-growth', social equity, alternative forms of finance, housing cooperatives, sustainable energy production, taxation, social welfare, full employment and so on can be found in many places. Philanthropy cannot substitute for concerted action within and between nations. Far from putting their hands in their pockets, what we see is ever more elaborate forms of social and fiscal evasion, plans for financial architectures that privilege corporate actors and disembed them from social responsibility as well as the increasing escape attempts realised through gated communities and fortress homes. Social science must name these projects for what they are without fear of being described as political, leftist or 'critical'. It should name its allies as those who are weakest and damaged by the daily operation of systems that allow those who do best to feel as though they owe the world nothing for their privileges.

The second step is perhaps more concrete and relates to the spatial aspects of social injustice outlined above. If we accept that the refuges of the affluent allow an increasing disregard for the woes of the world around them, how might we begin to challenge the existence of these sites? I think the first step here is to acknowledge the basic willingness of most to accept that many social problems exist and that there is a desire to tackle them. There is no shortage of willing philanthropists and charities devoted to these issues. The real problem is that many of those who are the witting or unwitting beneficiaries of the system believe that they play no part in reproducing these outcomes, and that greater fairness will require the relinquishing of some privileges in order to face down many of the problems that they themselves would acknowledge.

Space is implicated in inequality through the basic condition of segregation. This suggests a need to re-engage and energise the moral capacities of planning frameworks at national, city and local levels in ways that connect with notions of social/spatial justice and the common good. A pre-requisite of planning should be that development and changes to the built environment operate in relation to the capacity and enhancement of the civic realm. Many developments of new tower blocks in London, for example, are being constructed with little or no wider benefits in terms of affordable housing or the creation of public spaces adjoining them. In places where the local economy is lagging there is little or no vision from central government, and every prospect of reduced forms of public spending. Regional policy has few advocates while some urbanists laud the extension of urban agglomerations and enhanced investment in those places already doing well. These patterns of regulation, spending and political advocacy are doing little to counter long-established inequalities. Dormitory suburbs, an archipelago of gated communities and domestic fortresses, are liberally sprinkled around and within London and the richer districts of the urban north. Many cities and neighbourhoods contain depressed localities and anxious residents in precarious or non-existent labour markets, whether or not they pursue debt-financed education programmes. The disparities are stark but are so often glossed over by pronouncements that economic growth, or its prospect under reduced taxation burdens or the largesse of corporations, can be encouraged if the system is, broadly speaking, left intact and unadjusted.

These two proposals form the basis of significant debates and commentaries that are beyond the scope of this chapter or volume to tackle directly. Yet what we can say with confidence is that there is a need to think about how towns and cities are planned, and how the housing system generates winners and losers who occupy different, and often mutually invisible, positions. Wealth must be assisted to help with the problems we have, the wealthy encouraged to advocate for their own greater contributions and for fairer economic and finance systems lest their position be viewed as illegitimate by the wider population. The good news in this respect is that there is no shortage of ideas as to how we can rejuvenate societies which recognise the need to contract our economies, to form stronger socially connected communities in which common wealth enhances the wellbeing of all rather than the few.

Conclusion

Perhaps the rich, like the poor, will always be with us. What has been particularly remarkable is that in recent years the rich, not just the middle classes and social elites of other kinds, have become more visible to society at large. Social research is doing more to shed light on how finance works, on how the wealthy live, and on how the economic system operates to privilege the few. All of this generates a key question, and this relates to how the wealthy see their role in something we call society and questions of contribution and reciprocity. How do the rich see the state of the world, their place in it, and consider whether they might be part of some drive to address these problems? Despite this we know that the gap between the wealthy and the rest of society is too large and needs addressing in the name of social justice, on the one hand, and to address the deficit in public spending, on the other. One way to address these issues is to consider forms of direct taxation, but another important way forward is to closely examine long-run patterns of heritable wealth and the systems that generate such a significant number of winners and losers. All of this is in no one's interest since, as we continue to see politically, new divisions and forms of social polarisation are generated that threaten the position of elites. In this sense inequality is destabilising, as we know from numerous assessments of social problems, but such instability also returns to haunt those who preside over the system itself. This is felt in fear of even modest political proposals for redistribution, within residential life that becomes more insulated and encapsulated, and within fears of social violence and dissent that becomes more explosive as gaps in power and wealth grow wider.

What kind of research agenda should a non-fat cat sociology address itself to? At a time of austerity and social crisis a vital function of social science is that society should know itself and thereby be offered ideas as to how we might move forward. The worst thing for sociology at a time of social catastrophe and distress is to offer a complacent or essentially conservative view which suggests that everything is well with the world. It has taken decades for social analysts to offer a firmer grasp of elite life and the beginnings of an account that is capable of narrating and explaining forms of economic crisis, revealing the significant beneficiaries of finance and regional chaos and the deeper mechanisms by which wealth and power are enlarged and reproduced over time. Yet there is much work still remaining to be done.

We have to assume with good faith that the bulk of social scientists and the wider population believe that social unfairness and rampant inequality are a problem. From this assumption flows a significant programme of research and public conversations informed by social research. Yet we also know that there are many defenders of the system as it stands, and some of these because they do not understand its consequences, or worse, understand that they are either the direct beneficiaries or hang from the coat tails of the rich themselves. The role of critical social science is no less than unmasking these various positions and offering accessible accounts that reveal how the system operates and who benefits from it as well as who is damaged.

In the context set out in this chapter and others, the role of politics is never less than contentious because it is increasingly clear that there are significant limits to action where mainstream political parties are being splintered by a spectrum of political thinking and identity politics. Even when political parties offered more coherent programmes and enjoyed popular support we did not see a significant challenge to the neoliberal, or market-oriented, politics that has presided for the past 40 years over its triumph as the post-war political project that generated the welfare state and other social/public programmes has been slowly unpicked to restore wealth to a superclass of international financiers, oligarchs, billionaires and ultra-wealthy cadres who feel little allegiance to nations, cities or communities. Such points return us to the role of place in shielding the wealthy from social distress and difference. At the same time as the very wealthy and the finance sector lobby for preferential tax treatments or whine about any form of property tariff, it is important to recognise their historically unprecedented position. Social scientists and populations cannot allow the project of sociology to be, by default, the handmaiden of these excesses by turning a blind eye, or by suggesting that this situation is tolerable or without competition from other blueprints for social organisation and prosocial endeavour.

Notes

[1]   The full speech is available at www.colorado.edu/Sociology/gimenez/fatcat.html
[2]   Britain is home to 840,000 high net worth individual (HNWI) dollar millionaires with £660,000 or more in assets, excluding their main home. Their combined wealth is US$3.5 trillion (£2.3 trillion).
[3]   See www.london.gov.uk/sites/default/files/cfal_oct_2016_fa_rev1.pdf

References

Atkinson, A. (2015) *Inequality: What can be done?*, London: Harvard University Press.

di Muzio, T. (2015) *The 1% and the rest of us: A political economy of dominant ownership*, London: Zed Books.

Davis, M. and Monk, D.B. (eds) (2011) *Evil paradises: Dreamworlds of neoliberalism*, New York: The New Press.

Meek, J. (2014) Private island: Why Britain now belongs to someone else, London: Verso.

Piketty, T. (2014) *Capital in the twenty-first century*, London: Harvard University Press.

Sack, R.D. (2003) *A geographical guide to the real and the good*, New York: Psychology Press.

Sayer, A. (2015) *Why we can't afford the rich*, Bristol: Policy Press.

Sennett, R. (1992) *The conscience of the eye: The design and social life of cities*, New York: Norton & Company.

Shaxson, N. (2012) *Treasure islands: Tax havens and the men who stole the world*, London: Random House.

Wilkinson, R. and Pickett, K. (2009) *The spirit level: Why equality is better for everyone*, London: Allen Lane.

FOURTEEN

The uses of catastrophism

Simon Winlow

The long sleep

Let's be honest with ourselves. We face today a broad range of truly monumental problems. It is clear that we remain grossly unprepared for many of the challenges that lie in front of us. Rather than acknowledging their huge scale and interconnectedness, and the hard work and sacrifice needed to overcome them, we tend to display a collective form of what psychoanalysts call 'fetishistic disavowal'. We know what we would prefer not to know, and so we continue on as if we were, in fact, not in possession of this disturbing knowledge. This knowledge strikes us as too difficult to deal with, too threatening to be faced head on, and so it is disavowed and forced from consciousness. Having convinced ourselves that we do not know of the problems that lie before us, or that we lack the capacity to do anything about them, we are granted leave to blithely stumble onwards with our own lives, absorbed in our own struggles and idiosyncratic preoccupations. We carry only the vague hope that others will act on our behalf, or that some mystical force might intervene to ensure that everything continues to rumble on in the normal manner. Despite the cacophony of criticism levelled at governments and elites, we appear still to have a general faith that those in power have the skills and information needed to guide us on to the best path forward. Given time, we hope, our political elites will see sense, shake off their lethargy and formulate a plan to prevent the various catastrophes that appear to await us in the near future. Let me be absolutely clear about this: they will not. At least, not without being forced to do so.

Let me begin this brief contribution with a preliminary and rather basic observation: if our goal is to *rejuvenate the social* – to make it real and vibrant to the extent that people are compelled to abandon solipsistic individualism and fight their way free from the prevailing culture of depressive cynicism before once again investing in collective projects, goals and identities – there must be a corresponding *rejuvenation of the political*. The supremacy of neoliberal political economy in the West, tied as it is to a doctrine of asocial liberalism and the stupid pleasures of 24-hour hyper-consumerism, has depoliticised our cultures and fragmented and individualised our society. It makes no sense to argue otherwise.

There are one or two signs of life at the margins, but millions across the country now recognise that our political system is banal, stage-managed and profoundly alienating. On the surface, our political system seems dedicated to openness, fairness and inclusivity, but huge swathes of the population feel entirely cut adrift from those who purport to represent them, and those who claim to govern in the best interests of all. The very things that our parliamentarians agree on and take for granted are the very things that a properly political culture would debate and discuss. Alternatives to the present orthodoxy, especially with regard to political economy, are noticeable only by their absence. The effects of this long-standing political inertia are legion.

We tend to assume that it is the presence of objects, forces or ideas that produce negative social consequences. However, absence, or lack, can also be causative. When things could and perhaps should be present, but remain absent, there is an effect. The failure of our culture and our politics to produce inspiring, understandable and appealing alternatives to the present produces effects that can be seen around us all of the time. We continue to live in the shadow of a stalled dialectic. We cannot move forward with purpose because we cannot imagine appealing alternatives to liberal capitalism and parliamentary democracy. Even now, with the first signs of epochal crisis coming into view, we cannot countenance the prospect of deep structural intervention. We refuse to consider the curtailment of consumer lifestyles. We cannot disconnect ourselves from the lures and enticements of consumer society. Every attempt to improve things at a fundamental level will, we are told, prove to be an utter disaster for all of us.

The commonly identified positive features of consumer capitalism outweigh its increasingly stark negativities. Our investment in the system is so long-running, so complete, that we cling to its structures, codes, promises and rhythms, despite the fact that knowledge of capitalism's dark side is widely dispersed throughout our culture. We cling to the hope that the system can be rehabilitated, that it can be made moral by the compassion of those people who work within its structures, that the will of the people will be acted on and that the avarice of profit motive will soon be forced into a cage of social democratic regulation.

The lengths we go to avoid doing what we know is necessary gives us some indication of just how successful the ruling ideology has been in its drive to integrate all into its project of endless renewal and continuity. Surely, with a little adjustment here and there, we can continue to move incrementally toward the civilisational ideal? Surely, given time, the government will listen to reason and begin to utilise serious social scientific evidence in the formulation of social policy? Surely it remains possible for us to harness the raw power of the market and to use it in the best interests of all? Tragedy, we are told, accompanies fundamental change. Any attempt to make things better will make things worse. Isn't it true that all alternatives to parliamentary capitalism are repressive, inhumane and totalitarian? Shouldn't we just move forward in a progressive direction using incremental adjustments to policy? Won't the simple strategy of accentuating the positive and eliminating the negative take us in the right direction?

I am often told that my desire to see fundamental social change is idealistic. I am told to be pragmatic and focus on achievable goals. This strikes me as quite odd, given the scale of the problems we face. Isn't it idealistic to believe that what exists can be rehabilitated? Isn't it idealistic to believe that our leaders will soon guide us away from the precipice? Isn't it idealistic to imagine that myriad technological fixes will magically emerge from the corporate sector to head off the worst effects of climate change? What we need now is a cold realism, a realism that acknowledges the absolute necessity of jumping into the driver's seat and attempting to steer the juggernaut in another direction (see Hall and Winlow, 2015). The fundamental realist question today is this: what kinds of intervention can be made, and just how deep do these interventions need to go in order to significantly alter what appears to be our destiny?

The failure of academia and politics to equip people with a positive vision means that we leave the door open for the politics of negativity and hate to wander in and make themselves at home. Fear and anxiety are everywhere these days. But the absence from the political imagination of positive alternatives to our present way of life also feeds into the cynicism and depressive hedonia – a 'hedonism' infused with sadness and dissatisfaction rather than joy – that are such important features of life in the real world, away from the glittering metropolis, away from the university campus, away from the corporate office, beyond the corridors and meeting rooms of Westminster. When we believe that no one really cares, that nothing much can be done, and that nothing will ever change, we tend to beat an understandable retreat toward hedonism and gratification. However, such activities fail to yield any genuine sense of satisfaction or joy. Rather, there is a palpable sense of lack, of absence, a perennial sense that something is missing (Winlow and Hall, 2013).

Part of this is to do with the fact that consumer culture now issues an injunction to enjoy. We are instructed to chase after hedonistic experiences, to indulge beyond reason, to never miss an opportunity to revel in excess, to transgress every boundary placed in front of us. The problem is that the pleasures of transgression are no longer experienced as they were in the past. It is difficult to enjoy that which we are instructed to enjoy. This absence, this sense of cynicism, irony and depression tied to insubstantial consumer indulgences, can be seen throughout our culture by anyone who has a mind to look. If we are to identify the fundamental causes of these feelings of atomisation and dissatisfaction, we must dig beneath empirical reality and talk honestly and openly about the powerful forces and stark processes we find there (see Hall and Winlow, 2015). Our political systems appear unable to produce appealing and comprehensible alternatives to our present way of life, and this is having a corrosive effect on both our culture and our society.

There is a tendency among many liberal social scientists to deny all of this. Many appear to find comfort in optimism and dismiss such critique as overly generalised and reductive. They want to discuss those minority groups whose lives remain animated by politics and those who can still utilise a functional symbolic order. They want to direct our attention to the young who, they believe, are the bearers of a gleaming banner that will in the near future replace darkness with light. However, the compulsory optimism of liberal social science actively prevents us from taking the steps that must be taken if we are to do what needs to be done. The compulsion to continually strive to identify difference has had a paralysing effective on the social sciences. It has led to the continual postponement of conclusions, and an absolute refusal to acknowledge those things that bond us all together, those things to which we are all subject, and those things that are shared by all. Our culture has also been subject to a corresponding process that has sought to denigrate and lampoon intellectualism. We have seen the rise of a deeply regrettable base populism that is closely tied to ongoing processes of marketisation and commodification.

To drag the social free from its moorings in political economy is a profound mistake, and it is a mistake made with alarming regularity by social scientists today. Given the scale of our problems, we must now be honest enough to recognise that the social cannot and will not be rejuvenated, reconfigured or made ethical by some nebulous movement of the spirit, or by the sudden and magical appearance of a new cultural imperative to abandon selfishness and intolerance and adopt an open and altruistic attitude to others (see Winlow et al, 2015, 2016). To do what needs to be done to set us on a better course we must move beyond the sphere of culture. There can be no quick and easy fix. We cannot simply shame, encourage or cajole the people into setting aside their differences. We cannot simply instruct the people to be a little nicer to each other and hope against hope that our edicts are acted on. There is no slight adjustment we can make, and no simple story we can spin, that will get us back on track. If we truly hope to rejuvenate the social, rather than simply cover up its continued disintegration with shallow, presentational displays of charitable fellow-feeling, we must recognise that the roots of the problems we face today go much deeper. If social scientists remain dedicated to the pursuit of truth, they must start digging down through the various sedimentary layers of reality until they can locate and accurately identify fundamental causes.

Facing up to reality

We should start by facing up to this stark fact: social life today cannot return to full bloom if in our economic life we remain fetishistically attached to a market logic that actively cultivates social competition, anxiety and envy, and reallocates money and resources from mainstream civil society upwards towards a plutocratic elite that has already amassed a staggering proportion of global wealth (see Piketty, 2014). We cannot recreate the social if the economic platform on which we must build it forces us all to pursue our own interests at the expense of almost everything else. If we clear away all the ideology and all of the detailed analysis of capitalism and its history, we find at its core a fundamental exchange relation that compels economic actors to attempt to take from the other more than they are willing to give in return. This basic logic has shaped the West's cultural life for hundreds of years, but, because the defence mechanisms erected during the post-war social democratic settlement have been abandoned, we sense, in a general and imprecise manner, its growing power and proximity. We recognise the growth of individualism and the decline of collectivism, and, if we are honest with ourselves, we can see the decline of community life and the growing prevalence of narcissism, envy and anxiety in our cultures. Indeed, the culture industries have for decades attempted to convince the masses that these processes are positive, and that we should celebrate and revel in the opportunities and freedoms that have arisen as the old 'repressive' social order has splintered and decayed. Altruism survives, of course, but its continued existence does little to challenge the dominant ideology. The continued existence of charitable impulses should not be taken as evidence that the people remain essentially good, kind and sympathetic, or that capitalism's attempt to occupy and control our cultural life is forever destined to fail. Rather, charity these days acts to cushion the hammer blows of economic restructuring, and it allows the titans of the free market the opportunity to assuage their guilt while encouraging 'economic development' and the expansion and evolution of markets. Charity is increasingly tied to the logic of the market; it is in no way antagonistic to it. One of the key distinctions between the liberal left and the radical left is relevant here: do we want to live in a society in which there is more charity and in which more care is shown towards the poorest, or do we want to live in a society in which charity isn't necessary and in which poverty as we know it today has been eliminated?

We must be honest enough to acknowledge that the degeneration of the social is connected to the total dominance of global capitalism and its ideological support systems, and the absence of any conceivable alternative to what already exists. The changing characteristics of markets, and the gradual evolution of social and political attitudes towards the profit motive, inevitably inform our culture and the general character of our shared social life.

It is a profound mistake to believe that we can reconstruct a vibrant and nourishing social life without controlling or replacing the raw asocial imperatives that lie at the core of our economy. We are now living through a period of quite profound social and political turmoil, and much of this turmoil stems from the total domination of markets over people and the attachment of our elites to the neoliberal economic model, which has been stripped of its ideological character and repackaged as pure economic pragmatism. There once existed the political will to regulate and constrain the profit motive, and to use its herculean power to secure social goods that benefited all. As the social democratic consensus gave way to the current neoliberal consensus, the common good was abandoned as a fundamental political concern. In fact, over time, such ideals were mocked and pilloried to such an extent that even politicians on the mainstream left found it necessary to utilise the language of the market to construct a positive image of the future. These political and economic changes had an impact on society and culture in ways we are only now beginning to get to grips with. The collective identities of the modern age were broken apart and splintered into a dazzling array of subject positions. Thatcher famously claimed that society did not exist. Her political successes and the longevity of the consensus she helped to establish made this antisocial libertarian proclamation a reality.

Now is the time to push past the dead ideas that clutter the field of the contemporary social sciences and to think anew about what the continued supremacy of markets will mean for our shared life together. We need new ideas now more than ever, and we should not be afraid to offer a measured dose of economic determinism when it is appropriate to do so. Only when we recognise and begin to come to terms with the interconnectedness of politics, society and economy can we construct reasonable accounts of the mess we're in and how we might begin the process of extracting ourselves from it.

The problems that exist today cannot be fixed with carefully calibrated policy interventions. I am often told by colleagues on the left that activist movements can win significant concessions from government, and that the accumulation of a broad range of small and pragmatic reforms can set our society back on a more equitable footing. There is a small measure of truth in this. Small victories can be achieved. However, the overall trend is quite clear. Activist movements may win small skirmishes here and there, but these minor victories are as nothing when underneath our feat a grinding tectonic realignment is separating us from the very things that make civil society possible. Piecemeal adjustments here and there simply will not do. Things are trending downwards. Our economies look set to experience a prolonged period of low or no growth, and, of course, further crashes remain highly likely. There is a shocking lack of reasonably remunerated productive jobs for young people right across the deindustrialised countries of the West, and there is little sign that our politicians are willing to act to realign global trade flows. We are already seeing the first signs of resources wars, and an unseemly corporate scramble to secure mineral wealth is well underway. Energy and food and water security are now of significant concern to Western governments, and climate change and geopolitical turmoil are driving millions away from their countries of origin and towards what seems like the wealth and tranquillity of developed Western states. The influx of migrants to the Eurozone has already fuelled nationalist politics across the continent, and this trend looks set to continue. Problems of this magnitude cannot be fixed by carefully calibrated policy interventions. The roots of these problems are buried deep, and messing around with surface changes will be of little use to us.

Our national economies are now so intertwined that, even if a radical leftist party were to win office, it would be difficult for a national government to genuinely transform things. We need new forms of intervention that challenge and move beyond the powerfully restrictive framework of global political economy. I am told repeatedly by my colleagues on the left that small interventions add up, and that small adjustments are better than no adjustments at all. However, I remain convinced that we must look towards the bigger picture if we are to avoid the gradual degeneration of those things we value about the present. As I see it, the key question for sociologists now is not what practical measures we can take that will improve things slightly for those who suffer most. Rather, it is how we can intervene, and just how deep we need to go, in order to create a sustainable social world that values and includes every citizen. Of course, to answer this question we need to free ourselves from the constraints of empiricism and once again grant ourselves license to interpret and imagine. We must also free ourselves from the dead ideas of the 20th century and construct our own intellectual frameworks that are capable of coming to terms with the world as it is now.

Left-leaning sociologists often believe that 'speaking truth to power' has the capacity to transform our social and political future. They believe that if they can prove a policy doesn't work, or that the policy is, in fact, counterproductive, power will be forced to change tack. Sociologists will then have used their expertise to correct an injustice or overcome an impediment to human flourishing. However, it is now high time to think again about concentrated power and its willingness to engage in democratic negotiation. Perhaps the injunction to 'speak truth to power' always sent the committed sociologist on a fool's errand. The fact is, power already knows the truth. After many years of engaged social research, it is perfectly clear to me that injustice is not an aberration. It is not a sign that the system is failing to function adequately. Injustice is an unavoidable outcome of our global political economy. These injustices are not signs of some kind of blockage in the system that needs to be addressed and removed; rather, they are concrete indicators of the logic of the system itself. Contemporary global capitalism continues in its present form by gradually withdrawing from modernism's various social commitments. Injustices continue to stack up on top of each other, and this will not change until we become capable of reanimating our political systems and using them to stage a fundamental intervention that changes our future by setting us on a new course.

Historic challenges

As others in this collection have already noted, the gap between rich and poor in Britain is now as wide as it has been for over a century. This gap has a huge effect on civil society. It foments envy. It breeds antagonisms. With every year that passes it becomes harder to maintain the pretence of an inclusive social order that values and welcomes all. Of course, and despite what the media tell us, Western societies remain very rich indeed. The problem is that this wealth is increasingly concentrated in the hands of the few. The rich have successfully cast aside any obligation they might once have felt to mainstream civil society (see Chapter Thirteen, this volume). They have abstracted themselves from the social, and tend to look back at it with a mixture of fear and contempt. They do not live in real neighbourhoods, and they rarely make forays into public space. Their interactions with others are often contractual, and these interactions always take place in the shadow of their own abundant wealth. The super-rich today, it appears, exclude themselves from the social. They set themselves apart from it, and imagine themselves to have transcended its rules and responsibilities. They are sovereign individuals who recognise no external authority that might force them to abandon the pursuit of their own economic self-interest.

At the other end of the social scale we have growing numbers of people who cannot access the things that appear to symbolise full social inclusion. Traditional working-class work has all but disappeared. Production has been shifted to low-wage and low-regulation economies in the developing world, and members of Britain's old industrial class have been forced to compete with one another for insecure jobs that are often completely devoid of the positive symbolism usually associated with traditional working-class work. Working in a shipyard, in a factory or down a coal mine could be difficult and demanding, but, for the most part, it paid enough to raise a family. Industrial jobs were often quite secure. Workers could plan for the future. They could set down roots and live a life free from the perpetual anxiety and insecurity that hangs like a cloud over contemporary labour markets in the de-industrialised West. Sociological studies of life on the shop floor tell us that the industrial worker was often able to retain the belief in the value of their own labour. Skills were considered important and worthwhile, and it was possible to imagine contributing to a workplace community composed of others with whom they shared a great deal. In some cases the industrial worker also carried with them a vague sense that in their daily labours they were doing their bit to drive the nation forward and out of the gloom and want that enshrouded the first third of the 20th century.

During the 1950s and 1960s, things improved rapidly for the working class. Work became safer and wages rose to the extent that the worker and his family were able to access the new forms of consumerism that were transforming the nation's cultural life. Of course, this progress was not a gift bestowed on the lower orders by a magnanimous modern capitalism. This progress was won by the political organisation of the working class and its steadfast refusal to capitulate to the interests of capital. During these years it remained possible to imagine an alternative to capitalism. Left-wing radicalism still existed across the continent, and it was in capital's best interests to take a seat at the negotiating table. Capitalism was forced to abandon the aggressive asocial accumulation of the pre-war years, it was forced to contribute higher taxes, and it now had an interventionist state to deal with. However, capitalism survived, and, as the system rumbled onwards, social democracy integrated the radicals at the margins. Capitalism's fundamental exchange relation did not change in the middle third of the 20th century. Modern capitalism was not kinder and more considerate. Rather, politics constrained capitalism's inherent drive to commodify reality and squeeze from it every last drop of surplus value. The organisational logic of capitalist markets was used to drive development and generate tax revenues that enabled the state to pursue positive social ends. None of this happened naturally. It required human energy and commitment, and a functioning political culture that encouraged people to think through their position in the market and the interests they shared with others.

The working class of today face a very different economic reality. Our political culture has grown sterile. Liberal individualism has achieved unprecedented success on the field of culture. The collective identities of the modern working class have fragmented into a multitude of subject positions, and the institutions that enabled working men and women to educate themselves about capitalism and their place within it have all but disappeared. Despite what many optimistic social scientists claim, Twitter and Facebook are not capable of filling the gap they have left. All are enjoined to see themselves as unique individuals who must fight hard to secure their own interests. Our politicians appear totally divorced from the reality faced by ordinary working and non-working people. They show no willingness to intervene in our economy to set us on a new course. From time to time they acknowledge the problems that have been created by our commitment to the free market, but they always then seek to trade these problems off against the supposed benefits of an unregulated market. Now, it seems, all politicians must be committed to ensuring that capitalist expansionism continues unimpeded. Above all things, we must ensure that our gross domestic product returns to growth.

The power of labour unions has declined enormously and the Labour Party has, for many years, been utterly dedicated to the basic principles of the free market. Few of those who work in working-class jobs are able to access the positive workplace symbolism that existed during the modern epoch. Short-term contracts are increasingly the norm, and those working in the lower reaches of the service sector expect to move quite regularly between employers. Pay is down in real terms, and growing numbers of people find themselves incapable of adopting the forms of life that signal full socioeconomic inclusion. This group is often described by sociologists as 'socially excluded', but this phrase doesn't quite capture the reality of their position. Of course, consumerism lies at the core of what we mean by a 'socially included lifestyle', and many of this group remain committed if poorly resourced consumers. They do not create fundamentally different forms of culture, and they do not adopt fundamentally different values to live by. There is no stark gap between the included and excluded. Rather, they form part of a large and growing pan-continental, multi-ethnic and economically redundant social group that are forced to compete against one another for the forms of low-level service work that keep Western economies ticking over while abstract financial markets continue their mad dance. Global capitalism no longer needs them as a productive force. Capital needed them as consumers, and it welcomes their involvement in new forms of digitised capital accumulation.

Sociologists have produced a number of interesting accounts of this particular marginalised group, but the vast majority of these accounts are predicated on the assumption that the best thing to do would be to re-include those who are currently excluded. But what good does this do if the fundamental mechanisms that drive 'exclusion' in the first place remain in place (see Winlow and Hall, 2013)? Most of the social exclusion literature in Britain displays a commitment to social democratic reform, and there is not too much wrong with that. However, most analysts tend to direct their ire at the Conservative Party, as if the government of the day had it within their purview to magically produce new forms of well-paid labour capable of re-establishing security and stability for the majority. Only very rarely do accounts of social exclusion wrestle with the thorny problem of global political economy.

Only an intervention of historic proportions would be capable of creating stable and rewarding forms of working in Britain's thoroughly de-industrialised and marketised economy. We cannot 'fix' social exclusion with small-scale adjustments to social policy. To create meaningful labour in Britain these days would involve stepping out of global trade flows that ensure that most production takes place in established surplus economies and debt-financed consumption continues in the de-industrialised West. Taking this course of action would be monumental, and the effects of such a move would, in the first instance at least, negatively affect the consumer lifestyles of the majority of Britain's citizens. These are big issues that require serious intellectual and political engagement. If we truly hope to revitalise our society and produce the forms of work that guarantee inclusion, we must honestly appraise the world as it is today. We cannot continue to occupy a restricted and sterile intellectual space that encourages us to focus only on small-scale adjustments to our welfare system, or directing a little more public funding towards those who suffer most. What would it mean to truly commit to economic inclusion? Could a new commitment to green energy and ameliorating the effects of climate change produce the new jobs needed to reintegrate those at the economic margins? What would a new social democratic project look like today? Can we introduce a new basic citizen's income? How would we fund such an intervention? Might state-funded national and regional investment banks begin to revitalise the economies of de-industrialised zones in Northern England, Scotland and Wales? Can new technologies enable us to think again about central planning? How might we begin to nationalise key economic sectors without causing yet further economic distress? How can we fund a welfare system that gives us the services we want? How can we create global accord on issues related to the management of climate change? These are, I think, some of the questions we need to be wrestling with. There are no easy answers.

As we begin to think through how we might change our future, we can at least draw strength and motivation from the absolute certainty that the path we're on leads to catastrophe. If we stay as we are, if we remain wedded to the reductive logic of the market, if we risk nothing and turn away from our most pressing problems, much that we value and much that we take for granted these days will disappear, and life will get a lot harder for the vast majority.

An enlightened catastrophism

I conclude only with the basic claim that we must ditch unworldly optimism and adopt an approach that stresses an enlightened catastrophism. But what does this mean? First, we must consciously accept the titanic scale of the problems we face. Without concerted action now, these problems will grow and mutate and drive the production of new problems that are, at the moment, difficult to identify with clarity.

In an exercise shorn of sentiment, we must imagine what it will be like to occupy a future in which the problems we face now have been played out, a future in which, as it were, all our chickens have come home to roost. This is a future shaped by the unwillingness of our generation, and our political leaders, to act now to prevent these problems coming fully to fruition. What if we continue to do very little to prevent the incremental rise in global temperatures? What if the polar ice caps continue to melt, and methane continues to be released into the atmosphere? What if we continue to stand by as an ever greater proportion of global wealth is taken by the 1%? What if the political left continues to atrophy and new nationalist movements continue to absorb the anger and frustration of ordinary people? What if the power of global corporations continues to grow? What if we continue to fail to fund research into clean energy? What if we refuse to take on the work of rebalancing our economies and integrating those currently at the margins? What if we remain fetishistically tied to oil, gas and coal? What if the possessive individualism of today continues to advance, and we fail to construct new forms of collectivism? Think about it. Discard the old trope of incremental progress, and ignore the comfort of assuming that a range of easy solutions will appear. Imagine yourself and those you love occupying that world.

Once we have imagined this future – a future that will come into being if we continue on as we are – we can begin to think again about what can be done in the here and now to set us on a different course. The shock of recognition and conscious acceptance must compel us to begin to do what needs to be done. So, ignore those who tell you to cheer up and look on the bright side. Face the future and look it square in the face, and then join with others to fashion the forms of intervention that can arrest our slow descent into the chaos of the future.

References

Hall, S. and Winlow, S. (2015) *Revitalizing criminological theory: Towards a new ultra-realism*, London: Routledge.

Piketty, T. (2014) *Capital in the twenty-first century*, Boston, MA: Harvard University Press

Winlow, S. and Hall, S. (2013) *Rethinking social exclusion: The end of the social?*, London: Sage Publications.

Winlow, S., Hall, S. and Treadwell, J. (2016) *Rise of the right: English nationalism and the transformation of working-class politics*, Bristol: Policy Press.

Winlow, S., Hall, S., Briggs, D. and Treadwell, J. (2015) *Riots and political protest: Notes from the post-political present*, London: Routledge.

Conclusion

FIFTEEN

Thinking prosocially

Rowland Atkinson, Lisa Mckenzie and Simon Winlow

If you have a credit card, a smart phone and a health plan you have everything you need.[1]

When we started this project we wanted to do something slightly different. Our main aim was to enable researchers to write in a different voice, less constrained by academic convention, and more directly applied to the question of how their knowledge could be used to help make societies better places for more people. Writing like this is often difficult for academics because, while of course they have their own political beliefs and ideas, they follow conventions that compel them to use dispassionate modes of expression, and frequently worry about providing readers with a sufficiency of convincing evidence. To offer a judgement more clearly shaped by ideological conviction is often believed to suggest a deficit in intellectual objectivity and academic rigour, and to believe too passionately or to argue too forcefully are often considered rather uncouth in the genteel world of academia. Polemical argumentation, no matter how cogent and convincing, often remains fairly marginal to the intellectual cultures of the social sciences. Carefully evidenced claims written in dry and uninspiring prose is a firmly established norm that is subtly reproduced in each new generation of academics by those that preceded it. But talking in different voices and to different communities who often seek a more active response from universities and their researchers is critical to addressing the kinds of concerns raised in this book.

We accept that carefully evidenced analysis should remain a defining feature of social scientific writing, but we are also arguing that it is important to make more room in our disciplines for forthright political critique and impassioned discussions. A significant motivation for many social researchers is the possibility that our work will act on and improve the world, even if this may only be in a small way. The push to work with and for business in academia in many countries suggests that debates will continue over the question of who and what publicly funded research is for. To identify and understand problems that require resolution is a key aspect of the ethos and function of social science, but again and again we see this undermined through funding cuts to research programmes, their consolidation into larger grants that are more often won by elite institutions, and by a continuing push to identify efficacy as that which benefits commercial partners. Outside of these ongoing concerns many social scientists have detailed knowledge of society's most egregious injustices, and yet the established norms of academic writing remain in place, with the additional worry that without evidence of connecting such work to policy-makers or companies, it will not be valued. In short, this agenda does little to encourage constructive and critical thinking that is designed as a form of circulation, of a need to influence and engage with social conversations.

In this context academics and social thinkers act in ways that are self-disciplining, if not self-defeating – we are constrained by institutional and disciplinary pressures, forced to worry about how our work will be received by our peers and senior administrators in our universities. If we want our careers to progress, the received wisdom is that we must attenuate critique and dispense with impassioned rhetoric and continue to hold out a glimmer of hope that, no matter how bad things appear to be, there is always the possibility that things can improve, that injustices can be overcome, and that, with a little hard work and one or two perfectly pitched policy interventions, we can quickly correct problems in the system. It is therefore often quite difficult to speak honestly and openly about what we, as social scientists, understand to be important or evident. Our journals are filled with fence-sitting articles that offer only tentative conclusions and suggestions for further research, framed as problems that new datasets may throw light on. Often we bite our lip. We hold back and refuse to identify and talk honestly about the bleak reality of social conditions. Rather than dedicating our working lives to producing the forms of knowledge that might make the world a better place, our disciplines are beset by careerism, anxiety and competition. We wanted to push off in a different direction in this book, and we have encouraged those who have contributed to abandon the usual protocols and tell it like it is. We face staggering levels of inequality, perennial economic instability and a gradually unfolding ecological crisis, and all of these things will shape the future in ways that are difficult to predict. Now is the time for social researchers to draw on their evidence and to intervene more forcefully than interior debates within disciplines via expensive journal subscriptions will allow. Elite universities crowing over their positions with regard to grant funding or publication activity could do more in this context to act more strongly to criticise and even side-step involvement in rankings and systems of institutional closure (such as the UK Russell Group) and help to facilitate pressured staff to be brilliant on a wider range of dimensions than banal measures of 'excellence' can capture.

At a time of national economic and social crisis and the terminal endpoint of our global ecological condition, the role of social sciences must be indexed by its capacity to engage and resolve. Writing in this historical moment we need to acknowledge the need for urgent action to tackle rising inequality, environment and climate catastrophes, globally organised criminality (often woven into economic and political life) and the lack of action within the political domain to tackle many problems. Here it seems incumbent on those with significant research experience and expertise to offer messages, ideas and answers in a variety of voices to help facilitate the possibility of new blueprints, maps and diagrams that offer us a way forward to a more socially just, inclusive and much less divided and enriched social condition. We need to be problem-driven, to be creative and to think self-consciously about what the pressures and privileges of academic life bring to academics faced with these challenges.

In the world around us there are significant social divisions. So what? Well, aside from the social injustice that many people feel about rising inequality there is enormous concern about the fact that the wealthiest are doing even better, running away from society at a time of increasing hardship for those at the bottom. Yet the respective positions of the rich and poor are not unrelated. In many cases poverty is the direct result of efforts by the wealthy to avoid making full contributions to society through tax, or of the low pay or poor conditions imposed by those with economic power. In addition, the wealthiest live in ways that insulate them from the social problems and distress around them. Were we to be particularly cynical (and, of course, we leave you to be the judge) we might also argue that those who are doing well live in ways designed to help secure their advantages in life and to maintain the kinds of systems that have delivered good things to them while denying opportunities to others. For them to acknowledge this would, of course, be far too confronting – it would invoke the need for a much deeper ethic of connection and responsibility for the tragedies unfolding globally. Here the use of philanthropy can only be seen as the very slightest of actions when we know that it is the systemic production of inequality, poverty, ill health, poor education and other forms of exploitation that will remain if the structures of these systems are not tackled in more concerted ways. The kind of actions that could be taken include choices relating to voting, schooling, healthcare, leisure, even to driving and other forms of social circulation and processes of social exclusion. Today these choices are further facilitated on the one hand, by new providers of core services like health and education and, on the other, by the defunding or closure of public services provided by the state, despite these being the hard-won outcomes of political contests in the early post-war period. Even as we write this volume we can see proposals for the re-introduction of selective schools in the UK, a crisis in funding for the National Health Service and care for the elderly and vulnerable, and the state brokering of contracts for nuclear power infrastructure awarded to state and corporate bodies from other countries. The common denominator here is that political and corporate power, more than ever before, works in the name of (more) money, and is freed from the perceived moral or social constraints in that would be imposed should the common good be considered.

These changes tell us something very clear about the direction of travel for those services that enabled the flourishing of human potential and which offered insurances against risks in our lives. The social, conceived as an alliance or partnership between the individual, and a legitimate state body that offered services and provisions for all, is firmly in a crisis phase. We have been told that such provisions are too expensive, that there is no money for these services or that people are choosing private services and more private lives for themselves. Yet, underlying these messages lies an enormous dissatisfaction, a gnawing social anxiety that fills everyday life – essential services like policing and probation are privatised alongside public space itself, local governance has become a stripped-back procurer of private services, middle-class children find post-university employment in sectors governed by short-term contracts, and algorithms dictate the work of numerous self-employed workers using rent-seeking infrastructures such as Uber or Deliveroo. The idea that something larger is helping, coordinating, healing, repairing and policing has become almost anachronistic. The council, police, postal worker, refuse collector and countless other public institutions and key workers see their public and accountable functions eroded or withdrawn in many cases. What we may now see as the public social realm is in fact a display of care mixed with force by corporations whose ultimate motivation is profit, extracting value for shareholders who are themselves drawn from the wealthier sections of society. Similarly, those on high incomes are able to select from the winners of contests to provide services and goods as cheaply as possible.

Despite the extent of privatisation and the self-destruction of the state led by its political executive, we are seeing more popular reactions and contests to rule of the social by profit and the invocation of efficiency. Alongside the observation that many private services are poor value, low-quality, dangerous or ill conceived lie a broader set of contradictions whose impact is increasingly visible. One critical area for such questions to be raised lies in the way that market motivations are introduced to areas of social life to which they are, at best, ill suited. Here we can mention again forms of healthcare, policing and security, but also the extension of security as a mode of private provision within such areas as migrant housing.

In the deeper background to these changes lies the ecological limits to humanity's spaceship earth. The extent of climate change, even within our own lifetimes, and fossil fuel dependency of a growth economy is undeniably destabilising and unsustainable, and yet the bulk of political debate and economic commentary is founded on notions not of steady-state service but of growth. As these changes deepen and climate catastrophe impinges on us, these positions will seem not only irresponsible, but in reality, callously linked to the needs of the globe's most affluent to secure their lifestyles in denial of the harm that they or their agents have enacted. While much of this volume has been devoted to arguments for greater social justice and better outcomes for all, it would be wrong to think that such results might include all or most of us living up to the same kinds of material excess of the very wealthy. This doesn't simply mean that we can't all live like oligarchs; rather, it means that economic and social life needs to find methods for de-growth, for people to adopt different diets and reduced ambitions for mobility, consumption and leisure if we are not to fry the planet and uproot a third of humanity. The worst-case scenario in light of this is, and we are already seeing this right now, that physical boundaries are built around the richest nations while refugees fleeing the consequences of climate change, economic collapse and persistent but low-intensity warfare are prevented access to the world's safer zones.

These concluding comments suggest that notions of the social still tend to be restricted to our position as subjects within a nation-state. We need to adopt a truly global and human consciousness in order to engage with the challenges ahead, and to realise that market motives are very often the enemy of the social or are not sufficiently harnessed to questions of responsibility and the public good. Now more than at any point in our recent history we appear locked into a declining trajectory. Given the growing gap between rich and poor, given the ecological catastrophe that lies just ahead, given impending resources wars, given the surfeit of anger and enmity that sloshes around our cities, and given the absence of a genuine alternative capable of capturing the hearts and minds of everyday people, it seems unlikely that we're in for a soft landing.

Much of the ideological divides that focus on questions of public and private make distinctions based on the degree to which social relationships, reciprocity and altruism are needed in daily social life. The problem with this divide is that it falters as soon as we acknowledge how these features of social life are critical to humane existence for all. We cannot suggest that care and responsibility are ideas or actions that can chosen or rejected. A denial of the essential qualities and restorative needs of social life is leading us into deeper social divisions, anxiety, crime, homelessness, social neglect and impoverishment.. However, the good news is that acknowledging community life and social relations is capable of generating greater, not less, potential for personal enrichment, health, wellbeing and the development of a more private and self-assured mode of individual existence. An informational and neoliberal mode of capitalism has given us zero hours contracts, rising crime, unending war, destabilising economic conditions and the uneasy sense that we, as individuals, are increasingly the shallow co-constructs of a diet of social media, news and on-demand television services. We are all diminished by this slow death of the social. We are more able to be ourselves for being in the safe company of others, and we all gain where the market is placed in our service rather than being the means by which wealth is generated for the few.

Note

[1] Adapted from the aphorism attributed to Cicero: 'If you have a garden and a library you have everything that you need.'

Index

A

academy
  neoliberalism in 22–3, 34–5
  polemical argument in 195–7
  see also co-production of knowledge
activist movements 185
    see also protest
Addams, J. 20–2, 23, 24–5
Alinsky, S. 143
altruism 183–4
antisocial
  concept of 9
  neoliberalism as 83–4
  political system as 8–9
  urban design as 130
anxiety 6, 7, 86, 155, 198
architecture 129–31
arts-based projects 81–2, 87, 89–92,
  99–102, 103, 104–6
Atkinson, R. 1–11, 165–77, 195–200
austerity measures 3, 47–8, 49, 117

B

Back, L. 88
Barnett, C. 30
Bauman, Z. 82, 83, 84, 86, 147, 156
Bentley, D. 158
blackout bombs 70–1, 76
blame 32, 33–4, 37
Body-Gendrot, S. 141–52
Brazilian City Statute (2001) 75
Brown, M. 99–100, 106
Burawoy, M. 17–18, 22
Burgum, S. 127–38

C

capitalism 6, 65, 85–6, 188
  see also consumer capitalism; market
  orientation; neoliberalism
caregiving 22, 25
catastrophism 190–1

change
  hope for 103–5, 162–3
  lack of alternatives 127, 180, 181,
    182
  need for fundamental 185–6, 189–90
  protest leading to 151–2
  resistance to 131, 180, 181
charity 183–4
Child Benefit 161
childcare 160
children
  and community knowledge 103,
    104–5
  and insecurity 159–60
choice 117, 118–19
cities *see* urban
civil society 2, 157
climate change 199
co-production of knowledge 81–2,
  89–92, 96, 97–103, 105–6, 107
collective identity 134–5
Collins, M. 88
communication, and protest 148,
  149–50, 151, 152
communities
  co-production of knowledge 81–2,
    89–92, 96, 97–103, 105–6, 107
  relationship with universities 95
community, de-valuing of 44–5,
  49–50
community knowledge 100–1, 103–4
community-based research
  and academic sociology 23–4
  see also co-production of knowledge
consumer capitalism 83, 180, 189
consumer culture 182
contractualism 116
Corbett, S. 111–23
Coward, M. 67–77
creative practice *see* arts-based projects
crime statistics 57, 58

crisis
  and catastrophism 190–1
  concept of 29
  financial 3, 47
  need for fundamental change 185–6,
    189–90
  and political inertia 179–81
  in welfare state 16
    see also urban crises
Critchley, S. 35

D

Dahl, R.A. 142, 151
de Certeau, M. 90
Debord, G. 90
defensiveness 33–4
dérive 90–1
design of urban space 129–31
Dewey, J. 21
disability 117
disorder 149–51
dissatisfaction 181–2, 198
  see also anxiety
dissent 5
  see also protest

E

early childhood education and care
    (ECEC) 160
education 6, 39, 160
Ellis, A. 55–66
empowerment 117, 120, 122, 143,
    148, 149
enclaves
  and urban violence 77
  of wealthy 168, 171–2
Enroth, H. 30–1
European Union (EU) policy-making
    119
exclusion 97, 98–9, 100, 189

F

fairness/unfairness 8, 173–4
  see also inequality
Featherstone, D. 31
financial crisis 3, 47
financial system 167, 171
food insecurity 16
France 144–6, 149
freedom of choice 117, 118–19
Freire, P. 6
Friends of the Earth 159

Frosh, S. 33–4

G

Gibson-Graham, J.K. 31–2, 36
global urbanisation 67
Good Right, The 159, 162
Gough, J. 84
Grad multiple-barrel rocket launchers
    (MBRLs) 69–70, 76
Gurney, P. 103

H

hardworking people 40, 41
Harvey, D. 74
health inequalities 15–16
hedonism 181–2
history 97, 103–4
home ownership 39, 144, 159
  wealthy neighbourhoods 168, 170–2,
    175
Hong Kong 149
housebuilding 144, 159
housing 4, 39, 144, 145–6
housing insecurity 7, 43, 44–5
  redressing 158–9
Huddersfield 96, 98–9, 101–2
Hull-House settlement 21–2, 23
humanitarianism 73–4
Hurcombe, M. 104, 105

I

idealism 181
identity
  and male violence 59–62, 63
  and neighbourhood 81–2, 89–92
  of protest movements 134–5
Imagine project 95–6, 98, 104
immigration 145, 146
inclusion 120, 146–9
income inequality 15
  see also wealthy; working class
income insecurity 44, 155, 160–2
individualism 1, 41, 111, 115, 116–18
inequality 8–9
  addressing 173–5, 176
  extent of 15–16, 155–6, 186–7,
    197
  impact of 39, 59, 118
  of neoliberalism 1–2, 6
  and opportunity 168
  within protest movements 135–6
  see also wealthy; working class

infrastructure 70–1, 72, 73, 76
insecurity *see* socioeconomic insecurity

J

Jacobs, K. 27–37
Jessop, B. 29
Judt, T. 29

K

Kane, E. 24
Khan, S. 168
Kirklees Local TV 99–100
knowledge *see* co-production of knowledge
KPMG 159

L

law/legislation 75, 76
Lefebvre, H. 74, 129
Levitas, R. 30
life expectancy 15–16
living standards 16
London
  inequality in 168–9, 170
  insecurity in 44–5
  Occupy movement 128–37
  property in 41–2
  wealthy in 167
low-income neighbourhoods
  socialisation in 84–5, 92
  and urban crises in France 144–6
  see also arts-based projects; poverty; socioeconomic insecurity; working class

M

Mckenzie, L. 1–11, 39–50, 195–200
male violence 59–63
market orientation 3, 10, 199
  dominance of 183–4
  of urban space 129–31, 132
  see also capitalism; neoliberalism
market value 41–2, 49–50, 82–3
Marshall, T.H. 113
Massey, D. 28–9, 31
media
  neoliberalism supported by 4
  violence in 55, 59
  working class in 42–3, 49
methodology 87–8
  see also co-production of knowledge
military strategy 69–71, 76

military weapons 68–71, 76
Mills, C.W. 6, 16–17, 18–20, 24, 85–6
moral indignation 35, 136
multiple-barrel rocket launchers (MBRLs) 69–70, 76

N

National Living Wage (NLW) 161
National Minimum Wage (NMW) 161
NATO 70–1
neighbourhoods
  and French urban crises 144–6
  socialisation in 84–5, 92
  of wealthy 168, 170–2, 175
  see also arts-based projects
neoliberalism
  in academy/universities 22–3, 34–5
  alternatives to 162–3
  approach to social policy 114–19
  concept and critique of 1–2, 28–30
  impact of 2, 82–4, 111, 156, 184
  normalisation of 2, 28, 86, 115, 127, 129–30, 179–81, 184
  responses to 30–5
  strategy of 3
  as system 29–30, 31–2
  and urban design 129–31
New Labour 116–17
Nicolaus, M. 166

O

Occupy movement 128–31, 148, 149
  limitations and possibility of 131–7
offshore investments 171, 173
O'Hara, M. 49
order and disorder 150–1
Orton, M. 155–63

P

Pahl, K. 95–107
parks 147
participation 5, 97, 119–20, 122
  see also co-production of knowledge
Paternoster Square (London) 130–1
Pick, D. 32
Pickett, K. 59
place
  and wealth 168–73
  see also neighbourhoods; public space; urban space
place making 41–2
pluralism 142, 151

plurality of cities 72, 74, 77
polemical argument 195–7
policing 132, 150
political inertia 179–81
political participation 5
political system
  and inequality 8–9
  see also neoliberalism; social democracy
politique de la ville 145–6
Pool, S. 104, 105
popular culture 42–3, 49, 55, 59
poverty
  attitudes to 5–6, 40, 48
  causes of 43
  extent of 15, 16
  neoliberal definitions of 118
  see also low-income neighbourhoods;
    socioeconomic insecurity; working
    class
poverty stigma 83–4, 87–8
powerlessness 136–7
pragmatism 20, 157
precariousness see socioeconomic
  insecurity
property market 41–2, 43, 44–5
  see also housing
prosocial forms of engagement 35–6
prosocial response to urban destruction
  73–7
prosocial thinking/ethos 10–11, 82,
  84, 85, 86–8, 92, 195–200
protest
  Occupy movement 128–37, 148, 149
  potential of 133, 151–2
  and public space 147–9, 150
  and urban crises 142, 145
psychoanalytical perspective 32–4
public sociology
  Addams' work 20–2, 23, 24–5
  current call for 17–18, 22–4
  Mills' work 17–20
public space
  and inclusion 146–9
  loss of 4, 144
  market orientation of 130–1, 132
  political use of 147–9, 150

R
Rafiq, Z. 99
Rancière, J. 132–3
Rasool, Z. 96, 98, 100–1
realism 181
reality effects, of research 87–8
rents and renting 158, 159

reputation 62
residents' perspectives 81–2, 89–92
resistance 32, 33–4, 37
  see also protest
responsibility see blame; rights and
  responsibilities
rich see wealthy
right to the city 74–5
right to sell and stay 159
righteous indignation 35, 136
rights and responsibilities 116–17
riots 142, 145, 169, 170
romanticisation of protest 135
Rose, J. 33
Rotherham 96, 97–8, 99, 104–5,
  106
Rustin, M. 31

S
Sack, R. 170
Samuel, R. 104
segregation 77, 168–73, 175
Sennett, R. 165
Shae, J. 70–1
Shah, M. 104
Shelter 159
site-specific art 89–92
Skeggs, B. 41
social administration 112–13
social bonds 7–8
social class 40, 41
  see also wealthy; working class
social cohesion 120
social democracy 2–3, 20–2, 29, 112,
  114
social empowerment 120, 122
social exclusion 97, 98–9, 100, 189
social fragmentation 5, 7–8, 84
social inclusion 120, 146–9
social media 5, 148, 149–50, 151
social mobility 39
social policy
  concepts of welfare 111–12
  neoliberal approach to 'social' 114–19
  'social' in post-war welfare state
    112–14
  and social quality 119–22
  to redress insecurity 158–62
social quality 119–22
social question
  current context 15–16
  historical context 15
  and public sociology 17–25

social realm
  erosion of 198
  wealthy insulated from 169–72, 187
social science
  invisibility of wealthy in 166
  polemical argument in 195–7
  and prosocial thinking 10–11,
    195–200
  role of 9, 176–7, 182–3, 197
  see also sociology
socialisation 84–5, 92
society, importance of 1, 2
socioeconomic insecurity
  extent and effects of 7, 16, 155–6
  housing insecurity 7, 43, 44–5,
    158–9
  redressing 156–62
  of working class 39, 40, 44
socioeconomic security 120
sociological imagination 16–17, 18–20,
  30–1, 85–8
Sociological Imagination, The 6, 17
sociology
  Addams and public sociology 20–2,
    23, 24–5
  call for public sociology 17–18,
    22–4
  impact of neoliberalism on 22–3
  Mills and public sociology 17–20
  role of 176–7, 186
sound system culture 101–2
soundscapes 104–5
space
  and financial system 171
  market orientation of 129–31, 132
  see also place; public space; urban
    space
state, decreasing role of 1, 39, 40
stigma/stigmatisation 45–6, 49, 83–4,
  87–8
symbolic violence 42, 43
systemic violence 63

T

tax avoidance 171, 173
Taylor, G. 81–93
television 42–3, 49, 99–100
Thatcherism 115, 116
Third Way politics 116–17
Thompson, E.P. 103
Titmuss, R.M. 113
Townsend, P. 113–14

U

universities
  and community 95
  see also academy; co-production of
    knowledge
urban crises
  France 144–6, 149
  and public space 146–9
  USA 141–4
urban disorder 149–51
  see also urban protest
urban fabric
  categories of 72
  destruction of 68–73, 76
  protection of 73–7
urban parks 147
urban planning 175
urban protest
  and crisis 142, 145
  Occupy movement 128–37, 148, 149
  and public space 147–9, 150
urban renewal 145
urban space
  market orientation of 129–31, 132
  right to city 74–5
  and urban crisis 146–9
  wealth and segregation in 168–73
urban violence
  military weapons 68–71, 76
  prosocial response to 73–7
  riots 142, 145, 169, 170
  urbicide 71–3
urbanisation 67
urbicide 71–3
US urban crises 141–4
utopian thinking 30

V

value
  de-valuing of working class 42–3,
    44–5, 49–50, 83
  as market-related 41–2, 49–50, 82–3
  working class narratives 43–9
violence
  of capitalism 65
  concepts of 56–7, 63
  function of 63, 64
  historical context 57–9
  in/against cities
    prosocial response to 73–7
    urbicide 71–3
    weapons 68–71, 76
  intervention and rehabilitation 63–4

in popular culture 55, 59
role of inequality 59
social context of male violence 59–63
ubiquity of 55
virtual communities 5, 149–50, 150

W

wages 161
Walker, A. 111–23
walking as art 81–2, 90–1
War on Poverty 143
Ward, P. 95–107
Warner, M. 34
Warr, D. 81–93
wealthy
  insulated from social 169–72, 187
  invisibility of 166
  places of 168–73
  position of 176, 187
  profile of 167–8
  and social bonds 7–8
weapons 68–71, 76
welfare 111–12
welfare benefits 46, 48, 161
welfare state 16, 112, 114
Wilkinson, I. 15–25
Wilkinson, R. 59
Williams, A. 35
Williams, R. 81–93, 96
Winlow, S. 1–11, 179–91, 195–200
working class
  changing nature of 187–9
  de-valued 42–3, 44–5, 49–50, 83
  narratives of 43–9
  precariousness of *see* socioeconomic
    insecurity
  see also low-income neighbourhoods;
    poverty
Wright, E. 36

Y

young people, and community
    knowledge 103, 104–5
Yugoslavia (former) 70–1

Z

Zizek, S. 33, 63